TRANSATLANTIC TIES
IN THE SPANISH EMPIRE

TRANSATLANTIC TIES
IN THE SPANISH EMPIRE

Brihuega, Spain,

&

Puebla, Mexico,

1560–1620

IDA ALTMAN

Stanford University Press ～ *Stanford, California* 2000

Stanford University Press
Stanford, California
© 2000 by the Board of Trustees
of the Leland Stanford Junior University

Printed in the United States of America

Library of Congress Cataloging-in-Publication Data
Altman, Ida.
    Translatlantic ties in the Spanish empire : Brihuega, Spain, and Puebla,
Mexico, 1560–1620 / c Ida Altman.
        p.   cm.
    Includes bibliographical references and index.
    ISBN 0-8047-3663-4 (cloth : alk. paper)
        1. Spandiards—Mexico—Puebla—History—16th century. 2. Brihuega
(Spain)—Emigration and immigration—History—16th century. 3. Puebla
(Mexico)—Emigration and immigration—History—16th century. 4. Puebla
(Mexico)—Relations—Spain—Brihuega. 5. Brihuega (Spain)—Relations—
Mexico—Puebla. I. Title.

F1391.P6 A48 2000
972´.4800461—dc21   99-047891

♾ This book is printed on acid-free, archival quality paper.

Original printing 2000
Last figure below indicates year of this printing:
09 08 07 06 05 04 03 02 01 00

Typeset by Robert C. Ehle in 10/12.5 ITC Galliard

For Jeanne Weinberger Altman
in loving memory

Acknowledgments

Research for this project was conducted in archives in Madrid, Brihuega, Toledo, Valladolid, Simancas, Seville, and Granada in Spain as well as in Mexico City and Puebla. I am most grateful for a fellowship from the National Endowment for the Humanities during the academic year 1994–95, which funded the major portion of my research in Spain and Mexico. I also thank the Program for Cultural Cooperation between Spain's Ministry of Culture and U.S. Universities of the University of Minnesota for a supplemental grant that allowed me to complete work in Seville in the summer of 1995. Participation in a National Endowment for the Humanities Institute directed by Frances Kartunnen in the summer of 1992 provided an excellent opportunity to become acquainted with Puebla and its region, and a travel grant from the College of Liberal Arts of the University of New Orleans allowed me to finish research in Puebla in the summer of 1996. I greatly appreciate the efforts of Arnold Hirsch and Joseph Caldwell, successive chairs of the UNO history department, who helped make it possible for me to spend an academic year conducting research and provided other support toward the completion of this project.

I have benefited considerably from the generosity and advice of colleagues and friends. James Lockhart, Sarah L. Cline, John E. Kicza, James Boyden, and David J. Weber read the manuscript at various stages and made valuable suggestions and observations. Juan Javier Pescador also read the manuscript and helped me with some of the genealogical data. David Metzger introduced me to the Archivo General de la Nación (AGN) and much more in Mexico City, Leticia Gamboa provided support and encouragement in Puebla, and Sara T. Nalle turned my attention to the Inquisition documents of Toledo and accompanied me to the Chancillería archive in Valladolid. Linda Arnold and William Taylor provided helpful advice in the AGN. Rosalva Loreto and Francisco Cervantes offered assistance and kind hospitality in Puebla, and Günter Vollmer graciously sent me his data on the marriages of immigrants from Brihuega in Puebla. The students in my seminar at Tulane University in the spring of 1998 helped me to focus my thinking on certain questions. I am grateful to Norris Pope for his encouragement even before this project was well launched, and to Anna Eberhard Friedlander for seeing it through to publication. Barbara H. Salazar was a meticulous and perceptive copyeditor. Jeanie Taliancich did the excellent work on the maps.

My thanks also to Daniel J. Hubbell for his companionship as well as computer expertise, patience while I was off doing research, and assistance in transcribing the tax lists from Simancas and proofreading. Preston, my dog, reminded me that intellectual pursuits need not preclude other ones. My family's love, steadfastness, sense of humor, insight, and common sense have seen me through this book, as through so much else. I dedicate the book to my mother, whose shining spirit will always light my path.

I.A.

Contents

Illustrations

Figures

Maps

TRANSATLANTIC TIES
IN THE SPANISH EMPIRE

Introduction

This book represents an effort to understand the experiences of a group of people from a middling-sized town in New Castile who went to New Spain in the years from around 1560 to 1620. During those six decades probably 1,000 or more people emigrated from Brihuega, a textile-manufacturing town near Guadalajara with a population of around 4,000. Nearly all of the emigrants settled in Puebla de los Angeles, early colonial Mexico's second most important city. They played a crucial role in making Puebla the colony's leading textile producer.

My principal objective here is to trace the connections, continuities, and discontinuities between the socioeconomic, cultural, and institutional patterns of a town in Castile and those of a city in New Spain as they can be discerned through the lives of the immigrants. In so doing I hope to offer a detailed and concrete basis for understanding the process and implications of the transference of these patterns within the early modern Hispanic world. I use the experiences of the immigrants from Brihuega, known as *briocenses*, as the basis for considering society in Brihuega and Puebla, drawing direct as well as indirect comparisons between the two places. The book examines the context, in Castile and in New Spain, in which the briocenses conducted their lives, working, marrying, and raising children, socializing, participating in religious activities, arguing, and confronting crises and opportunities for change.

In the seventeenth and eighteenth centuries Puebla's historians were well aware of the presence and significance of the immigrants from Brihuega. Modern scholars, however, have paid little attention to Puebla's history in the middle years of the colonial period or to the briocenses' contributions to the city's development. Among the depositions of prospective emigrants in the Indiferente General section of the Archivo General de Indias in Seville, the historian Enrique Otte found a series of letters that Spaniards living in Puebla wrote to their relatives in Castile in the last third of the sixteenth century and the early years of the seventeenth, which he published in the 1960s.[1] Letters from the briocenses and their kin and close associates in neighboring towns in the Alcarria figured prominently in this collection, and Otte devoted a considerable portion of his discussion of the letters and their context and implications to the activities of the emigrants from Brihuega.

While conducting research in the Archive of the Indies in the late 1970s, I came across the series of depositions from which Otte had extracted these letters. In contrast to the project on which I was working at the time, the case of the Brihuega emigrants seemed to offer the possibility of realizing a rather tidy and limited two-sided study of people in both their community of origin and their new home in the Indies. Some years later, when I began to read the full depositions, it became clear that the movement of people from Brihuega to Puebla was far more substantial than the letters alone had indicated, involving not just a few dozen but possibly hundreds of people and continuing in full force over several decades. Rather than simply providing the basis for a scholarly article, the topic seemed to merit full-scale, book-length treatment.

The migration from Brihuega to Puebla very likely was a unique phenomenon in the movement of people from Spain to the Americas in the early colonial period by virtue of both its size (in relation to that of the place of origin) and its rather astonishingly concentrated focus. Certainly no comparable example has surfaced to date, either in the published compilations of emigrants or in the scholarly literature on early modern Spanish emigration.[2] In my work on Extremadura I identified approximately 1,000 individuals from the city of Trujillo, hometown of the Pizarros, who departed for the Indies during the sixteenth century.[3] Although more than half of the people from Trujillo ended up in Peru, substantial numbers went elsewhere in the Spanish empire, and even in Peru immigrants settled in a number of locales. In around 60 years probably at least as many people left Brihuega as left Trujillo, although the town was less than half Trujillo's size, and nearly all of them went to one place. Their common destination allowed them to maintain their friendships, kinship ties, and economic associations, if not intact, then certainly at a highly functional level.

The contrast to the movement from Cáceres and Trujillo, the two cities I studied in Extremadura, is striking in other respects as well. The *extremeño* emigrants and their families were closely associated with the "heroic" age of early Spanish American history. They included larger-than-life individuals such as Francisco Pizarro and his brothers; key officials like fray Nicolás de Ovando, early governor of Hispaniola and relative of Lic. Juan de Ovando; powerful *encomenderos* and representatives of important families of the provincial nobility who were much aware of (and concerned about) their privileged status; and influential artisans such as the architect Francisco Becerra, all of whom had entourages of relatives and retainers, many of them from their hometowns and "tierra." The briocense emigrants—artisans, entrepreneurs, and farmers—were thoroughly ordinary people. They lacked powerful connections at court and in New Spain; they missed entirely the Conquest period in the Indies. Although a few achieved office in Puebla and many had participated in local government in Brihuega, there were no high officials of church or state among them, no encomenderos, and very few *hidalgos*. The town's hidalgo families were not particularly wealthy, distinguished, or numerous, and the activities of the briocense hidalgos who did go to New Spain differed in no discernible fashion from those of their commoner compatriots. Like the rest of the briocenses in Puebla, the handful of hidalgo immigrants became involved in textile manufacture and other commercial and industrial enterprises, intermarried with other briocense families that did not necessarily belong to the privileged group, and took up residence in the same neighborhoods. As late arrivals in New Spain, the briocenses were on the whole modest and practical in their ambitions, and to a great extent they achieved the economic security and social stability they sought.

Before the early eighteenth century, when a battle fought at Brihuega in December 1710 gave King Philip V a crucial victory over the British and gained for the town a royal textile factory as a reward, perhaps Brihuega's greatest distinction lay in this large contingent of its native sons and daughters who left home to live in Puebla de los Angeles in the last third of the sixteenth century. Up until then the town's historical experience was largely unremarkable—at least, no one bothered to remark on it. Although at one time Brihuega, having been from the Middle Ages one of the more important towns in the archbishopric of Toledo, could lay claim to a certain status, no one ever wrote a real history of the town. The nineteenth-century historian Juan Catalina García López treated Brihuega's medieval history in some detail in the introduction to his study and transcription of the town's *fuero,* or code of laws and privileges. He paid scant attention, however, to the sixteenth century—a particularly unfortunate omission, because he clearly had access to the town's notarial records, which have since disappeared.[4]

In general, then, sources on Brihuega are scarce. The town was not included in the "Relaciones geográficas" of the sixteenth century, perhaps because it was under the jurisdiction of the archbishop. It probably is fair to assume, however, that in many ways Brihuega substantially resembled other towns of its region, the Alcarria. The location of its fortress attests to the town's uneventful history; in contrast to most other such structures built in medieval Castile, Brihuega's castle sits below the town, descending the hill, a location that renders it all but useless for defensive purposes. Apart from the eighteenth-century addition of the imposing textile factory, which dominates the ridge along the town's northern edge, internal and external events appear to have affected the town very little. The same families that were economically and politically active in the sixteenth century figured prominently two centuries later. Today Brihuega, which attracts few visitors despite its tranquil charm, its proximity to Madrid and Guadalajara, and the recent extensive restoration of its historic buildings, is probably somewhat smaller in population than it was in the late sixteenth and early seventeenth centuries.

In the latter part of the sixteenth century Brihuega's economy was faltering, while Puebla prospered. Puebla was founded only a decade after the Spanish conquest of Tenochtitlán. Its early years have been well documented, as have some other notable periods of its history, such as when Juan de Palafox was bishop.[5] Situated in a fertile, well-watered region close to the new Spanish capital of Mexico City and accessible from the ports on both coasts, Puebla generally did well from the time of its founding in the 1530s, and by the late sixteenth century, industry, trade, and agriculture were flourishing in the city and its region. From early on it was one of the colony's leading ecclesiastical centers. Brihuega's decline and Puebla's increasing prosperity in the last third of the sixteenth century were not entirely coincidental. Although emigration probably did not hurt Brihuega economically—if anything, it provided an important alternative for people who sought to escape difficult circumstances and brought welcome remittances from successful emigrants to family and kin back home—the briocenses contributed significantly to Puebla's economic development.

I do not pretend to offer a complete history of either place during the period in question but rather to consider the milieu in which the immigrants functioned primarily as it touched and was touched by their lives. In any case, without the notarial records Brihuega's history remains sketchy at many points. These key local records consist primarily of legal and financial transactions (rentals, sales, partnership and employment agreements) along with wills and dowry contracts. Their absence limits the detail in which it is possible to document some important aspects of the town's economic life, from the organization of the textile industry to the impact and level of remittances that townspeople received from relatives in the Indies. In one sense, however, the impossibility of consulting the town's notarial records yielded unanticipated benefits, for it made the search for potentially relevant documentation elsewhere all the more crucial. Sources that I otherwise might have neglected, such as Inquisition records, not only proved to be quite rich but also suggested ways in which material that principally has been used for one purpose—in the case of Inquisition records, the study of religious practice, belief, and dissent—can be of considerable value in understanding local history.[6] The effort to find material relevant to the briocenses and their history and milieu took me to archives and collections in Madrid, Simancas, Toledo, Valladolid, Seville, and Granada. The varied perspectives offered by the documentation in these archives made it possible to draw a fairly detailed and balanced picture of Brihuega in the context of Castile and the empire, notwithstanding the absence of key primary records and little in the way of secondary literature.

Perhaps more surprising, given Puebla's importance today and especially in the first century and a half of the colonial period, is the relative lack of scholarly work on the city. Documentation is abundant, and much of it is readily available outside the archives.[7] Although only one notarial series is reasonably complete for the sixteenth century, that series, together with another one or two that are partially preserved, offers ample material that has been little used to study the city. The records of the city council have been used more extensively.[8] Puebla's surviving judicial records for the period are fairly limited in both quantity and accessibility, but they are of considerable interest, and virtually every section of the colonial documentation in the Archivo General de la Nación in Mexico City contains material relevant to Puebla. On the whole, however, scholars have taken a greater interest in Puebla's region than in the city itself.[9] Although I do not offer here a full-scale study of the city in the period under consideration, the activities of the immigrants from Brihuega and the context in which they took place do shed much light on the history of a city that played a prominent role in the development of New Spain. The focus here, however, is more on people than on place, although the real premise of this book is that the two are inextricably linked. My general intent is to describe the personal and human dimensions of socioeconomic, political, and cultural institutions and forms of organization and to examine how immigrants individually and collectively maintained and modified these patterns and preserved a distinctive sense of community and identity as they moved from one locality in the Spanish empire to another.

This book clearly bears a close relationship to my work on emigration from Extremadura. There are some obvious parallels and connections between these studies, particularly in terms of the basic mechanisms by which people emigrated and the crucial role that family and kinship relationships and objectives played in shaping and facilitating the movement from Spain to the Indies. This book is not, however, just another version of my earlier one in a new guise; rather this study of the people of Brihuega and their experiences in New Spain complements and extends my earlier work. The focus of *Emigrants and Society* was the impact of the movement of people to Spanish America, and their consequent involvement in the Indies enterprise, on local society in Extremadura. Here the principal emphasis is almost reversed. I consider local society in Brihuega in order to understand how it shaped the activities and expectations of the briocenses who departed. These people in turn had a significant impact on the way Puebla developed, while at the same time their choices and experiences reflected the process of adaptation to their new home.

Like *Emigrants and Society*, this study of Brihuega and Puebla is offered as a contribution to a growing literature that is concerned not only with emigration but also with the larger, and arguably more interesting, question of the relationship between early modern European societies and the developing societies of the Americas. This topic is so complex and until recently was so relatively neglected, at least by historians of Spain and Spanish America, that it readily accommodates a variety of approaches. George Foster's *Culture and Conquest*, published in 1960, has by no means been superseded, and it continues to be quite relevant to the question of how to understand the process of transference and transformation of material culture in the expanding Hispanic world. Historians of Britain and the British colonies of the Americas have taken considerable interest in the connections between the societies of the metropolis and the colonies. Earlier scholars who addressed this topic, such as Sumner Chilton Powell, may have benefited from the nature of the available records and the relative advantages of scale in looking at a small region such as New England.[10] More recent work, such as James Horn's on the seventeenth-century Chesapeake, *Adapting to a New World*, is far more ambitious and complex, requiring painstaking research in varied sources on both sides of the Atlantic. The study of the relationship between Spain and Spanish America, by comparison, is still at a fairly early stage. Recent work by Juan Javier Pescador on the long-term impact on local Basque society of its involvement with the Indies and by Amanda Angel on women emigrants to New Spain in the sixteenth century represent significant additions to a field that offers a host of possibilities for scholarly research.[11] It is my hope that this study of the relationship between a modest town in the Alcarria in Castile and a thriving city in Spanish America is a worthwhile contribution to the historical literature on how people forged and experienced the connection between the distinctive parts of the Hispanic world.

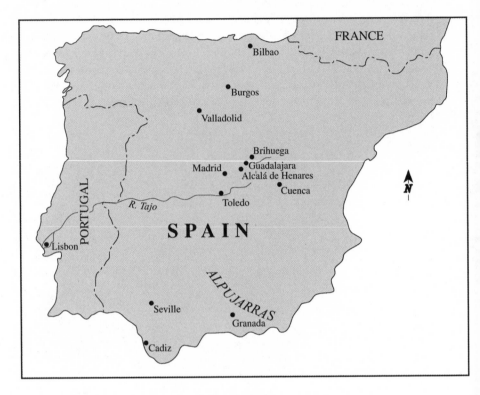

MAP I. *Spain*

CHAPTER ONE

Settlement, Space, and Mobility

In the latter part of the sixteenth century, developments in Brihuega, a town of approximately 4,000 inhabitants located some 30 kilometers northeast of Guadalajara in New Castile, propelled perhaps 1,000 or more of its residents to central New Spain, where nearly all of them remained. They made their home in Puebla de los Angeles, the rapidly developing city that was second only to Mexico City as a center for Spanish society in New Spain. There most of them attained a degree of prosperity that almost certainly would have eluded them had they remained in Brihuega. The very considerable influx of artisans, entrepreneurs, and their families left its mark on Puebla. This sizable immigrant community contributed substantially to the expansion of Puebla's textile industry, and frequent marriages within the group, extensive kinship and *compadrazgo* relations, joint business undertakings, and strong participation in Puebla's commercial and industrial sector enabled it to maintain a visible and fairly coherent presence in the city for at least two or three generations.

The experiences of some of these people shed much light on the nature, sources, and implications of the migration to New Spain when they are considered in the context of the circumstances in which they took place and to which they responded. The story of one fairly modest emigrant and his family can serve to initiate this examination of the interplay between individual and collective experience, and between specific circumstances and the broader context of local society, Castile, and the Spanish empire.

A Family in the Empire

In March 1581 a cloth shearer (*tundidor*) named Sebastián de Pliego from Brihuega wrote from New Spain to his wife, María Díaz, urging her to make the necessary arrangements to travel with their daughters in the company of her brother and one of his own to join him in Puebla de los Angeles. He also wrote to his brother Pablo de Pliego, repeating many of the instructions he had given his wife regarding the sale of property in Tendilla, a town south of Brihuega, and legal and other preparations for the journey.[1] Earlier letters he had written to both of them right after he arrived in Puebla have not survived. The lengthy and detailed directives in the letters to his wife and brother included the suggestion that a husband might be sought for one daughter, but in writing to his brother, Pliego of course omitted some clumsy if touching verses meant to express his loving devotion to his wife.

Sebastián de Pliego and María Díaz probably had been apart for only about a year, a relatively short interlude by the standard of many marriages interrupted by the emigration of one partner in that era. Unlike many husbands thus disencumbered of spouses and families and content to let supposedly temporary separations stretch on for years, Pliego yearned for a speedy reunion. His affection for his wife pervades the letter: "I will say no more than that I wish to see you with my eyes before I die. All that there is would not pay for the tears I have shed for you day after day. Say, I would like to see you count, to be sure you wouldn't say 30 is more than 40."[2]

If the warmth and strength of Pliego's sentiments seem unusual, certainly his objective and the means by which he proposed to carry it out were commonplace in the sixteenth-century movement of people between Spain and the Indies. Almost from the outset it was standard (although not, of course, invariable) for a man first to go on his own and settle in before sending money for other family members to join him, or returning to get them himself, or entrusting the responsibility to a relative or close acquaintance. Relatives typically traveled together for convenience and security. Pliego probably went to New Spain with his brother Francisco de Pliego, also a cloth shearer; in 1580 Francisco obtained a license to go to the Indies with his wife, Quitería de Ubeda, also a native of Brihuega, and their children, Francisco, Sebastián, and Mariana.[3] His brother-in-law Juan Martínez, another cloth shearer, husband of his sister Floriana de Pliego, was in Puebla by 1583 and possibly had accompanied them as well, although without his family.

Sebastián de Pliego's move and his effort to bring other members of his family to Puebla were unusual in one way, for when he wrote to his wife in

1581, she was living in the town of Mecina de Buen Varón and his brother Pablo was a *vecino* (citizen) of the neighboring town of Yator, both in the Alpujarras. This was an isolated, mountainous region east of Granada, some 400 kilometers due south of Brihuega. In the early 1570s several members of the family—Sebastián de Pliego and his wife, his brother Pablo and his family (but apparently not their brother Francisco), and his wife's father, Hernando Díaz, and her brother Baltasar Díaz—had departed Brihuega as part of a substantial group headed not to Seville and from there across the Atlantic to America but rather to the Alpujarras, which until recently had been a stronghold of Morisco settlement and silk production. As was true for the people who left Brihuega for New Spain at almost exactly the same time, the families that went to the Alpujarras intended to relocate there permanently, or at least for the foreseeable future. The participation of people from Brihuega in the resettlement of the Alpujarras after the expulsion of the Moriscos offers an intriguing parallel to the simultaneous formation of the briocense immigrant community in Puebla de los Angeles because of its timing, its dimensions, and the strikingly collective nature of the two phenomena.

Sebastián de Pliego was born around 1542. Probably in the early 1560s he was examined in the cloth shearing trade and set up his own shop in Brihuega.[4] The town's economy was far from flourishing, and the same must have been true of Pliego; many years later, in 1612, his wife noted in her will that neither of them had brought anything to the marriage: "Neither he nor I had any property because we married in poverty in the said town of Brihuega."[5] After a decade or so of work, the couple perhaps judged their prospects to be no better than when they had started. They joined more than 50 other vecinos from Brihuega who decided to relocate in the Alpujarras, doubtless in response to an official campaign to resettle that region, which had been virtually depopulated after the expulsion of its rebellious Morisco inhabitants.[6] Brihuega may have attracted the attention of recruiters because of its reputation as a textile producer, since the preservation of the silk industry of the Alpujarras was central to the crown's resettlement policy. Brihuega's textile manufacturers, however, almost exclusively produced woolen cloth, with perhaps some linen on a limited scale.[7] Despite the likelihood that the briocenses had no experience in silk production, the terms offered to potential colonists clearly were sufficiently appealing to attract many of them. Settlers were to be assigned property that at a minimum would include a house, irrigated land with vineyards and mulberry trees, and land for cultivating wheat. They might also receive draft animals and tools with which to begin cultivation and in return would pay an annual *censo perpetuo* to the royal treasury in the amount of one real per house and a percentage of the harvest.[8]

Most of the briocense recruits settled in the town of Mecina de Buen Varón, which they colonized almost single-handedly, although there were a few vecinos from other places. In June 1572, 54 individuals were listed as having agreed to pay the censo perpetuo; the group included two widows (probably with children), but the majority no doubt were married men, the kind of settlers who were sought in particular.[9] The repetition of surnames within the group suggests that many of the colonists shared kinship ties, and not surprisingly, the scanty evidence available shows that the children of relocated briocenses intermarried in the years after they established themselves there.

After the initial agreement to relocate was signed, some adjustments and substitutions were made, but they do not seem to have affected greatly the overall number of prospective vecinos. Fifty-seven individuals signed the final "carta de censo y tributo" prepared in Mecina de Buen Varón, including Sebastián de Pliego and his father-in-law, Hernando Díaz. Blas Mateo, whom Pliego mentioned in his letters to his wife and brother, saying that Mateo's brother in Puebla urged him to come and would pay his passage ("his brother says he should be a man, and venture to come"), was one of the town's *regidores* (a member of the town council). Other briocenses became vecinos of the smaller neighboring village of Yegen, including two who received quite substantial allotments of three *suertes* each. In 1576 Sebastián's brother Pablo de Pliego became a vecino of the village of Yator, which was contiguous with Yegen and Mecina and had 23 vecinos; very likely he arrived in the Alpujarras after the group that went mainly to Mecina. Mecina had "211 casas de moriscos" and two ovens for baking bread, as well as mills for grinding wheat and pressing olives. Sebastián de Pliego's allotment included a house next to an *alberca* (pond or reservoir) that supplied water for spinning silk, an orchard behind the house next to one assigned to his father-in-law, and other irrigated orchards with mulberry trees as well as land for grapevines and fig trees and unirrigated land.

Despite the attractions of the Alpujarras, a few years there apparently convinced Sebastián de Pliego that he would be better off elsewhere; he must not have been practicing his original trade, and the adjustment to a quite different way of life probably proved difficult. His brother Francisco, who had remained in Brihuega, surely was aware (as nearly everyone there must have been by that time) of the successful experiences of their compatriots in the textile trade who had gone to Puebla; possibly he persuaded Sebastián to move on to New Spain. Since Francisco took his family with him in 1580, he must have felt fairly confident about his decision to leave Castile. Their brother Pablo seems to have had more ambivalent feelings about making a second move. In October 1581 he appeared with his sister-in-law María Díaz in the town of Ugijar, near Mecina de Buen Varón, where she made the deposition she needed to secure a license to go to New Spain with her children. At that time Pablo stated that he was a vecino of Mecina de Buen Varón (rather than Yator); one month later he was in Brihuega to make his own deposition and apply for a license to go to New Spain with his wife and children, accompanying Sebastián's wife. Yet he did not go to the Indies for at least another twelve years, during which time he probably continued to live in the Alpujarras. In Puebla in 1593 his brothers Francisco and Sebastián and brother-in-law Juan Martínez authorized Hernando de Carmona, a vecino of Seville, to provide Pablo de Pliego 300 pesos to cover the cost of traveling to the Indies with his family.[10] No record of his presence in Puebla has been found, however, nor did he return to Brihuega,[11] so perhaps he remained in the Alpujarras. Certainly other briocenses did, relocating within the area but not necessarily abandoning it, a process that seems to have gotten under way almost from the time they first arrived, as settlers attempted to find the most favorable situation. Members of the intermarried Arroyo, Manzano, and Peregrina families, for example, were living in Mecina, Yegen, and Lanjarón in 1585.[12] In his letter of 1581 to his wife, Sebastián de Pliego sent greetings to "everyone in Mecina in general" and "everyone in Ahudia, may God watch over them."

In addition to Sebastián de Pliego's wife and five daughters, one other member of the family went to New Spain in the 1580s: Sebastián's sister Floriana de Pliego, the wife of Juan Martínez, petitioned for a license to go to New Spain in 1584, stating that her husband had sent money for her and their children to join him. One witness in Brihuega described her and her children during her husband's absence as "poor and very needy."[13] Floriana de Pliego was in Puebla with her husband by 1586.[14]

Both Sebastián and Francisco de Pliego worked at their trades from the time they arrived in Puebla. Sebastián spent his first two years working for Diego de Pastrana and Francisco del Castillo, two *obraje* (textile workshop) owners from Brihuega, and by the fall of 1583 had his own cloth shearing shop in the arcades of the city's main plaza. In September 1583 the two brothers, along with their brother-in-law Juan Martínez and three other men (one of whom, Pedro Martínez, probably was Juan Martínez's brother and shared a shop with him), were in prison, having been denounced by Diego de Pastrana for practicing the cloth shearing trade without being properly examined and for being in violation of other ordinances regulating their trade.

Upon paying a bond they secured a speedy release but had to show proof they had been examined. Francisco de Pliego showed his *carta de examen*. Juan Martínez stated that his was in Mexico City and he would send for it. Sebastián de Pliego claimed his was lost—perhaps not surprising, given that he had made two major moves in under ten years—so another briocense testified on his behalf.[15]

Why Diego de Pastrana tried to make trouble for his compatriots is not known. Perhaps resentment of the competition posed by the increasing number of individuals arriving to work in the textile industry was a factor in his decision to bring charges. Pastrana may have been happy enough to have Sebastián de Pliego working for him but less enthusiastic about his going into business on his own. A few years later Francisco de Pliego got into a dispute with another *obrajero*, Rodrigo García, over the terms by which Pliego had agreed to go to Mexico City to buy from their compatriot Mateo de Peregrina 100 "papelones" (probably cardboard forms of some sort) for pressing certain kinds of cloth for García. Pliego claimed that García had agreed to sell him the papelones, and Pliego had agreed to work for him exclusively until he had repaid the equivalent of 100 pesos; García denied any such agreement.[16] Rodrigo García was Diego de Pastrana's nephew. This second dispute suggests that there was bad feeling between these men that possibly stemmed from personal rather than economic issues. Newcomers were constantly arriving from Brihuega from the 1570s through the 1590s, after all, and apart from these episodes there is little indication that they were resented by earlier arrivals; on the contrary, better established immigrants normally provided assistance and employment to newcomers, and many of them recruited relatives and acquaintances to come to work for them.[17] Nonetheless, disputes between members of the immigrant community, especially over financial matters, were not uncommon. The Pliegos seem to have remained somewhat on the margins of the briocense community in Puebla, although the wealthy obrajero Alonso Gómez acted as *padrino* (godfather) at the baptisms of Sebastián de Pliego's children Sebastián and Mariana, born in 1585 and 1587. Alonso Gómez's parents were from Tendilla, the town where the Pliegos owned property, so they may have had kinship ties.[18]

On the whole, Francisco de Pliego appears to have been a more successful businessman than his brother Sebastián. By 1590 he owned an obraje and during the subsequent decade contracted with apprentices and Indian workers, bought and sold African slaves, and in January 1593 made an arrangement with the briocense merchant Juan de Pastrana in Mexico City for Pastrana to sell all the cloth that Pliego sent him from his obraje, in return for which he would pay Pastrana a commission of 400 pesos a year.[19] In addition to obligating himself for at least part of the passage for his brother Pablo and his wife in September 1593, he authorized another vecino of Seville, probably a native of Brihuega, to provide 250 pesos to cover the expenses for the passage of his niece Isabel de Ubeda, a vecina of Brihuega, and her husband and children.[20]

Sebastián de Pliego's economic progress was less impressive. He became a vecino of Puebla in 1584 and served as a *portero* (porter or doorkeeper) for the city council in 1585; in the same year he received a lot on the "street that goes to San Francisco" next to a lot granted to his brother Francisco. He and his wife owned a house in San Francisco, a very commercialized neighborhood northwest of Puebla's main plaza, where many other briocenses also lived and worked. In the 1590s their daughter Magdalena de Pliego and her husband owned a house next door to her parents' house in San Francisco. In 1598 Sebastián de Pliego served as the *mayordomo* of the *cofradía* of María Santísima Nuestra Señora; this image of the Virgin, known as La Conquistadora, was in a chapel of the monastery of San Francisco. María Díaz asked to be buried in the monastery.[21]

Sebastián de Pliego and his wife had seven children—five daughters and two sons—who survived to adulthood. Their daughter María de Pliego received a modest dowry of 200 pesos when she married. In December 1602 her brother Sebastián de Pliego, who was seventeen years old, entered into an apprenticeship with Nicolás Postigo, a silk weaver in Puebla, for a year and a half. The arrangement was made by the briocense Diego del Río as the boy's "tío y administrador."[22] This somewhat surprising choice of apprenticeship suggests that after his father's death little or nothing remained in the way of a family business, or in any case that the younger Sebastián had not been trained in the cloth shearing trade. In 1612 María Díaz stated that her possessions consisted of the house in which she lived, "una negrilla" named Esperanza who was nineteen years old, "and nothing else."[23]

The Pliegos' experiences reflect the kinds of possibilities that the Spanish empire could offer to rather humble townspeople in the latter part of the sixteenth century. Stymied by unfavorable economic circumstances at home but possessing skills and training that could be put to use elsewhere, Sebastián de Pliego and his family were able to take advantage of two quite different opportunities to relocate in search of a more secure existence. In doing so they faced hardship, uncertainty, and separation, all of which they were fortunate enough to survive with their family nearly intact. In Puebla, Sebastián de Pliego and his wife lived near relatives and acquaintances from

Brihuega. If their economic situation did not represent a radical improvement over what they had left behind, their new home at least seems to have afforded them a modicum of comfort and security.

Brihuega in Castile and the Empire

The experiences and choices of the members of this modest and only moderately successful family suggest something about the position of the town of Brihuega and its inhabitants in the region of the Alcarria, the realm of Castile, and the Spanish empire in the last third of the sixteenth century. Brihuega was a point of both attraction and dispersion within these units. It was part of a complex network that tied it to neighboring towns and villages, where briocenses had kin and business dealings and sometimes had originated or would relocate; to more important urban centers such as Toledo, seat of the archbishopric to which it belonged, Alcalá de Henares, site of the university where briocenses sent their sons to study, and Guadalajara, members of whose noble families played some role in local affairs; to the resettled towns of the Alpujarras, one of which, as seen, briocenses colonized almost entirely; and to Puebla de los Angeles, the second most important city of colonial New Spain and the nearly exclusive destination of briocenses who went to the Indies. Much as anthropologists map out a person's kindred by identifying a network of relationships centered on that individual, making Brihuega the focal point of the concentric entities of region, kingdom, and empire sheds light on how its multiple and overlapping relationships functioned. Of course Brihuega did not play a crucial or dominating role in any of those units, but by examining the interactions between the town and its people and the different contexts in which they figured from the point of view of Brihuega, one can better understand the dynamics that shaped society and daily life in that era.

Brihuega lies north of the Tajo River in the Alcarria, the mostly arid plateau east of Madrid dotted by dozens of towns and villages that belonged to a confusing—and in the sixteenth and seventeenth centuries, changing—array of jurisdictions that seem to have had little to do with geographical location as such.[24] Because of its location on the Tajuña River and several local springs, Brihuega's site was attractive and well watered, making it a favorite of some of the archbishops of Toledo, who chose to spend their summers in this "garden of the Alcarria." King Alfonso VI gave the town, where he had once taken refuge from his brother, to the archbishop of Toledo in 1085, and by the thirteenth century it was the head of a district that included six villages.[25] In the sixteenth century that district included

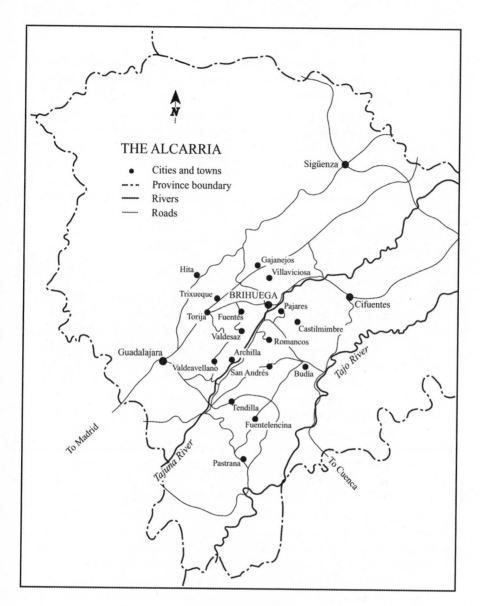

MAP 2. *The Alcarria*

Villaviciosa, Valdesaz, Castillo, Gajanejos, Pajares, Romancos, and San Andrés and the *arrabal* (outlying hamlet) of Malacuera, but although Brihuega remained part of the archbishopric until the mid-1580s, the burgeoning sales of towns to enrich the royal treasury reduced its jurisdiction even before the town itself was directly affected. In 1564 Romancos paid the crown 8,800 *ducados* to separate from Brihuega, although it still belonged to the archbishop. In 1578, however, the crown sold Romancos to Juan Fernández de Herrera, who then sold it to the briocense returnee Diego de Anzures; Anzures owned it only until 1585, when the town opted for self-purchase for another 12,000 ducados. Pajares separated itself from Brihuega in 1579 and San Andrés subsequently did so as well.[26]

During the period from the Middle Ages through the sixteenth century, then, the extent of Brihuega's district varied but over time diminished; a series of suits with the monastery of San Blas in Villaviciosa and the towns of Romancos and San Andrés over property and the rights to collect certain taxes underscore the town's losses in revenues and holdings that accompanied the reduction of its jurisdiction. From the point of view of Brihuega's inhabitants, however, these jurisdictional adjustments probably had little if any impact on their ties to other towns and villages, which in any case seem to have had almost nothing to do with the legal arrangements that defined relationships among towns, villages, and the holders of at least nominal governing authority or with geographical proximity strictly speaking. Place of origin, kinship ties, and economic activity above all seem to have shaped the relations between the vecinos of Brihuega and other places.

The most obvious indication of Brihuega's connections with other towns and cities is the existence of surnames that are place names. *Apellidos* such as Alcalá, Angón, Cifuentes, Guadalajara, Pastrana, Pajares, Torija, and Trixueque were common in Brihuega, and at least in the late sixteenth century vecinos of the same surname as a rule resided in the same parish, strongly suggesting that they had a common origin in another town, or were related, or both.[27] Furthermore, certain surnames that were not place names apparently might be closely associated with particular places. One witness in a deposition on the genealogy of a man from Brihuega who was living in Tlaxcala in New Spain in 1633, for example, claimed that "the surname of the Condados came from the village of Yela and he knows this because he is married in that village."[28]

In themselves surnames are, of course, an unreliable indication of origin or kinship and therefore of little use in analyzing patterns of migration as such. Their presence is not, however, necessarily insignificant. For one thing, the place-name apellidos most commonly found in Brihuega pertain not to the places nearest at hand but rather to fairly good-sized towns lying within the region but at some distance and in different jurisdictions: Guadalajara, Pastrana, and Cifuentes were all better represented among the apellidos of briocenses than were the names of such nearby villages as Pajares and Gajanejos. Doubtless a small village lacked the prestige or at least name recognition that adhered to a city the size of Guadalajara and so might not appeal to a migrant as a surname. Even so, the substantial presence of people who at some point probably came from one or another of these more removed but larger places may imply that Brihuega itself functioned as something of a regional magnet. These place-name surnames also rather roughly define the boundaries of the region within which Brihuega and its people most commonly functioned. That region extended west to Alcalá de Henares, north and east to around Sigüenza and Cifuentes, south to Pastrana and the Tajo, and southwest to Guadalajara.

Brihuega's residents seem to have been most active within this area, commonly going from one town or village to another. They did business, visited friends and relatives, and participated in religious festivals and ceremonial occasions in other localities.[29] An Inquisition case of 1554, for example, involved charges brought against one of a group of vecinos of Romancos who had taken the parts of saints, an angel, Jesus Christ, and two Marías in a tableau staged during a fiesta for San Roque in the town of Retuerta.[30]

Permanent moves, or relocations that lasted for some years, most likely were related to economic opportunities and marriage. People in Brihuega and neighboring towns probably viewed the region as an essentially coherent milieu (notwithstanding jurisdictional distinctions) in which one could relocate with some ease. This perception no doubt helps to account for the many examples of siblings and other close relatives who lived in different towns but still in some proximity. Bach. Alonso Díaz of Fuentelencina, a priest who testified before the Inquisition in 1554, had siblings living in Tendilla, Peñalver, and Fuentelencina, a sister who was in a convent in Cifuentes, and relatives on his mother's side in Pareja. A man named Luis González, originally from Brihuega, was a vecino of Cifuentes when he was brought before the Inquisition in the early 1520s. One of his brothers, a physician, lived in Hita, and he had a sister in Cifuentes and brothers in Cogolludo.[31]

Most of the Inquisition cases of the early sixteenth century were brought against *conversos*, who were prominently associated with the kind of commercial activity that required a fair degree of mobility and thus had a wide circle of geographical contacts. In the Middle Ages, Brihuega had active communities of Jews and Muslims, with a synagogue (to this day the town has a "calle de la Sinoga" [*sic*]) and mosque. So essential were Jews considered to the commercial life of the town that one archbishop changed the market day from Saturday to Wednesday, not only so that people who came to market would be less likely to miss mass the following day but also (explicitly) to ensure that Jews would not be prevented from participating because of their Saturday observance of the Sabbath.[32] In 1436 the *chantre* (choirmaster) of the church of Sigüenza, acting as *visitador* (inspector) in the archbishopric of Toledo, contended that despite prohibitions against Jews, Muslims, and Christians living and working together, Jews and Muslims commonly worked for Christians in Brihuega and took their meals with them. His complaint suggests that in this period members of all groups interacted quite freely. García López notes that there is no indication of anti-Jewish violence in the towns of the Alcarria in the late Middle Ages.[33] This tradition of fairly peaceable relations doubtless encouraged many conversos to remain in the region in the late fifteenth and sixteenth centuries.

Inquisition cases involving some of these individuals provide insight into the kind of local and regional movement that must have been fairly ordinary, especially among the entrepreneurial groups. Luis González, who was called a "cristiano nuevo de judío," was the son of a trader (*tratante*), and one of his brothers, who lived in Brihuega, and an uncle in Cogolludo were also traders.[34] Some of the witnesses against González lived in Tomellosa, where González probably went on business. A lengthy case prosecuted in the years 1516–21 against González's father-in-law, Juan Beltrán, who was accused of heresy and apostasy and eventually "relaxed" (that is, handed over to the secular authorities to be executed), reveals similar kinds of connections and contacts within the region.[35]

Juan Beltrán was a merchant, said to be 85 years old at the time charges were brought against him.[36] Beltrán had a son named Francisco who was married and living in Cifuentes, a married daughter living in Uceda, and another married son in Puente del Arzobispo. One of the witnesses who testified against Beltrán was a woman married to a *labrador* (farmer) who was a vecino of Villaviciosa; she said she had lived with Beltrán and his wife, Leonor, for fourteen months, presumably as a domestic servant. Other witnesses who were vecinos of Valdesaz, Fuentes, Valconete, and Olmeda testified regarding Beltrán's activities in their towns. Witnesses that Beltrán presented on his behalf included vecinos of Hontanar, Valdesaz, Archilla, Budía, and Brihuega and a friar in Villaviciosa, and persons whom he named as possible enemies lived in Tomellosa, Valconete, and Valdesaz. Evidently Beltrán's circle of acquaintances included some prominent individuals, such as a "cardinal" who came to Brihuega and stayed in his house; among the people who testified on his behalf in 1518 were the parish priests of San Miguel and San Felipe in Brihuega, several of the town's hidalgos, and doña Luisa de la Cerda, a nun, who stated that Beltrán had received Franciscan friars in his home. The details of this case and its perplexing outcome aside,[37] the testimony shows that Beltrán maintained extensive contacts with people in other towns lying within a fairly circumscribed area.

Locality and Kinship

The kinship ties that linked people living in different places could have a continuing impact on personal and economic decision making and could survive for many years in memory even when contact was minimal. People sometimes managed to stay in touch to a rather surprising degree and in doing so created or bolstered the connections between places that might be fairly distant.[38] The lengthy investigation into the family background of Esteban Ballesteros of Tlaxcala in New Spain, who in 1623 hoped to attain the office of *familiar* of the Inquisition, suggests some of the connections that individuals who had relocated could forge.[39] Ballesteros, the son of Esteban Ballesteros and María Gutiérrez, left Brihuega for New Spain around 1613. His parents were labradores who lived in San Juan, the smallest and probably most agriculturally oriented of Brihuega's parishes. Toward the end of their lives they had gone to live in the nearby village of Trixueque, where one of their sons was serving as parish priest.

Much of the testimony elicited centered on the antecedents of Ballesteros's mother, whom many thought to have been conversos. Her father, Diego Gutiérrez, had been a labrador but also a collector of *alcabalas* (sales taxes) and tithes.[40] In Archilla, on the road to Brihuega, he and several vecinos of Romancos were co-owners of houses, vineyards, and wine cellars. Diego Gutiérrez's grandfather had been *corregidor,* or royal representative, of Archilla. Esteban Ballesteros's paternal grandmother, Catalina Martínez, also was from Archilla. After she married in Brihuega, according to a witness who was a vecino of Archilla, she often returned to the village to visit her relatives.

Diego Gutiérrez, Esteban Ballesteros's maternal grandfather, had served in various official capacities in Brihuega, including terms as *procurador general* (general representative) of the *pecheros* (taxpayers, or commoners), *jurado* (representative of a parish) of the general town council, and *alcalde* (magistrate) of the council of the parish of San Miguel; Diego's brother, Alonso Gutiérrez, had been a *regidor* (town councilman).[41] In Brihuega in

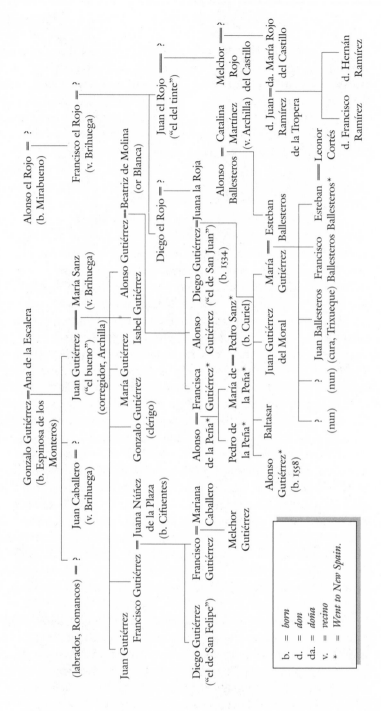

FIGURE 1. *Family of Esteban Ballesteros*

b. = *born*
d. = *don*
da. = *doña*
v. = *vecino*
* = *Went to New Spain.*

1592 Diego Gutiérrez called himself a "vecino de Valdeavellano y desta villa" (Valdeavellano is very close to Archilla) and stated that his son Alonso Gutiérrez had gone to New Spain twelve years before. In 1580, at the age of 22, Alonso Gutiérrez, the brother of Ballesteros's mother, had presented an *información* (deposition) in Brihuega in 1580 with the intention of securing a license to go to the Indies.

Esteban's brother, Juan Ballesteros, the *cura* (parish priest) of Trixueque, furnished a copy of this uncle's deposition to the officials conducting the inquiry into Esteban's family background. He also submitted the *información de limpieza* (deposition of purity, i.e., of blood) compiled by Melchor Gutiérrez, a great-grandson of Juan Gutiérrez "el bueno," which he had prepared when he was trying to enter the monastery of San Francisco in Cifuentes. Juan Gutiérrez el bueno, Esteban's great-great-grandfather, had served as the mayordomo of the archbishop of Toledo and corregidor of Archilla. Juan Gutiérrez was born in Espinosa de los Monteros, a town near Burgos. He accompanied his father, Gonzalo Gutiérrez, a master builder, when the latter went "to do construction and work in his trade of stonecutting [near Guadalajara], where he [Gonzalo] left him [Juan]."[42] At least one person said that the work that Juan's father undertook was in Brihuega itself. Juan Gutiérrez, also called "maestro de cantería" (master stonecutter), stayed on after his father returned home and married María Sanz, said to have been quite wealthy. At some point other family members joined him; one of his sisters married in Romancos and another in Brihuega.

Some of the information on Juan Gutiérrez el bueno comes from testimony compiled for the información of yet another family member who in 1552 apparently intended to go to the Indies, Esteban Ballesteros's grandfather Diego Gutiérrez, who was born in 1534.[43] One of the witnesses in the deposition recalled that 40 years earlier he had accompanied Juan Gutiérrez back to his hometown, where he saw him talk with his relatives and other vecinos of Espinosa. Pedro Durón, who at 76 had been a contemporary of Juan Gutiérrez, also said that Gutiérrez had gone to visit his hometown and that he had seen him with people from Espinosa who came to Brihuega. A witness in Espinosa, in his 80s, testified in a deposition compiled by Esteban Ballesteros's brother and brother-in-law in the 1630s that he had heard that Juan Gutiérrez had gone to live in "the district of Guadalajara" and was a master stonecutter and that he used to come to Espinosa to visit his family. Another witness recalled that when Juan Gutiérrez visited his parents, "he came very well dressed because in the construction projects [*obras*] that his father had left him he had profited considerably."

Witnesses in Espinosa also knew that a vecino of the town named Pedro de Velasco had arranged for one of his daughters to marry either a son or a grandson of Juan Gutiérrez. He did so because "as natives of this town they [the families] had dealings with each other and stayed in touch and married one another." Another witness confirmed these ties between the families: "he heard it said that they had made the said marriage because they were all natives and descendants of the same place ["de una tierra"] and because people of one name ["apellido"] would commonly marry in order to conserve [the lineage] and because they were from the same place." Another stated that when María de Velasco married a son (or grandson) of Juan Gutiérrez, "compatriots and people from the same place had married, conserving their origins."

There is evidence, then, that Juan Gutiérrez's descendants maintained some ties with his place of origin. By staying on in Brihuega when his father returned home to Espinosa de los Monteros, Juan Gutiérrez el bueno created a branch of the family that in the future would be associated with a new locality. Kinship and other traditional relations (as between the Velasco and Gutiérrez families) attracted others from his hometown to the area around Brihuega as well—Juan Gutiérrez's sisters in addition to a daughter- or granddaughter-in-law and visitors from Espinosa. Gutiérrez's activities in and around Brihuega also set precedents for the family's future. His relationship with the archbishop of Toledo, whom he served as corregidor and mayordomo, probably resulted from his work as a master builder; it in turn fostered a connection between the Gutiérrez family in Brihuega and the nearby village of Archilla, where they had property (Archilla is on the Tajuña River, about halfway between Brihuega and Guadalajara) and other places such as Romancos and Valdeavellano. Eventually the family would extend itself again, this time much farther, to New Spain. Esteban Ballesteros went to New Spain 30 years after his uncle Alonso Gutiérrez, whose father, Diego Gutiérrez, may also have gone to the Indies; certainly he considered going. In the interim between the departure of Alonso Gutiérrez and his nephew Esteban Ballesteros, a family who were probably their cousins also relocated to New Spain.

The inquiry made in 1662 into the antecedents of another individual whose roots were in Brihuega vividly demonstrates how contacts and memories endured even when families relocated to far distant places. The case involved a man who was born in New Spain, Dr. don Joseph de Carmona Tamariz, *racionero* (prebendary) of the cathedral of Puebla, and his brothers. Their maternal grandparents, Alonso Gómez and Catalina de Pastrana,

FIGURE 2. *Family of Alonso Gómez*

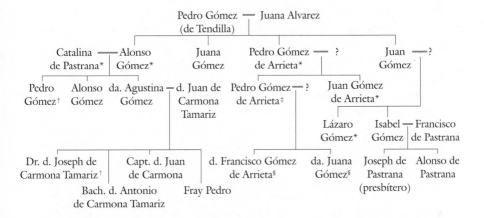

---

*Went to New Spain.   ‡Went to New Spain and returned to Castile.
†Born in Puebla, visited Brihuega.   §Born in Puebla, went to live in Brihuega.

had immigrated to Puebla from Brihuega nearly a century before.[44] The investigation carried out under the auspices of the Inquisition of Toledo focused on the antecedents of Dr. Carmona's grandparents. An 84-year-old vecino of Brihuega named Melchor de Lucio recalled that Alonso Gómez's father was from Tendilla.[45] Pedro Alvarez de Castro also testified that "he heard his parents who are now dead say that Alonso Gómez was a native of this town and had his origins in Tendilla by reason of his father having come from there." Another witness stated that he had heard of Dr. Carmona's mother, doña Agustina Gómez, "from many people from this town who live in the said city [of Puebla] who are natives of this town who go [there] and come [back]." Alonso de Alcalá, a 37-year-old notary of Brihuega, stated that "he has heard it commonly said in this town both from very old people who are now deceased and from others who have come from the Indies that the said Alonso Gómez and Catalina de Pastrana his wife were from this town." In Tendilla a man named Pedro Hernández Ballestero testified that he recalled his deceased parents saying that "one Gómez" who was a close relative of his own grandmother (although he did not know in what degree) had gone to live in Brihuega with his wife, Juana Alvarez. He had heard that they had children; he did not know their names, only that they had left Brihuega to live in the Indies. A vecina of Tendilla who was originally from Romancos testified that her mother-in-law, Ana Hernández Gómez, had said "many times" that she had relatives in the Indies. Another woman recalled hearing her father say that relatives of his had gone to live in Brihuega and that one of their sons went to the Indies and "was very rich," but she did not know his name or where he was. Another witness, named Alonso Gómez, had heard almost the same from his father, who seven or eight years before had gone to Brihuega and spoken to a descendant of the Gómez who went to the Indies who was visiting in Brihuega, and "they treated each other as relatives."

Many people in Brihuega recalled Dr. Carmona's visit, as it had occurred quite recently. As would be expected, he had sought out his relatives; Felipe Tartajo, a 78-year-old labrador, said that Carmona had come to Brihuega "to meet his relatives" ("reconocer a sus parientes")." Probably these were mainly people on his grandfather's side, with whom the family in New Spain maintained much closer contact than with his grandmother's relatives. One of his grandfather Alonso Gómez's brothers, Pedro Gómez, also had gone to New Spain, where one of his sons (also Pedro Gómez) later joined him. The younger Pedro Gómez subsequently returned to Brihuega with his children, two of whom testified in the información. One of them, Francisco Gómez de Arrieta, said he had been born in Puebla and as a child he had known Dr. Carmona there. Dr. Carmona visited and spoke with many other people in Brihuega as well. Lic. Cristóbal de Soria y Velasco, the town's archpriest and vicar, met Carmona and said he had heard about Carmona's mother and grandparents from people who had come from New Spain to Brihuega. A merchant named Cristóbal Alvarez Viñuelas knew Dr. Carmona during the five years that he had spent in the Indies, having lived for seven months in Puebla in 1648 in the house of Lázaro Gómez, a first cousin of Carmona's mother, doña Agustina Gómez. Doña Agustina's brother Pedro Gómez at one time visited Brihuega and took Lázaro Gómez to New Spain with him when he returned to Puebla.

This family kept alive the memory and knowledge of people who had moved from Tendilla to Brihuega and then from Brihuega to the Indies through letters, word of mouth, visits, and the return of people who had lived or even been born in New Spain. Although inquiries into the family of Dr. Carmona's maternal grandmother, Catalina de Pastrana, took place at the same time as those regarding Alonso Gómez, they did not yield anything like the detailed information that vecinos—many of whom were in fact relatives—provided about members of the Gómez family. Witnesses failed to agree on whether there were one, two, or even as many as five distinct Pastrana families and to which one Carmona's grandmother had belonged. Nor did there emerge any clear indication of the origins of any of the Pastranas or how long they had been in Brihuega. The very different kind of information elicited about the two families suggests that in the absence of some effort to maintain family ties and contacts, any awareness of them and recollection of family history faded rapidly from individual and collective consciousness.

Relocation and Separation

In the two cases just discussed, relocation apparently benefited not just the individuals who made the initial move but a number of their relatives and members of succeeding generations as well. These were migrant success stories. Leaving his hometown brought Juan Gutiérrez el bueno profitable employment, a fortunate marriage, and a prestigious association with the archbishop; the grandsons of Alonso Gómez and Catalina de Pastrana entered into the highest ranks of society in Puebla, attaining key positions in the cathedral chapter and the city council. Migration and relocation, however, did not always equate with progress and success. The separation of spouses and families could cause great stress, economic as well as psychological, for migrants, and probably was even more stressful for family members left behind. One can sympathize with Sebastián de Pliego's loneliness when he was separated from his wife and children by thousands of miles, but the difficulties that María Díaz must have experienced in making two major moves with her children within a decade—the second of them perhaps mainly on her own, since there is no evidence that either her brother or her brother-in-law accompanied her to New Spain—surely were far more severe than anything her husband endured.

Considerable disruption and uncertainty could arise from a family member's decision to migrate. The departure of someone who may have been a family's primary source of labor or income, the uncertainties of communication, and the possibility that distance and new circumstances and opportunities would erode marital and familial bonds of affection, obligation, and loyalty all meant that people could find themselves stranded or abandoned (even if only temporarily), forced to fend for themselves and to make decisions on their own, rather than with the support and cooperation of other family members. Women whose husbands departed for the Indies and who were barely able to support themselves and their children at home would hardly be likely to find the means to emigrate unless their husbands came or sent for them.

Certainly the seeming abandonment of women and children did not necessarily mean a callous denial of responsibility on the part of male migrants but rather in many cases resulted from an effort to find some long-term solution to intractable economic difficulties.[46] When Francisca Gutié-rrez petitioned for a license to go to New Spain to join her husband in 1590, for example, she explicitly stated that he had left because he could not support his family in Brihuega. He did well enough in Puebla to send for his family after several years, but while he was absent she and her children, according to witnesses, suffered great deprivation.[47] The situation of Juana Gutiérrez and her husband, Cristóbal de Pastrana, was similar. Pastrana went to the Indies in the early 1570s on some unspecified business and stayed on in Mexico City as a merchant. By 1577 Audiencia officials had initiated proceedings against him to force him to leave for Spain to live with his wife. Pastrana, however, claimed that he had left Brihuega with his wife's consent "because they were poor and burdened with children." Juana Gutiérrez herself protested that it would be a hardship on the family if her husband were to leave Mexico, as he would return with little money. Pastrana sent money and his wife's nephew to bring her and their three daughters and two sons to New Spain.[48]

Relocating family members when resources were limited could create serious problems, as in the case of two women from Fuentelencina. One of them, Catalina Rodríguez, was the sister of Melchor Rodríguez, who went to Puebla in 1594 and essentially functioned as a member of the briocense community there.[49] In 1601 Catalina and her sister-in-law Ana López, Melchor Rodríguez's wife, petitioned for a license to go to the Indies with Catalina's daughter Agustina, Ana's son Juan, and their nephew Juan Rodríguez.[50] At that time they had been waiting in Seville for over a year and had been unable to secure a license to depart.[51] According to witnesses, they also had been unable to get the money that Melchor Rodríguez sent them for the passage; the person holding the money would not hand it over until they had the license. Catalina and her sister-in-law had gone to Seville with Catalina's husband, Alonso Rodríguez,[52] who decided that because of their difficult circumstances ("porque pasaban hambre y malaventura") he should travel to New Spain by himself to get help ("por socorro"), leaving the women and children in Seville. Caught in this bizarre situation where they could not depart without money but could not get the money that was rightfully theirs to live on until they obtained authorization to leave, they asked for permission to emigrate in 1601 to resolve their dire situation ("atento que pasan extrema necesidad"). With both their husbands already in New Spain, joining them must have seemed preferable to the alternative of returning to Brihuega with no support or relief in sight.

Some immigrants, of course, were perhaps unwilling rather than unable to send for their spouses. In 1575 Gracia de Pliego applied for a license to go to the Indies with her seven children to join her husband, Alonso Díaz, a cloth shearer who had left Brihuega two years before and had sent for them. Her son-in-law Andrés González was to accompany her with his wife and child.[53] González and his family went, but Gracia de Pliego did not. In 1587 her husband, Alonso Díaz, stated that eight years earlier the authorities had wanted to send him to Castile for his wife because of his unruly behavior ("andaba inquieto"). Although Díaz did go to Spain as ordered, he apparently still did not bring his wife back with him. When she finally arrived, in 1580, Alonso Díaz did not go to meet her but instead left the arrangements for her journey to Puebla in the hands of his son or son-in-law,[54] suggesting an indifference far removed from Sebastián de Pliego's anxious anticipation of his wife's arrival.

Not only spouses but children also suffered from the stress and turmoil of separation and abandonment. In the early 1570s Diego de Pastrana said that he had received a license to go to New Spain with his wife and children and to take with them the four children of his brother-in-law Juan García Rodrigo, who was already in the Indies. Juan García Rodrigo had been married to Diego de Pastrana's sister Mariana Lagúnez, who must not have been living when he left for the Indies around 1571.[55] Diego de Pastrana subsequently requested that his license be modified to include only two of Juan García Rodrigo's children; one son had left, his whereabouts unknown, and Pastrana's parents had their little granddaughter living with them and refused to let her accompany their son.[56]

Rodrigo García, the missing son, had worked for three years for a man named Hernando de Machuca, but he left Brihuega without completing his term of service. Witnesses testified in 1573 that he had been gone eight or nine months. Francisco de Brihuega said he had run into Rodrigo García in Oropesa, "40 leagues from this town," and wanted to bring him back with him, but he would not agree to come. Another witness, Francisco de la Carrera, said that in June 1572 he encountered Rodrigo García "on the other side of San Bartolomé de Lupiana" and that García had gone with him to Corche. When he inquired where he was going, Rodrigo told him "he was going to work somewhere around there and if he didn't find employment he would go to Seville to look for his father." After that Carrera never saw him again. Eventually he reached New Spain, possibly having rejoined his uncle in Seville, as this undoubtedly was the same Rodrigo García who eventually became a wealthy obrajero and a regidor on Puebla's city council.[57] Children whose parents were absent or deceased were likely to be neglected or exploited if there was no one to look out for them. When Gonzalo Díaz applied for a license in 1573 to go with his wife, Isabel de Molina, and their children to New Spain, where two of his brothers were living, he asked permission to take his brother Gil Díaz, "considering that he is young and in this country he will be lost, and going to New Spain to be with my brothers he will be protected because he doesn't have a father or mother."[58]

Migrants often went to considerable effort to look after children or siblings and used their circle of contacts in both Castile and New Spain to try to ensure their well-being. In 1605 María de Valhermoso, born in Puebla to Cristóbal de Peñarroja and Elvira de Ortega of Brihuega, left New Spain to go to Castile with her husband, Pedro Martínez de Santiesteban. He was a vecino of Tlaxcala who was originally from the town of Budía, near Brihuega. According to Martín de Lezcano, a bread baker from Brihuega who had become a vecino of Seville, María's father had written to him saying that she and her husband were traveling to Spain and asking him to look after them. Peñarroja later wrote other letters asking them to come back. Gil de Pliego, a vecino of Budía who had lived in Brihuega, said that Peñarroja had written asking him to do anything María and her husband required. Peñarroja sent 1,000 pesos with the briocense Miguel Pérez de Angulo, who was traveling to Castile in 1605 at the same time as María de Valhermoso, instructing him to give the money to his daughter only when she arrived. In 1607 Diego de Sahelices, a vecino of Budía who was originally from Brihuega, said that Pedro de Santiesteban, María's husband, had left Budía ten or eleven years earlier and returned about a year and a half ago with his wife and child. Another vecino of Budía, Alonso Díaz, said that his brothers had written him from the Indies that María and Pedro had married and that they were coming to Spain, and his cousin Melchor Caballero had told him the same when he came from the Indies. María, who was only eighteen years old in 1607, when she and her husband were in Seville trying to get a license to return to New Spain, by then had two children, one of them born in Seville.[59]

María de Valhermoso's father thus did a great deal to ensure a smooth transition for her and her husband when they went to Spain, sending money and letters to people in Budía and Seville, informing his friends of their imminent arrival, and asking them to look out for his daughter. If anything, given that she was already a married woman—albeit a very young one—who was traveling with her husband, Peñarroja's concern seems almost excessive. Yet his uneasiness may have been well founded. One witness in

1607 said that María and her husband wanted to return to New Spain because they were quite poor and she had "very wealthy" relatives there, so perhaps her father had good reason to suspect that they would not be able to make a go of it in her husband's hometown, where they had stayed only about a year and a half.

This episode underscores again the vitality of connections between people in Brihuega and other nearby towns and the way they figured in actions and decisions at home as well as in Puebla and its environs. Brihuega seems to have had close ties to the town of Budía, which was about twenty kilometers to the southeast, although Budía was never part of its jurisdiction and lay within the bishopric of Sigüenza. Some witnesses for María de Valhermoso and her husband had lived in both towns. In testimony related to the paternal grandmother of Pablo Carpintero, an immigrant from Brihuega who was a vecino of Tlaxcala in 1633, one vecino of Budía said he had known her by virtue of having been in her house in Brihuega "many times."[60] Kinship and probably economic activity as well connected the people of the two towns. Melchor Caballero, mentioned by his cousin as having come from the Indies, was the son of Isabel de Brihuega, a woman from Brihuega who had married Francisco Caballero in Budía. Melchor and three of his brothers and a sister went to New Spain. On their mother's side they had relatives from Brihuega who also were in Puebla and with whom they had close ties. Like many of the briocense immigrants, they owned obrajes in Puebla. In most senses the immigrants from Budía functioned as part of the briocense community in Puebla, working together, forming business partnerships, and intermarrying. In 1608, for example, Isabel de Morales, the daughter of Melchor Caballero's sister Ana, married a man from Brihuega, Alonso Caballero, in Puebla.

The same was true of people from other towns of the Alcarria. In 1572 Martín Hernández Cubero wrote from Puebla to his nephew in Fuentelencina mentioning Alonso Hernández and Alonso de Ribas of Brihuega (who had returned to Spain), saying that "we went around together while they were here and were great friends, being all from the same country" ("por ser como éramos de una patria"). María de Pastrana, an immigrant from Tendilla, married a man from Brihuega. Her "tío" Pablo de Pastrana, a prominent obrajero and merchant in Puebla, was originally from a town in the bishopric of Sigüenza and had gone to live in Brihuega, where he had relatives, when he was twelve years old.[61] The sense of identification with the place of origin proved quite enduring. In 1662, for example, a 65-year-old man named Diego de Pareja, who said he was both a vecino and a native of

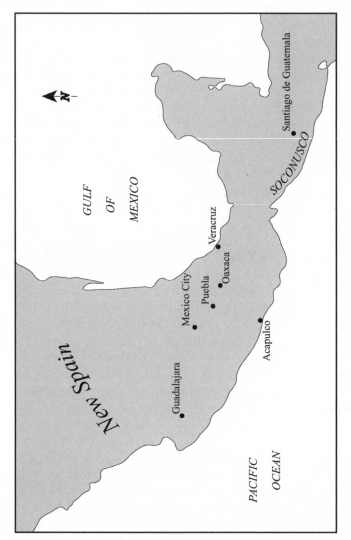

MAP 3. *New Spain*

Puebla, testified that he had known Catalina de Pastrana (wife of Alonso Gómez and grandmother of Dr. Joseph de Carmona Tamariz and his brothers) and had heard that she was from Brihuega; "for that reason and being all from one *patria* they communicated especially for more than 50 years until she died."[62] Born in Puebla but part of the briocense community, Pareja still thought of Brihuega as his homeland.

Settling in New Spain

The immigrant community in New Spain was remarkably cohesive, not only in the network of economic, social, and kinship ties they maintained but geographically as well. The emigrants from Brihuega and their close acquaintances and relatives who left other towns of the Alcarria such as Fuentelencina and Budía overwhelmingly went to New Spain; only a handful of people appear to have chosen Peru as their destination, and some who said they intended to go to Peru nevertheless ended up in New Spain.[63] With few exceptions they made Puebla de los Angeles their home virtually from the outset. A small number of emigrants settled in Mexico City, where they mostly worked as merchants, shopkeepers, and obrajeros. This much smaller group stayed in touch with their compatriots in Puebla, establishing business partnerships, acting as agents for them in a variety of transactions, and selling cloth the obrajeros sent to them, as Juan de Pastrana did for Francisco de Pliego and for other people as well. The reliance of briocenses in Puebla on the services of their compatriots in the capital suggests that the briocense group in Mexico City functioned almost as an extension of the community in Puebla, a variation on the pattern whereby economic enterprises frequently were based in the capital city and extended out from there to secondary and provincial cities.

Some people from Brihuega and other towns of the Alcarria settled in the larger indigenous towns near Puebla, such as Tlaxcala, Cholula, Tepeaca, and Huejotzingo, or in the valley of Atlixco; a few who established estates lived in pueblos nearby.[64] These briocenses, too, maintained ties with the immigrant community in Puebla; for example, Jorge de la Hoz of Brihuega was a vecino of Tlaxcala in 1599 when he married the daughter of the briocense immigrants Martín de Viñuelas and Mariana García, who lived in Puebla. In 1642 Pedro del Molino, a vecino of Totomehuacan originally from Brihuega, married Isabel de Merino, the daughter of briocense immigrants who lived in Puebla; witnesses to the marriage were three other briocense vecinos of Puebla.[65] In the 1590s Isabel Bautista's nephew Benito Sanz

Bautista bought an obraje in Cholula after working for some time in the obraje of her husband, Martín de la Fuente, in Puebla. He would visit and stay with his aunt when business brought him to Puebla, and she and other family members visited Benito Sanz Bautista in Cholula as well. In these towns, as in Mexico City, however, the numbers of immigrants from the Alcarria were small in comparison with the briocense community of Puebla.

Why did the first wave of emigrants from Brihuega decide to make Puebla their new home? Certainly the choice was not inevitable. In retrospect it is clear that the success of the earliest migrants to New Spain in the 1550s and 1560s led them to encourage their relatives and other compatriots to join them. They returned or sent for their own families and recruited other relatives and acquaintances as well. While the momentum that the movement attained and the volume of migration are impressive, given Brihuega's size and location, the way this considerable transfer of people took place was standard for the period. The success of the first migrants, together with the assistance and employment they could offer relatives and compatriots, probably sufficed to make Puebla the first choice of most subsequent emigrants.

Why, though, did the early migrants settle there in the first place? Unfortunately, they did not explain their choice, at least in the records that survive. Possibly the first briocense to establish himself in Puebla was Diego de Anzures, who would become extremely successful and attract a number of other emigrants, including several of his siblings and many other relatives. He went to New Spain in 1555, when he was in his early twenties, in the company of a family friend from Brihuega, Cristóbal Escudero, who had been living in Seville for about ten years. Escudero went to New Spain as a merchant and stayed on in Mexico City, where he became an obrajero. Anzures, however, decided to live in Puebla, where he owned obrajes and also fairly early acquired public office. He served as the notary of the city council (a position he would pass on to a younger brother, Pedro de Anzures) and went on to hold other influential positions in the city. During the nearly 25 years that Diego de Anzures lived in Puebla he remained close to Escudero; he married in Escudero's house in Mexico City in 1561. Possibly on Escudero's advice or even with his backing, Anzures decided to test Puebla's potential for textile manufacture. Puebla, of course, already was producing textiles, yet arguably it was the arrival of the briocenses, especially in the last 30 years of the sixteenth century, that transformed the city into New Spain's leader in the textile industry. Most of the briocenses who went to Puebla in the 1550s and 1560s—including Diego de Anzures and his brothers Macario and Pedro de Anzures, his brother-in-law Juan de Roa, the brothers Alonso and Cristóbal de Ribas and their brother-in-law Andrés de Angulo, Juan de Pastrana, and Juan de Brihuega—were obraje owners.

The decline of the textile industry in Brihuega must have encouraged the town's artisans and entrepreneurs to seek new arenas in which to practice their trades; in Puebla they discovered precisely the kind of opportunity they sought. The migration of people to the Alpujarras in the early 1570s doubtless was a response to the same problems that underlay the move to New Spain. Yet despite its greater distance from home, Puebla offered a much more attractive solution to the briocenses' problems. It had considerable potential for producing woolen cloth (rather than silk, as in the Alpujarras) and an almost ideal location near fertile agricultural land and pastures, as well as on key routes for trade and transportation that connected it to Veracruz, Mexico City, and the Pacific ports and the south. Not only did emigrants find promising economic opportunities in and around Puebla, but the city seemed able to accommodate far more newcomers than the small and isolated villages of the Alpujarras. When after a decade or so this enormous potential became clear, people began to leave Brihuega for Puebla in large numbers and continued to do so for the next half century; the movement tapered off only in the second decade of the seventeenth century. Well beyond that time, however, people in Brihuega continued to look to Puebla as a destination, either temporary or permanent.

Approximately 800 people are known to have left Brihuega for the Indies in the years from the mid-1550s to around 1630.[66] The actual numbers probably are a good bit higher, but the figure excludes individuals whose origins cannot be documented for certain. Starting out with just a handful of early arrivals, probably exclusively male, in the 1550s, the movement gained momentum in the 1560s. In that decade some men who had initially gone to New Spain on their own returned home and brought their families back with them to Puebla. During each of the following four decades an average of around 150 people left for New Spain, the numbers increasing each decade to a peak of 165 emigrants in the 1590s.[67] The composition of the emigrant group changed during those 40 years; the percentage of single young men was highest in the 1570s, although their absolute numbers did not vary a great deal until after 1600, suggesting that Puebla continued to be a significant destination for young men seeking employment and opportunity.[68]

As was the case for the move to the Alpujarras, the notable clustering of departures for New Spain in some years underscores the collective nature

FIGURE 3. *Ribas Family*

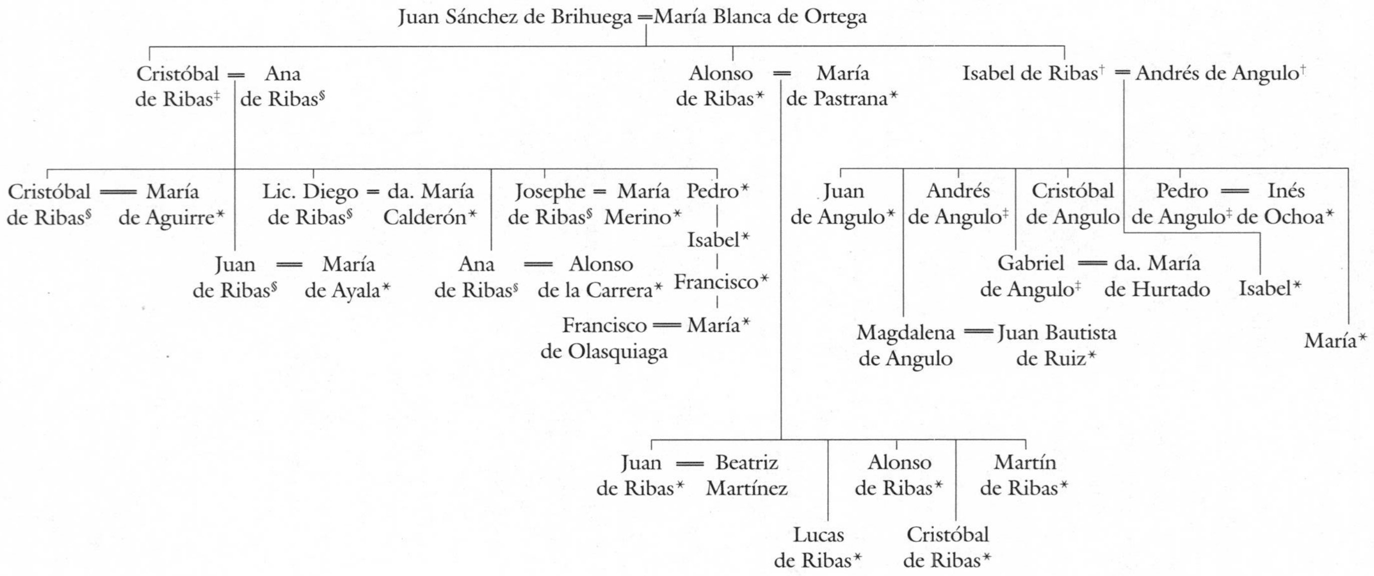

*Went to New Spain.
†Went to New Spain, returned to Brihuega.
‡Went to New Spain, returned to Spain, went back to New Spain
§Born in New Spain, went to Spain, returned to New Spain.

of the movement from Brihuega. More than 60 people went to Puebla in 1573. Many of these emigrants shared kinship ties, and many went to join relatives who had preceded them; a substantial number, in fact, were part of an extended kinship network related to the Anzures family through blood and marriage.[69] At least 30 people departed Brihuega in 1580, nearly that many in 1583, and more than 30 in 1590. In 1593 the entourage of Cristóbal de Ribas, who had returned from Puebla in the early 1570s and decided to go back there, formed the nucleus of another very large migrant group (see Figure 3). That group included Ribas's wife and five unmarried children; his son Cristóbal de Ribas "el mozo" and his wife; another son, Lic. Diego de Ribas, with his wife and daughter; yet another son, Juan de Ribas, with his wife and three children; his daughter Ana de Ribas and her husband, Alonso de la Carrera, and their two children; Alonso de la Carrera's brother Lope de la Carrera with his wife and daughter, who also took his brother Cristóbal as *criado* (servant or retainer); and two other criados from Brihuega, Juan de Córdoba, who accompanied Alonso de la Carrera, and Gabriel de Hita, who went with Lic. Diego de Ribas. Another 28 people joined this group in 1593; 30 more went the following year. Thirty-five migrants departed in 1601 and 30 in 1608. The coordinated departure of such substantial numbers of migrants can have resulted only from deliberate planning and organization. It reflects the intensity and extent of communication of information both in Brihuega and other nearby towns and between the briocenses in Puebla and their relatives and acquaintances back home, and probably the availability of considerable financial support from immigrants already established in Puebla as well.

As in villages, towns, and cities throughout Spain, returnees from the Indies played an important role both in facilitating this flow of information and in directly and indirectly encouraging others to migrate. As suggested, in the case of the Brihuega-Puebla nexus this process began almost immediately; Andrés de Angulo and Alonso de Ribas, for example, had returned to Brihuega and brought their families back to Puebla by the mid-1560s. Francisco González, who was a labrador in the valley of Atlixco, near Puebla, went back to New Spain in 1573 accompanied by his nephew Juan Ponce, a locksmith, and in the same year the Augustinian fray Alonso de Vera Cruz took his nephew Juan de Cifuentes and another young man from Brihuega back with him to New Spain as his criados; Juan de Cifuentes's brother Francisco followed soon after. Visits that resulted in the departure of other relatives occurred regularly throughout the decades in which briocenses were leaving for New Spain.

Some emigrants returned to stay, although other family members might depart subsequently. Three of the sons of Andrés de Angulo and Isabel de Ribas, who returned to Brihuega in the late 1570s, went back to live in Puebla, as did three sons of Juan de Roa and Francisca de Anzures, who had also returned to Spain. Then there were those emigrants such as Cristóbal de Ribas, who returned to Brihuega, stayed for a long time, and then left again. Some people may have felt equally at home in both places. Ribas's son Cristóbal de Ribas el mozo, who was born in New Spain, after returning with his family to Puebla in 1593 visited Brihuega in 1602 and went there again around 1618 with his wife and an orphan girl named Juana whom they had adopted. In 1622, when he and his wife were both around 60 years old, he petitioned for a license for the three of them to go back to New Spain.[70]

Hernando de Roa Anzures, the son of Juan de Roa and Francisca de Anzures, also spent many years in Castile. Born in New Spain in 1574, he must have returned with his parents to Brihuega as a very young child. In 1584 his brothers Juan and Diego went back to live in Puebla, and at some point Hernando must have done so as well. In 1600 he returned to Castile to collect the legacy left by his parents on his own and his brothers' behalf. Presumably he had planned just a short visit, since the next year he requested a license to go to New Spain and to take two criados from Brihuega with him. He received permission to depart in 1602 but never left and apparently did not request a renewal of the license until 25 years later, when he stated that he had been unable to leave earlier because he had married and then become a widower and because of business. He may have lived in Seville for much of that time. In 1627 he asked to take his fourteen-year-old daughter, who had been born in Seville, with him to New Spain to rejoin his brothers.[71]

The number of permanent returnees to Brihuega probably was fairly small. In general they do not appear to have stood out very distinctly, perhaps because the volume of movement between Brihuega and New Spain was so great that departures of emigrants and arrivals of visitors or returnees were commonplace events. Among the permanent returnees probably the most visible was the very individual who initially forged what would become the notably strong connection between Brihuega and Puebla, Diego de Anzures, who left Brihuega in 1555. Anzures, the uncle of the Roa Anzures brothers, returned to Brihuega at the end of the 1570s and spent the remaining twenty-odd years of his life there. Eventually he entered the order of San Juan to become fray Diego de Anzures y Guevara. Active in local political affairs, in which he worked closely with his brother Rodrigo de Anzures (the only one of the brothers who never left Brihuega for the Indies and a frequent officeholder), briefly the *señor* of the nearby town of Romancos, founder of an entail, and father of doña Catalina de Barrientos, who married into a well-connected noble family, Anzures was the most conspicuous of the returnees, just as he probably was the most influential person in shaping the immigrant community in Puebla. These accomplishments endowed his long life and career with an interesting sort of symmetry; he lived more than 80 years.

On the whole, however, most of the returnees appear to have settled in rather unobtrusively. In the 1585 *vecindario* no one appeared with the descriptive "indiano" or "perulero" (back from the Indies), and the 1595 *padrón* (tax assessment list) included only one such example, that of the wife of "Juan de Olivar indiano." Since both lists include individuals known to have returned from the Indies, the omission of the designation may indicate how relatively unremarkable the status was considered to be. Surprisingly, given the very high volume of traffic between Brihuega and Puebla, the town itself appears to have changed little. Returnees did not come to dominate briocense society, economy, or politics.

The briocenses in Puebla, in contrast, were highly visible, the impact of their numbers enhanced not only by their multiple interrelationships but by their residential patterns as well.[72] In the sixteenth century the Spanish population of Puebla was mostly concentrated in a fairly small geographic zone, the *traza*, which extended a few blocks in each direction from the main plaza, the site of the *ayuntamiento* (town hall) and the cathedral. Although Puebla was founded as a new Spanish town in the 1530s, unusual in that there was no preexisting indigenous town at the chosen site, by the second half of the sixteenth century a substantial Indian population resided in *barrios* to the west and east of the central traza. The briocenses, like other Spaniards in Puebla, sometimes lived, owned property, or had businesses in these barrios, but for the most part they concentrated in three areas within or just beyond the traza: the barrio of San Agustín, southwest of the main plaza; the area near the plaza itself, which on the southern side was more or less an extension of the San Agustín neighborhood, with which it shared some features (more substantial housing and less commercialization than on the north side, which was an area of inns and shops); and the barrio of San Francisco (officially an Indian district), east of the plaza, which because of its proximity both to the San Francisco River and to the plaza became a key industrial-commercial zone.

In pursuing their goals of establishing themselves and their families on a sound economic base, the briocenses transformed their chosen new home to a significant degree. The barrio of San Agustín, which could be considered their real center, evolved into a more substantial and prestigious neighborhood, and the indigenous barrio of San Francisco became an important commercial and industrial zone that included not only obrajes and fulling mills but bakeries, ovens, gristmills, tanneries, and a variety of mercantile and artisan shops. Although San Francisco undoubtedly had started to develop along those lines before the briocenses began to arrive in significant numbers, the ease with which early immigrants obtained good sites along the river suggests that the growth of the industrial-commercial sector was fairly limited before the entrepreneurs and artisans of Brihuega established themselves there.

Although apparently rather tranquil, Brihuega—no doubt like most of the towns and villages of early modern Spain—was the scene and focus of a great deal of movement in all directions, drawing people from the towns and villages of the fairly well defined region that surrounded it and in return sending its merchants and young people out to trade, work, study, and marry. In the last third of the sixteenth century this constant, often short-term and temporary kind of movement expanded into a very different sort of mobility that involved long-distance, collective relocation, to the Alpujarras and, on an even larger scale, to New Spain. As far as can be determined, this phenomenon was unprecedented in the town's recent history. It was also perhaps unmatched in the emigration movement to Spanish America in the period. Although in absolute terms Brihuega's migrant group was not especially large in comparison with the numbers of people who departed from other towns and cities, in proportion to the town's population and for the relatively short period of about half a century in which the great majority of the migrants left, the movement from Brihuega may have been the most substantial case of collective migration in the period.

Despite the movement's impressive proportions and its unusually focused direction—one town in the Alpujarras, one city in New Spain—the long-standing economic and social patterns that appear to have nurtured the phenomenon were in no way exceptional: physical mobility associated with trade, service, employment opportunities, and marriage choices; a considerable number of residents who had artisanal and commercial skills and experience that could be put to good use in the burgeoning economy of central New Spain; a population sufficiently small that the town's residents shared multiple ties of kinship, friendship, origin, and economic interest; a kind of fluidity that characterized the region of the Alcarria within which relocation of individuals and families and the maintenance of connections with kin and acquaintances in other places were common. Yet even if those patterns were in no way unique to Brihuega, one must look to them to find the keys to the great appeal and success of this collective shift in residence that focused above all on Puebla de los Angeles.

CHAPTER TWO

The Economic Sphere

The people who emigrated from Brihuega in the second half of the sixteenth century left behind a world that for many was defined by limited resources and deteriorating circumstances. Whether the economic situation of the town's residents worsened sharply in that period or a long-term decline coincided fortuitously with the appearance of attractive opportunities elsewhere cannot be determined definitively. The nature and timing of the briocense migration suggest that a combination of push and pull fostered the very substantial movement to New Spain. The economic resources and conditions in Brihuega and Puebla that played a crucial role in shaping the movement were closely related in some respects, as can be seen through a consideration of occupations and economic activities.

The Economy of Brihuega

In the latter part of the sixteenth century the economic prospects of many of Brihuega's vecinos appeared bleak. The profitability of textile production, the main commercial pursuit of the town's residents since the Middle Ages, apparently had diminished considerably, yet its importance in the local economy had not. As part of the verification of the padrón compiled in the mid-1580s, when the town was removed from the archbishopric and put up for sale, officials questioned several men about the state of textile manufacturing. When asked if the town had any business other than textiles, a cloth merchant–entrepreneur named Francisco Gutiérrez responded that "he does not know of any other trades because only this one is of any consequence and real consideration in supporting many poor people in the manufacture of cloth."[1]

Gutiérrez and all the other leading textile producers questioned drew a sharp distinction between the handful of entrepreneurs who produced between 30 and 60 *paños* (bolts of cloth)[2] in a year, generally selling at around 6,000 *maravedís* each, and the larger number of vecinos—they estimated perhaps 30—whose annual output averaged 10 or 12 paños. Within the group of small to middling producers, however, there was a good deal of variation, with some producing as few as five or six bolts and others eighteen or twenty. The members of this latter group, again according to Francisco Gutiérrez, "have very little capital because they get wool on credit and they work the said cloth according to their trade and also occupy their wives and sons and daughters in spinning and making the cloth because they have no other trade or business and with this they support themselves and their families." The bigger merchants who testified blamed the low profitability of cloth manufacture on the cost of materials and the number of middlemen involved in the trade. Brihuega's textiles had to be taken elsewhere to be sold at fairs, where they were liable for the alcabala (sales tax), because merchants did not come to buy in the town itself.[3] In April 1586, when the inquiry was conducted, one of the biggest merchants, Hernando Ruiz "el mozo" (said to produce 60 paños in a typical year), was about to depart for the "fair of Pastrana and other places." Although this situation hurt many of the town's cloth manufacturers, the well-to-do cloth merchants may have benefited from it, since very likely they took the cloth of the smaller producers to sell at the fairs. Thus they probably figured among the middlemen who profited from the production of the undercapitalized majority of local specialists in the textile trade.

The padrón listed well over 200 people as having an occupation directly related to textiles. The largest group (90) were people (over a third of them women) designated as working cloth ("labra paños"), a catchall category that included both large and small manufacturers as well as some who probably did not produce finished cloth on their own. Another 19 vecinos (including 2 women) were listed as being in the cloth trade ("trata en paños"). Of the specific trades mentioned, the largest category was the carders (47, all men), followed by weavers (32, about half of whom, including 1 woman, had their own looms) and cloth shearers (10). In addition 6 men owned fulling mills (*batanes*) and 5 others rented them, and 3 vecinos owned dye shops.

Four merchants and four shopkeepers were not specifically described as participating in the cloth trade, but they probably did. Francisco Gutiérrez by no means exaggerated the degree to which the town concentrated on textile manufacture. While in the 1580s Brihuega had the basic range of trades one would expect to find in a town of middling size, with several carpenters, masons, blacksmiths, and sixteen tailors, probably only the tanners and shoemakers (nine and nineteen, respectively) were sufficiently numerous that they might be expected to have served a larger market than just the town itself. Twenty-one people (twelve of them women) were involved in bread baking in some degree, no doubt almost exclusively for the local market. Three people owned gristmills and another four rented them.

The dominant role of textile manufacture in the town's commercial sector may be further inferred by what the padrón omitted. There were no spinners, for example, so probably spinning was a common domestic activity, even in families that were not primarily oriented to cloth production. The familial basis of textile production seems fairly clear but must largely be inferred in the absence of the town's notarial records, which surely included sales, rentals, and work contracts of the kind that would shed light on the local organization of the cloth business. The comments of the entrepreneurs who testified in connection with the padrón, occasional notations in the tax list that sons or daughters worked with the head of household in a particular occupation, the inclusion of women (mainly widows) among cloth producers, and the abundant evidence that siblings or parents and children shared the same trade all suggest an industry that was principally domestically based, although probably few households encompassed all phases of production. [4] Fulling and dyeing probably were separate operations in most cases.[5] The widow of Bartolomé Barbero, for example, owned a dye shop in which her two sons worked. *Batanes* required a plentiful supply of water, so they were located on streams or rivers on the outskirts or even at some distance from town. Their locations may have made them popular places for socializing or romantic trysts, especially in the warm summer months; perhaps that is the reason for a municipal ordinance prohibiting young people from sleeping at the fulling mills.[6]

Artisans and merchants in the textile trade maintained shops in which they employed apprentices and other workers. The deposition of Andrés de Ortega, a first cousin of the Anzures brothers in Puebla, who also planned to emigrate in 1573, conveys a sense of the scale of a typical enterprise in Brihuega. One witness stated that Ortega had married a couple of years before and since then had maintained "a shop for merchandise and for making cloth in his house, and for said business he [the witness] has always seen him have a boy and girl who serve him and other artisans who make cloth."[7]

Paulino Iradiel Murugarren has suggested that the merchant-entrepreneur played an important role in organizing both the production and marketing of cloth.[8] In the 1520 Inquisition trial of the merchant and accused Judaizer Juan Beltrán, a 50-year-old wool carder named Juan de Carmona, a vecino of Brihuega, said that "for a long time here . . . he has worked in Beltrán's house and he knows and has seen that Antón Cubero and Pedro Cubero and their father Pedro Martínez Cubero also have worked in the said house."[9] His statement about the Cuberos (who also testified) underscores the typical, but certainly not invariable, pattern of familial concentration in one trade. Juan Caballero "el mozo," one of the men summoned to verify the 1585 padrón, was the son of a merchant of the same name, and he and his brother-in-law Francisco Gutiérrez apparently together were responsible for the production of around 60 paños of varying quality a year.

The vecinos who worked primarily in agriculture and transport were about as numerous as those involved in some aspect of textile production and marketing— approximately 200 labradores (only 5 of them women) as well as a few other specialists (five shepherds and two swineherds). Seven men were muleteers. Slightly over 100 people (1 of them a woman) were listed as laborers (*trabajadores*). Both they and the nearly twenty *jornaleros* (day laborers, also including one woman) probably did mainly agricultural work, although they may have supplied some of the less skilled labor needed for clothmaking. A labrador named Miguel Fino who testified in the Inquisition case against Diego de Anzures (the elder) in 1553 mentioned seeing Anzures "y muchos peones" when he passed by Anzures's vineyard.[10] The scanty evidence regarding the organization of economic enterprises in both town and countryside suggests no shortage of labor. Adolescents and adults of both sexes seem to have been readily available to provide additional labor at times of peak demand. City ordinances regulating the workday of rural laborers (basically sunrise to sunset) stipulated that they pertained to both men and women.[11]

Brihuega's farmers principally cultivated wheat and grapes as well as some hemp and *zumaque* (used in tanning leather and sometimes in dyeing cloth).[12] They also produced generally fairly small amounts of olive oil, nuts, and honey, the last being a specialty of the Alcarria. At least in the 1580s agriculture does not seem to have been flourishing any more than textile manufacturing was, a situation that resulted in significant local shortages.[13] Summoned to verify the padrón in 1586, Juan del Castillo, Diego Gutiérrez, and Asencio Cubero, "labradores and practical men with experience in farming in this town," claimed that the town's farmers collectively owned only ten teams of oxen and 59 yokes of mules. Asked about the recent past, they stated that "in the past years there were fewer, but since last year the harvest was a little better, the vecinos have been encouraged to buy animals to work with."[14] Perhaps so, but a labrador named Cristóbal de Espuela who applied for a license to emigrate to New Spain in 1590 gave as his reason for wanting to leave that "these years have been so sterile and difficult and not having harvested bread or raised cattle he has come into great need and poverty such that he and his wife and daughter cannot maintain themselves." Espuela claimed that his rich uncle, Juan Barranco, and siblings and in-laws who were living in Puebla had sent for him because they had found out that he "had lost his cattle and other goods."[15]

As elsewhere in Castile, people in Brihuega often combined agricultural, commercial, and other occupations. The surgeon Juan Martínez produced four or six paños a year; Juan Bautista made some cloth and had a bakery (a fairly common combination of activities); Pedro Barbero, a dyer, had a house and dye shop and also sawed walnut wood for sale; Juan de Mena ran an inn and made cloth; the returnee Cristóbal de Ribas had a mill and an oven and harvested wheat, grapes, and honey. The mixing of trades and occupations, both on an individual basis and perhaps even more significantly within families, provided the kind of economic flexibility that probably helped people not only to survive economic change and crisis but also to adapt to new circumstances and situations. In the inquiry into the background of Pablo Carpintero, a vecino of Tlaxcala who in 1633 aspired to be a *familiar* of the Inquisition, a witness in Brihuega named Pedro de Cifuentes testified that Esteban Condado, Carpintero's father-in-law, who also had emigrated to New Spain, "was a cloth weaver and he learned the trade of weaving in the house of this witness." Other witnesses testified that Esteban's father was a labrador who "plowed with oxen."[16] Esteban Ballesteros, a contemporary of Pablo Carpintero who also was a vecino of Tlaxcala, was a merchant in New Spain. In Brihuega his parents were labradores who made their living producing bread and wine. His grandfather Diego Gutiérrez (discussed in Chapter 1), however, was not only a labrador but also a collector of the sales tax and tithe and a merchant. Juan Fino said that Diego Gutiérrez and his wife were "labradores and dealers in wine" and that they owned vineyards and *bodegas* (wine cellars).[17] An economically diverse background of this kind doubtless helped to equip or at least predispose men such as Esteban Condado and Esteban Ballesteros to undertake varied economic pursuits, whether they remained in Brihuega or left.

The town's wealthiest residents, at least according to the assessment for payment of the alcabala, generally had more than one source of income.

Diego Gutiérrez, who was responsible for paying 12,600 maravedís (the highest assessment), manufactured "paños menores" but also kept 200 head of cattle, produced grapes and honey, owned three "pares de casas," and held 20,000 maravedís in censos in Brihuega and elsewhere.[18] The cloth manufacturer–merchant Hernando Ruiz el mozo, assessed 10,200 maravedís, owned a house and 200 head of cattle, held 20,000 maravedís in censos in Brihuega, and harvested wheat and grapes. Many vecinos, however, specialized primarily in a single trade, and some apparently did quite well. Blas de Ubeda, whose share of the alcabala assessment was 6,000 maravedís, had a pack train of six mules. Juan Ruiz, who paid 5,500 maravedís, owned a vineyard, but doubtless the major part of his income derived from his "botica de paños." Juan Rojo "el viejo," whose share was 7,000 maravedís, also had a house and vineyard but made his living chiefly by trading in wool. At the other end of the scale were those individuals who owned little or no property or capital and barely made a living practicing their trades. Blas de Andrés, a cloth weaver, was said to have nothing more than his loom, and Manuel de Andrés, a cloth shearer, also "has nothing more than his trade." Cristóbal Alvarez, who had "a loom with which he works," was described as poor, and Miguel Alvarez, who also worked at a loom, also was called "pobre."

The difficult economic circumstances of many of Brihuega's vecinos are underscored by the testimony of emigrants. The 1590 deposition of Francisca Gutiérrez stated that "about eight years ago because of experiencing much need and work and because her husband Alonso de la Peña could not support her or their children he went to the provinces of New Spain to be with relatives he has there in Puebla de los Angeles, for which Our Lady has shown him favor in that country by granting him much fortune in property and cattle."[19] Statements regarding dowries also reveal the limited means of many young people in particular. In a will made in Puebla in 1577, María de Pastrana, wife of Alonso de Ribas, stated that "I brought to him few goods of little value and my husband brought no goods whatsoever to me."[20] Isabel de Guadalajara stated in her will of 1595 that her second husband, Juan de Ortega, brought nothing to their marriage ("vino pobre a mi poder"). She, however, owned a house and tannery in Brihuega from her first marriage.[21] Certainly not all emigrants departed poor. Gonzalo Díaz, who went to New Spain in 1573 with his wife, Isabel de Molina (sister-in-law of Rodrigo de Anzures), to join his two brothers, took with him 500 ducados' worth of merchandise. His brother-in-law Bautista de Molina, who accompanied them, had permission to take merchandise worth 600 ducados. Díaz also asked to take two criados with them, "because in this country I have always been served by criados."[22] Many briocenses living in Puebla continued to hold property in Brihuega for years.

What appears to have been a crisis in the last third of the sixteenth century in both the town's commercial and agricultural sectors doubtless persuaded many vecinos to depart, to the Alpujarras or elsewhere in Castile (a number of briocenses settled in Seville) or to New Spain. Nonetheless, evidence from late in the seventeenth century suggests that Brihuega's commercial-industrial sector remained important and apparently viable. Witnesses in the depositions prepared for grandsons of the emigrant Alonso Gómez when they were trying to attain office in the Inquisition in New Spain in the 1660s included the following individuals who were called either *mercader* (merchant) or tratante:[23]

Name	Age	Occupation	Connection to Indies
Melchor de Lucio	84	Mercader	Nephew of Francisco de Brihuega, obrajero in Puebla
Joseph Díaz	60	Mercader	
Juan Alvarez	58	Tratante	
Gabriel de Brihuega	60	Tratante	
Cristóbal Alvarez Viñuelas	41	Mercader	Returnee
Pedro Alvarez de Castro	74	Tratante	
Baltasar de Mena de Cifuentes	59	Labrador, mercader	Brothers in Puebla
Cristóbal de Soria	40	Mercader	
Pedro de Aguilera	54	Tratante	
Juan de Alcalá	73	Tratante de paños	
Pedro Gómez Cifuentes	19	Mercader de hierro	

The age range of these men suggests that throughout the seventeenth century trade continued to provide a livelihood for a significant number of individuals.[24]

Briocenses and the Economy of Puebla

If information about economic organization and activity is scarce for Brihuega, the multiple economic involvements and interests of the briocenses in Puebla produced a mass of evidence. The record of their activities not

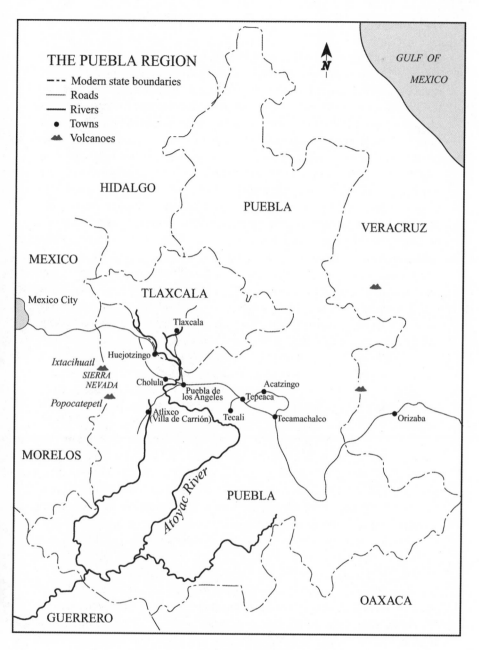

MAP 4. *The Puebla region*

only demonstrates their individual and collective success and the close connections between the immigrants' entrepreneurial activity in Puebla and their background in Brihuega but also points to their significant contributions to Puebla's development. In precisely the years when the briocenses were establishing themselves in increasingly large numbers in Puebla, the city evolved from a moderately prosperous secondary town of New Spain into a thriving center for commerce and industry as well as commercial agriculture. It appears that the briocenses' arrival in Puebla did not simply coincide with this period of increasing wealth and economic diversification; rather the immigrants from Brihuega played a crucial role in shaping and driving Puebla's economic development, especially as a manufacturing center.

Puebla came into existence a little over a decade after Mexico City was established as the capital of New Spain on the site of the partially razed city of Tenochtitlán. Located southeast of Mexico City in a well-watered, temperate region with nearly ideal conditions for agriculture, Puebla was one of relatively few Spanish towns that was not imposed on a preexisting indigenous community, although it was located near such important Indian centers as Cholula, Huejotzingo, Tepeaca, and Tlaxcala. The royal authorities who authorized Puebla's establishment hoped that it would act as a counterweight of sorts to the capital, with its conquistadores and wealthy encomenderos; Puebla's vecinos would receive urban plots and grants of land in nearby areas such as the agriculturally rich Atlixco valley, but no *encomiendas*.[25] Despite such plans, a number of encomenderos took up residence in Puebla, where they could not only live in some proximity to their encomiendas but also obtain desirable land grants. The city and its vecinos and clergy succeeded in gaining access to indigenous labor through other means, and almost from the outset Puebla attracted a substantial indigenous population that settled in barrios around the central traza.[26]

Although the city exercised no official jurisdiction over the Indian towns and villages in its vicinity, it nonetheless managed to achieve a considerable degree of unofficial control over the indigenous countryside and its resources in various ways. Its vecinos often served as administrative officials in Indian towns, and encomenderos and corregidores occupied seats on Puebla's city council. In the ecclesiastical realm also Puebla carved out a position of influence with the wealth to back it up; when it was officially named the seat of the diocese of Tlaxcala in 1543, it became the headquarters for a bishopric that would be much wealthier than the archbishopric of Mexico itself.[27] By the 1560s, when briocenses began to arrive in New Spain in some numbers, Puebla was well positioned to enter into what Guy Thomson has called its "golden age."[28] It had the human and natural resources necessary for diversified economic development and enjoyed an optimal location, close to Mexico City, the ports on both coasts, and several important Indian towns, as well as on the routes to the south.[29] The briocenses were quick to take advantage of virtually everything the city and its region could offer, and in doing so they put their own strong stamp on *poblano* economy and society.

The Manufacturing Sector

Puebla offered favorable conditions in which to develop textile manufacturing. Located near the convergence of the San Francisco and Atoyac Rivers, it had water to power mills, and the region produced wool, dyestuffs, and plentiful and cheap supplies of food. The city also had a substantial indigenous population that could provide labor. Although almost all the briocenses in Puebla varied their economic activities to some degree, and a substantial number had no direct involvement in textile manufacturing, nonetheless the production of woolen cloth was the central and predominant occupation of the Brihuega immigrants and many of their children as well in the second half of the sixteenth century and early decades of the seventeenth.[30] Even those individuals whose economic interests were most diverse seldom gave up their obrajes altogether, surely a sign that even if the profits were moderate, they were reasonably secure.

The briocenses who arrived in Puebla in the 1560s brought their expertise in the cloth trades and, over the next decades, their relatives and compatriots as well. Although probably fewer than 30 briocenses were in Puebla before 1570, most of the adult men who arrived in the early years established obrajes. Textile production in New Spain, however, differed so greatly in scale and organization from the industry back home as to constitute virtually a new kind of enterprise. Incorporating nearly all stages of the preparation of wool and manufacture of cloth, relying on large, mixed labor forces in which substantial numbers of workers probably were trained on-site rather than having progressed through the accustomed stages from apprentice to master, the obrajes had little in common with the small-scale, domestically based textile shops of Brihuega.

Although the training and skills of the immigrant artisans and entrepreneurs were crucial, success in the new-style manufacturing also had quite a lot to do with their access to capital and credit—much of it generated within the briocense community itself—that allowed them to invest and operate on a substantial scale. Over time, therefore, probably fewer obraje owners were themselves skilled artisans, although because of their normally close day-to-day involvement in the business, most of them were doubtless thoroughly familiar with all stages of cloth production. Still the shift in textile production from an occupation of fairly small-scale artisans in Brihuega to the much more capitalized and complex obrajes of Puebla signaled a notable change in the lives and activities of the immigrants, as many of them quickly became more entrepreneurs than artisans.

Textile manufacturing got its start in Puebla in the 1540s, but there seems little doubt that it received a major impetus when the briocenses established themselves in the city. The relatively limited development of the industry before their arrival is suggested by the ease with which immigrants in the 1560s and 1570s obtained grants to build fulling mills at key sites along the San Francisco and Atoyac Rivers. Although there were always other obrajeros in the city, at any one time in the years between 1565 and 1620 the majority of the obraje owners in Puebla were briocenses by origin or descent, and most of the others were closely connected to them by origin (such as the Caballero brothers from Budía and entrepreneurs from Fuentelencina) and business or marital ties. The briocenses set up their obrajes all over the city, often in the same houses in which they lived or right next door. By the end of the sixteenth century Puebla was the leading textile producer in New Spain, sending cloth to be sold in the capital and as far away as Peru.[31]

Although smaller shops always existed alongside larger ones, many of the obrajes of Puebla in this period were good-sized operations that might employ between 50 and 100 workers, the majority of them Indians, although workforces of over 100 were not uncommon.[32] In the sixteenth century and the first decade or so of the seventeenth century, before official efforts to curtail the practice of confining workers could be enforced very effectively, the workforce of a typical obraje was divided into several categories. Normally there were one or two managers or mayordomos, who usually were Spaniards or mestizos; slaves, who often acted as overseers or guards but could also be skilled artisans; and Indians, both men and women, who might live either inside or outside of the obraje. When Francisco de Brihuega's obraje was inspected in 1583 it had 30 "indios libres" (free Indians), another 54 who were "encerrados" (locked up), and 32 women. Brihuega stated that another 10 or 12 workers "enter and leave," and others worked in their houses; presumably these people were not present to be counted at the time of the *visita* (inspection). Apparently Francisco de Brihuega followed the practice of having husbands and wives exchange places.[33] The evidence from this and other visitas and records suggests that most of the encerrados were not from Puebla. Brihuega himself stated that the Indians who were confined were outsiders, who he assumed would run away if they could. Unfortunately, there is no consistent indication of the origins of the workers in the obrajes. Brihuega's suggestion that the encerrados were more likely to be outsiders is substantiated, however, by the surnames used. Thus among the group not confined in Francisco de Brihuega's obraje only one man had a surname indicating an origin outside of Puebla (Francisco Tlax-cala), but among the encerrados four were named Tlaxcala, four Tetela, two each Huejotzingo, Tepeaca, and México, and a few other places appeared at least once among the workers' surnames.

Inventories, sales, partnership agreements, and visitas all suggest that the labor arrangements in the obrajes were variable and perhaps more flexible than is sometimes assumed. Probably the majority of workers contracted their services voluntarily, although normally when inspections were conducted at least a few people would come forward to claim that they had been lured into an obraje and kept there against their will. A worker named Bernabé de Guatemala testified that the briocense Pedro de Angulo tricked Lorenzo de Tlaxcala into service. In 1584 Angulo had eighteen encerrados and a dozen other Indian men and women workers in his obraje "de saya-les" (coarse woolen cloth). He allegedly had run into Lorenzo on the road to Cholula and offered to hire him to accompany him to Veracruz to pick up some wine; instead they went only as far as Angulo's obraje, where Lorenzo de Tlaxcala was then detained. Angulo claimed that he had hired Lorenzo to work as a carter, but when he sold the cart, Lorenzo started to work as a spinner in the obraje, perhaps to pay off an advance on his wages. The situation of two boys with only very small debts found locked up in the obraje of Juan de Ribas in November 1583 doubtless seemed more clear-cut; the authorities sent for their parents to come get them.[34]

The case of an Indian named Mateo, a twenty-year-old native of Tehuantepec employed in the obraje of the briocense Juan de Ortega Prieto, who in February 1603 was accused of having "indios encerrados," also demonstrates how someone could unintentionally end up working in an obraje. According to Mateo, two months previously he had come from Tehuantepec

> serving Pedro Sánchez, muleteer, vecino of Tehuantepec, where he [Mateo] left his wife. And having arrived in the city of Mexico with the mule train, which was carrying cacao, a mulato named Francisco, the criado of Juan Ortega Prieto, arrived and deceived this witness and another Indian named Miguel who is now deceased and died in the obraje of the said Ortega, telling them to come with him to the obraje to work as muleteers. And he gave each a peso and with this they came with him and he took them to the obraje, where this witness had been locked up until now. . . . They made him card [wool] all this time . . . and

they gave him another eight pesos which Baltasar mestizo who was in charge of the obraje ["andaba mandando en al dicho obraje"] gave him.

Juan de Ortega Prieto explained the events differently: "Having sent the said Francisco mulato to Mexico to pick up Indians who had run off and bring others that wanted to come with him to work for him," Mateo and Miguel had voluntarily accompanied Francisco. He said that he paid Mateo three pesos a month.[35]

The status of at least some of the encerrados apparently varied over time, and some people spent periods living both within and outside of obrajes, depending on the amount of their debt or their perceived reliability. Damián Sánchez was one of several witnesses who testified that a mayordomo of Juan de Ribas named Salaíces beat and mistreated the workers. "When one of the Indians doesn't come to work . . . Salaíces goes to find them in their houses and brings them to the obraje and keeps them locked up for a week more or less."[36] When an obrajero paid off the debt of someone who was in jail or confined in another obraje, the individual contracted in this fashion normally would be confined, sometimes in chains.

By the time visitas were conducted in 1620, official efforts to enforce the ordinance of 1609 prohibiting the practice of confining workers had begun to have an impact. Indians in the obraje of Andrés de la Fuente, the son of Martín de la Fuente and Isabel Bautista and a second-generation obrajero, said they all came and went freely, "living as they live outside of it [the obraje] in the barrio and houses they have in this city and they all have contracts with Andrés de la Fuente their master that they made voluntarily and without any force." Nonetheless, the practice of confinement persisted. Tomás Baltasar, an *emprimador* (person who did the second carding of wool) in the obraje of Gonzalo de la Carrera, said he had worked for Cristóbal de Brihuega, and when he went to Carrera's obraje he had been locked up. Now, however, he was allowed to come and go freely because his brother had agreed to serve as his guarantor. He said he had been paid but had no contract. Gaspar Pérez, a native of Oaxaca who worked in the obraje of Cristóbal de la Carrera, said that they had locked him up for three years because his wife had run away. Two weeks before the visita they released him, and now both he and his wife could enter and leave freely and they had a contract. The testimony of a number of workers in the obrajes visited in 1620 suggests that many people were released just before the inspections. A worker in the briocense Miguel Carrillo's obraje, for example, stated that at present there were no encerrados because "before Easter they were given their freedom so they would go."[37]

Perhaps surprisingly, given the usual image of the colonial obraje as a coercive setting that workers would flee if they could, a number of the Indians who testified in the 1620 visitas voluntarily spent many years working in the same place. A carder named Matías de Luna from Cuautinchan "said he had worked for 35 years in the obraje [of Cristóbal de la Carrera] entering and leaving freely and he was locked up for three years and since a month ago he [again] enters and leaves freely and wants to stay there and work and he has a contract." Sebastián Hernández, a native of Tlaxcala, testified that he and his wife had worked for thirteen years in the obraje of Pedro Gómez (also a second-generation obrajero, the son of Alonso Gómez). Pascual Guanes, who was from the barrio of San Sebastián in Puebla, apparently had spent his entire working life in Gómez's obraje. He was 50 years old at the time of the visita and said he had worked in the obraje for 40 years; "all the time he has entered and left freely and his wife Francisca Luisa for some years [also has worked there]."

This kind of longevity suggests that the workforces of at least some obrajes may have been fairly stable, but one cannot assume too much from such anecdotal evidence. Obrajeros typically employed married couples, and some explicitly stated their preference for married workers. Among the 26 Indians working in a small obraje that Rodrigo García rented in October 1591 for a period of three years were ten married couples, the son of one couple, and the brother of one of the married men.[38] The intention in seeking married couples may have been primarily to exercise greater control by using the threat of confining one spouse to ensure the accountability of the other. An additional motivation may have been the hope that married men living with their wives, whether within or outside the obraje, would be more settled and less unruly than single men or married men separated from their wives. Equally important, women probably were a source of cheap labor. They almost invariably were employed as spinners and, at least as well as can be judged by the advances they received and debts they accrued, appear to have earned less than men. In 1611 in the obraje owned by Isabel Bautista, the widow of Martín de la Fuente, the debts of the shearers and carders (all men) generally were in the range of 40 to 60 pesos, and of the male spinners 40 to 50 pesos, whereas the female spinners' debts were considerably lower, between 20 and 30 pesos.[39] Of course this discrepancy could also indicate that women made a greater effort than men to limit their indebtedness. The two reasons together may have accounted for the lower debts of women workers. The preponderance of male labor in the obrajes reflects a change from the preconquest indigenous situation, in which women were solely responsible for cloth production.[40] A mixed male and female labor force is consistent with Spanish practice, however, and possibly the work that obrajeros contracted out on a domestic basis was performed primarily by women, who could thereby remain at home.

Wages paid to workers usually ranged from two or three to six pesos a month, depending on the nature of the work.[41] In April 1595 an Indian from Cholula named Diego Pastrana agreed to work for three years in the obraje of the briocense Bartolomé García Barranco in Puebla for 30 pesos a year; Miguel Gabriel, also of Cholula, in December 1600 entered the service of Pedro Gómez to work in his obraje as an *emborrador* (also a worker who carded wool for the second time) for three pesos and four tomines a month.[42] A free mulato named Pascual made a contract in December 1608 to work for Gabriel Caballero as a weaver for two years, earning either fourteen reales per piece of cloth or three pesos a month if he worked at spinning, plus food. He received twenty pesos in advance. Obraje owners hired apprentices such as Baltasar Conciencia, another free mulato who entered the service of Juan Bautista Ruiz in 1574 for three years. He was to learn the trade of tundidor (cloth shearer), earning sixteen pesos a year plus clothing and food. A 21-year-old native of Toledo, Juan Bautista de Fonseca, apprenticed himself to Francisco de Pliego in the same trade in October 1600.[43] Nearly all workers received either partial or full advances on their wages.[44] The outstanding debts of the workers constituted a substantial proportion of an obraje owner's capital outlay and would be included in the obraje's price if it were sold. Obrajeros also customarily included the debts of workers who had left. Since typically they had only limited success in retrieving absentees, a certain percentage of advances to workers really should be considered a normal operating cost.

The conditions in which people worked in the obrajes doubtless varied quite a lot. During the visitas workers complained about poor or insufficient food, inadequate sleeping accommodations, failure to provide medical care, and being forced to work overly long hours or to do additional tasks for no extra pay (in the case of those workers who were paid by the piece). Physical mistreatment also was common. Complaints about beatings and other kinds of abuse usually cited a particular individual as being responsible, and workers far more frequently accused the mayordomo or one of the slaves than the obraje owner. Since presumably the mayordomo and slaves who acted as overseers were in closer contact with the workers than the obrajero was, this difference in behavior is not surprising, although the evidence suggests that most obraje owners were closely involved in day-to-day operations and often lived and slept in the same building.

The close proximity in which obrajeros lived with their workers is suggested by a couple of criminal cases of the early seventeenth century. The *probanza* prepared by Benito Sanz Bautista when he was implicated in the stabbing of Francisco López, who was married to Benito's aunt Isabel Bautista's niece, included testimony by workers that he was present in his obraje in Cholula on the night in question. A weaver who had worked for him for two years said that he saw Benito arrive home, undress, and go to bed, and also saw him get up the next morning.[45] Cristóbal de la Carrera brought criminal charges against two of his Indian workers in February 1609. He stated that "Lucas Gaspar indio . . . owing me the quantity of 50 pesos and having made with me a contract five months ago . . . when I and all the people of the said obraje were gathered together one night around eight o'clock," Lucas Gaspar and Pedro Martín, both weavers, broke through a wall into a room where cloth and wool were kept and stole yarn and dyed wool worth more than 200 pesos. When some of the other Indians warned them not to steal the things, the perpetrators threatened to kill them if they refused to go with them. The result was that thirteen people fled and had not returned. One of the witnesses, a spinner named Alonso de Mapaluca, said that the incident took place while Carrera was "sleeping and in bed with all the people of his house." He claimed that Lucas Gaspar and Pedro Martín had broken through the wall with a *coa* (digging stick) and knives, and that when he tried to warn Carrera, Lucas Gaspar had stuffed some wool into his mouth and almost suffocated him. In his defense Lucas Gaspar claimed that he and Pedro Martín just happened to get up and, finding the hole in the wall, called to the others, and they all left carrying some wool and yarn. He said he had taken nothing but rather had gone to visit some relatives and then returned to the obraje. He received a sentence of 50 lashes and a fine of 50 pesos to be paid by working in Cristóbal de la Carrera's obraje in chains.[46] Perhaps conditions in the obrajes were not as uniformly grim and demoralizing as they are often painted. Nonetheless, given the proximity in which everyone lived and the sometimes large numbers of workers confined for long periods who routinely endured various forms of mistreatment and who had ready access to tools that in a pinch could serve rather effectively as weapons, it is notable that there were not more incidents of this kind.

Obrajeros generally had at least a few slaves of African origin or descent. They often were among the most highly skilled laborers, working as tundidores especially, no doubt because their permanence made it worthwhile to train them in the most skilled trades. The officials (*veedores*) who supervised the cloth shearers in Mexico City brought a case in May 1571 against the briocense Cristóbal Escudero, who lived in Mexico City and owned an obraje near Coyoacán, alleging that Escudero did not employ a master tundidor but rather used his slaves in that capacity. Escudero said that when his tundidor left several months earlier, the slaves he had supervised simply continued to do the work without him. He had paid the maestro 300 pesos a year plus room, board, and clothing, but "he didn't do anything except be present for what the said skilled blacks did." Escudero pointed out that the cloth his slaves had worked on had been approved by the inspectors of finished cloth.[47]

With increasing restrictions on the use of indigenous workers, the numbers of slaves rose in the early seventeenth century, at least in the larger obrajes. In July 1615 Isabel Bautista and her second husband, Juan de Mata (formerly the mayordomo of her obraje), empowered a vecino of Mexico City to sell 22 of their slaves, including fifteen men and women from Angola and one "chino."[48] The 1608 inventory of the estate left by Alonso Gómez included 20 slaves. A detailed list provides information on their origins, ages, and occupations;[49] most of them worked in the obraje his heirs inherited. In addition to several mulatos and people born in Mexico, Gómez owned several slaves each from Mozambique, Congo, and Angola. A 70-year-old man named Domingo Portugués apparently did general work ("ayuda en lo que se manda"). Antón from Angola served as portero. Five men were cloth shearers, two worked at sorting wool, and one was a spinner. A *criollo* named Diego Cortés, listed as a burler (*despinzador*), was working for a Baltasar de Pastrana in Mexico City. The list of slaves in Gómez's will of 1601 included three carders who were not included in the 1608 inventory. A woman named Juana worked as a spinner, and the other women were household workers; 55-year-old Francisca worked in the kitchen.

Alonso Gómez had been one of the most successful obrajeros; his estate was worth over 120,000 pesos. The 1608 inventory stated that the obraje had 188 "indios naborías," with 66 Indian women in the obraje and another 8 who washed wool outside of it. The large numbers of both slaves and Indian workers suggest that even obrajeros who could afford to use substantial numbers of slaves still relied primarily on indigenous labor, an indication that at least in the first decade of the seventeenth century the composition of the typical obraje workforce had not changed substantially.[50] Evidence from the visitas of 1620, however, does seem to show that obrajeros were shifting away from reliance on a confined labor force. Thus the change that was going on in the period was not the wholesale replacement of Indian workers by African slaves (which royal ordinances and officials had intended) but rather the increasing use of free wage workers who lived

outside the obraje. Twenty years after the confinement of workers was pro-
hibited, however, some obrajeros continued to lock up their workers. Very
possibly the practice resumed to some degree whenever official vigilance
relaxed.[51]

Although the obraje owner normally was closely involved in the operation of his enterprises, he also would employ a manager, who usually was
assisted by a slave or another employee; he might have a *capitán* for the
Indian workers as well.[52] Newly arrived immigrants from Brihuega often
worked for a time in established obrajes before setting up on their own.
This practice provided obrajeros with a fairly steady if somewhat transient
supply of managers and artisans who were their relatives or compatriots,
although certainly they employed people in this capacity who were neither.
Pedro de Anzures hired Juan de Olivera, apparently not a briocense, in 1570
for two years at an annual salary of 200 pesos, probably as his mayordomo.[53]

The arrival of a large group of immigrants from Brihuega in 1573 meant
a considerable increase in the availability of compatriots with the necessary
skills and background to work in the obrajes established in the 1560s. Many
of these people were specifically recruited for the purpose. Macario de
Anzures sent for his niece's husband, Juan de Iñigo, to work in his *batán*
(fulling mill), complaining that few people in Puebla had the requisite skills.
In 1576 he wrote to his brother Rodrigo de Anzures asking him to send his
son Diego de Anzures, saying he needed him in his "obrador de paños" and
would give him half the profits.[54] Juan de Pastrana offered his first cousin
Pablo de Pastrana an annual salary of 500 ducados to work in his obraje,
explaining that he preferred to hire a relative rather than someone he did
not know.[55] Pablo de Pastrana probably worked no more than a year for his
cousin; in 1575 he was called "tabernero" (tavern keeper), and by the 1580s
he was an established local merchant. In 1609 Juan Gómez de Arrieta, who
was 40 years old, was the mayordomo in the obraje of his brother Pedro
Gómez de Arrieta (they were nephews of the obrajero Alonso Gómez) and
had previously worked for a vecino of Carrión named Martín de Jáuregui,
a sometime partner of his brother.[56] Not all emigrants attained economic
independence. In April 1581, soon after Antón Torijano arrived in Puebla,
he wrote to his wife, Catalina Ponce, in Brihuega that he was working in
the "molino y batán" of his compatriot Macario de Anzures. In 1599 he
rented a batán from Cristóbal de la Carrera and Juan Gutiérrez de Salas for
two years, agreeing to treat 250 paños a year. In 1610, at the age of "over
70," Torijano said he was a "perchero" (teaseler) working in the house of
the briocense Juan Crespo Carrillo.[57] Apparently, then, Torijano never
became an independent entrepreneur.

Rentals offered another means by which immigrants in effect contracted to work for their compatriots even though strictly speaking they were not employees. Bartolomé García Barranco "rented" 30 Indians for his obraje along with four looms "de sayal" (for coarse cloth) from Lucas de Ribas (the son of Alonso de Ribas) for 700 pesos a year, beginning in January 1594. Part of the agreement was that Ribas would work in Bartolomé García's obraje and the latter would hire a boy to help him.[58] Partnerships could provide another solution to the problem of management, as the terms of the agreements often stipulated that one partner would take charge of the obraje. Juan de Brihuega and his brother Francisco de Brihuega formed a partnership for four years in 1579 in which Francisco invested 1,500 pesos in cash. Juan's much larger contribution included tools and equipment worth 1,150 pesos, a batán with five donkeys worth 5,000 pesos, five slaves (four men and a woman), a horse, and various dyestuffs. Francisco was to manage the obraje.[59] In 1594 Pablo de Pastrana and his nephew Hernando de Pastrana formed a "compañía" for two years with a man named Diego de Corona. The Pastranas invested 10,000 pesos, which represented the value of the obraje, wool, looms, and other equipment and the debts of the Indians. Corona's investment was 5,000 pesos, and he was to work in ("asistir en") the obraje. Half the profits would go to the Pastranas and the other half to Corona.[60]

Partnerships, rental agreements, and sales all point to some degree of fluidity and turnover in the ownership and management of obrajes. This turnover does not necessarily indicate a high rate of failure, although clearly some such ventures did not succeed. In November 1602, for example, Juan García del Castillo (the son of the briocense Rodrigo García, who would later serve as a regidor on the city council) and a vecino of Tlaxcala named Francisco Sánchez Calvo dissolved a partnership in an obraje they had entered into the previous year because of the "deaths and absences of Indians who have run off." Even so, the obraje apparently continued to be a going concern, as Juan García del Castillo bought out his partner and continued to operate the obraje on his own.[61] In 1605 Lucas de Ribas said he lost his obraje for similar reasons.[62] The involvement of briocenses of the second and even third generations in textile manufacture does suggest, however, that the industry continued to be profitable and viable well into the seventeenth century.[63]

The frequency of sales and the fairly short duration of most partnerships probably reflect their profitability rather than the opposite—that is, investment in the rental or ownership of an obraje typically paid off in a relatively short time. Usually the sale of an obraje included the building, equipment, wool, dyes, debts of the Indian workers, and a few slaves. In January 1591 Juan García Barranco (brother of Bartolomé García, mentioned earlier) and Juan de Cifuentes bought an obraje from their compatriot Pedro de Angulo for a total of 10,600 pesos. The price of the "casas para obraje," located next to the house of Cristóbal de Brihuega, was 5,500 pesos plus a censo of 1,400 pesos, and the sale price also included two slaves who must have been tundidores, since their price of 1,000 pesos included two pairs of scissors.[64]

A price of around 10,000 pesos was fairly standard for an obraje, although more modest establishments of course could sell for less. Benito Sanz Bautista[65] bought an obraje and "casas de morada" (houses to live in) in Cholula in 1599 for around 7,500 pesos, which included four looms, the debts of 40 Indians who owed 1,164 pesos, and a slave worth 250 pesos; he agreed to pay Marcos de Cepeda, a vecino of Cholula, in installments over three years. Pedro Gómez paid less—6,120 pesos 2 tomines—in 1594 when he bought an obraje from Bartolomé de la Torre, but the price did not include the building, since the obraje was located in a house owned by his father, Alonso Gómez. The debts of 130 Indians constituted nearly half the purchase price (3,000 pesos), and four slaves (two men and two women) were valued at 1,250 pesos. The obraje had ten regular looms and two for sayales.[66]

The ownership of fulling mills appears to have been more stable. They were usually good-sized establishments that included not only the mill but often houses for workers and an orchard or garden as well. Lic. Cristóbal García Barranco, a *clérigo presbítero* (ordained priest), in 1608 paid 2,800 pesos for a batán on the Amalucan River, next to one owned by Cristóbal de Brihuega, which included living quarters, a dovecote, and a stable as well as ten donkeys, a large cauldron, and other pieces of equipment. There were three "indios bataneros," a man and his two sons.[67] The mechanization of fulling with water-powered mills meant the labor needs for a batán were not great; the batanero generally had a slave or two, or a few Indian workers, to assist him.

A batán was more likely to be rented than sold, or the owner would keep it for his own use. Sometimes the person who rented paid in kind by treating the mill owner's cloth. Cristóbal Barbero rented his batán in Totomehuacan in 1593 to a vecino of Puebla named Luis Ascacio for one year for 800 pesos. Barbero agreed to provide him with three Indians to work in the batán, and he would take care of all major repairs. Ascacio was obligated to do minor repairs and to treat all the cloth from Barbero's obraje at a price of one and a half pesos per bolt of cloth. In February 1602 Barbero rented the batán to Bartolomé de Ribas for two years at 700 pesos a year; the rental included fifteen burros and the services of five Indians.[68]

Since fulling was an essential part of manufacturing most kinds of cloth, and batanes could be rented out at fairly high prices (usually between 600 and 800 pesos), the people who owned these mills generally kept them for many years. Alonso Gómez actually entailed his two fulling mills, one located in Totomehuacan, near the batán of Cristóbal de Brihuega, the other on the Atoyac River. The value of the first, which included two *caballerías* (over 200 acres) of land, was assessed after his death at nearly 14,000 pesos and that of the second at around 7,700 pesos.[69] Batanes did require constant maintenance. In 1603 Gómez's son Pedro Gómez brought a suit against Matías Pérez, who had rented the batán on the Atoyac River for three years beginning in January 1602 for 400 pesos a year. Pérez previously had rented a batán from the briocense Lope de la Carrera, also on the Atoyac. Pedro Gómez maintained that Pérez had neither maintained the mill nor informed him of repairs that needed to be done. He claimed that the "wheel with which the batán runs has been destroyed" and that leaks in the roof had caused the beams to rot; the damages amounted to more than 400 pesos. By the time he brought the suit, Pérez had gone to work for Cristóbal Barbero.[70]

Agriculture and stock raising in the region around Puebla, together with the city's commercial ties to the south and the capital, assured Puebla's obrajeros of reliable access to the materials they needed. Wool was plentiful in the region, and obrajeros usually made arrangements to purchase it in advance of shearing time. Probably some of the obraje owners supplied at least a portion of the wool they needed from their own estancias. The same was true for dyes. Macario de Anzures owned "estancias de pastel." He wrote to his brother-in-law Francisco Barbero, a labrador, in 1573 urging him to come take charge of them so he could use the dye "en mi tinte y obrador."[71] In the earlier years obrajeros may have had some problems obtaining supplies. When Diego de Anzures wrote to his cousin Andrés de Ortega, he asked him to bring 50 or 60 pounds of indigo and 50 or 100 pairs of "cardas desde Córdoba" (teasels for carding from Córdoba), assuring him he would make a good profit from those items.[72] Trade with Guatemala and elsewhere brought indigo and other dyes to the city. Puebla was an important center for the trade in cochineal, which the city's obrajeros used to dye high-quality cloth.

Obraje owners sold their cloth locally and in Mexico City and supplied it to merchants who took or sent it to Guatemala and elsewhere. In the will Rodrigo García prepared in April 1591 (he in fact lived many years after that) he stated that he had sent various kinds and amounts of cloth with a muleteer from Tecamachalco to Guatemala to be delivered to a man named Juan Martín de Mondragote, who was to sell the cloth and use the proceeds to buy *añil* (indigo).[73] Many obrajeros maintained shops in Puebla or the capital. The brothers Pedro and Macario de Anzures were selling "paños de la tierra" in 1568—575 varas for 1,150 pesos in November, another 26 varas in December. In July 1569 their compatriot Francisco Alvarez said he owed Pedro de Anzures 500 pesos for merchandise from his store. Around the same time Anzures purchased two slaves, a man and a woman, and 1,800 goats, for which he paid in part with 800 "varas de paños de la tierra" worth 15 tomines per yard.[74]

Obrajeros formed partnerships in stores or paid people to act as their dealers or agents. In November 1571 Andrés de Angulo and his son-in-law Juan Bautista Ruiz formed a company with a vecino of Puebla named Pedro Juárez de Mayorga for two years in a "tienda de paños de la tierra." Juárez was to sell in Mexico City all the cloth that his partners made in their two obrajes. He would pay half the rent for the store and receive half the profits. The agreement specified the prices at which various qualities and types of cloth would be sold.[75] In January 1593 Francisco de Pliego said he had made an agreement with Juan de Pastrana, a merchant in Mexico City who almost certainly was from Brihuega and was closely connected with the briocenses in Puebla, according to which Pastrana would sell all the cloth he manufactured and also would supply him with things he needed for his obraje, and Pliego would pay Pastrana a commission of 400 pesos a year. Several other obrajeros made similar arrangements with Pastrana at the same time.[76] In October 1602 in Mexico City Pastrana authorized Gabriel Caballero to pay Marcos Rodríguez Zapata, then *escribano del cabildo* in Puebla, up to 4,000 pesos for cloth he would buy for him, with Caballero acting as his guarantor; Caballero bought 50 bolts of cloth for him the following month.[77]

The other semi-industrial enterprise in which briocenses were involved was the ownership of bakeries, which produced both bread and biscuit, the latter primarily to be sent to the ports or sometimes south to Guatemala. As in Brihuega also women, usually widows, might operate *panaderías*, although in Puebla men owned the majority of these establishments. As in the case of the obrajes there was a marked tendency toward familial involvement. The briocense brothers Juan and Diego Llorente both had bakeries, as did their cousin Juan Carpintero and Juan Llorente's son-in-law Alonso del Moral.[78] The brothers Juan and Miguel de Angón also had bakeries in the late sixteenth century, as did Antonio and Diego del Río.

Few if any of these individuals, with the possible exception of the widows, limited their economic interests to the panaderías. Some owned obrajes as well, and many were involved in trade and transport; both Francisco el Rojo[79] and Jerónimo de Pastrana were called "panadero y mercader" in the seventeenth century. Francisco Carrillo, who made his will in 1599, listed among his assets 800 pesos' worth of wheat and debts of 600 to 700 pesos owed by the Indian bakers, as well as 44 oxen and two carts.[80]

Bakeries operated on a fairly substantial scale. Miguel de Angón, for example, bought 570 fanegas of wheat in May 1592. When his brother Juan de Angón made his will in 1603, he listed among his goods 800 fanegas of wheat and another 1,000 that he had paid for.[81] In October 1590 a carter from Mexico City said he had received from Hernando de Pastrana 239 *quintales* and 3 *arrobas* of "bizcocho bazo" and 49 quintales, 2 arrobas, 20 pounds of "bizcocho blanco," all of it in 161 sacks to be delivered in Veracruz to Juan de Torija, who was the brother-in-law of Pastrana's uncle Pablo de Pastrana. In the same year Juan Llorente sent 10 "tercios de bizcocho bazo" with a muleteer from Antequera to Soconusco to be delivered to his partner, Bartolomé Tartajo. In 1602 Antonio del Río sent 150 quintales of biscuit to be sold in Veracruz; Gabriel de Anzures Izquierdo, who was an escribano, sold 68 quintales of "bizcocho bazo" to a muleteer from Antequera in 1612.[82]

The labor needs of the panaderías in Puebla were far smaller than those of the obrajes. In his will Juan de Angón mentioned only four "indios panaderos" and five slaves (three of them women), and Isabel de Guadalajara listed the debts of only two Indian bakers in her will of 1595. Notwithstanding the small numbers required, workers with the necessary skills apparently were not easy to find and keep. In 1590 Diego del Río complained that he had paid an Indian named Francisco seventeen pesos to work for him as a baker, but Francisco had gone to work in Miguel de Angón's house; Francisco said he left because of an argument over "a certain amount of bread he said was missing."[83] Panaderos generally earned much higher wages and probably enjoyed better working conditions than textile workers. In 1609 Andrés Pérez de Angulo agreed to pay Pedro Pepense, a native of Cholula, eight pesos and two tomines a month as well as to provide food and "un sope cada día." Pedro Pepense received a hefty advance of 150 pesos. Andrés Pérez hired Baltasar Pérez, who was from the barrio of San Francisco in Puebla, and Francisco Hernández from Tepeaca under the same terms. Diego Llorente paid the same wages to several men he hired at the same time, as did Juan Carpintero.[84]

Trade and Transport

The close relationship between manufacturing and sales drew owners of obrajes and bakeries into an array of commercial activities, from retail sales to wholesale purchases of commodities—wine from Castile, for example, and cacao and indigo from Guatemala—to owning carts, oxen, and mule trains and maintaining inns or stores that offered a variety of merchandise, including locally produced goods (especially cloth) as well as items imported from Spain and China. Few briocenses functioned primarily as merchants and probably none did so exclusively, although quite a few individuals at one time or another were called "mercader," if not necessarily consistently. Even Juan de Pastrana, the merchant in Mexico City who maintained close ties with the briocense community in Puebla, owned an obraje and eventually a sugar estate and cattle ranches with his father, Cristóbal de Pastrana.

Trade with Guatemala accounted for a substantial part of the briocenses' mercantile activity. They participated directly in this commerce, traveling there themselves, and indirectly by providing merchandise or capital for partners who made the journey south, where they might remain for a year or more. A trip to Guatemala seems to have offered the means for young men or recently arrived immigrants to get their start, providing them with a stake that they could invest in an obraje or some other enterprise that would allow them to stay closer to home. In 1573 Andrés de Angulo sent his son Juan de Angulo to sell merchandise for him in Guatemala, Izalcos, and Soconusco. He was to invest in cacao or other items and send home money or merchandise.[85] Juan de Ribas paid a merchant named Jerónimo Rodríguez 360 pesos and Pablo de Pastrana 60 pesos for merchandise and "ropa de la tierra" for his ne'er-do-well brother Lucas de Ribas to take to sell in Guatemala in the early 1580s; in 1586 Lucas still owed his brother money from that trip as well as for other debts Juan had paid off for him, including payments he made to get Lucas out of jail.[86] In March 1598 Blas Carrillo and Martín de Viñuelas agreed that the latter would travel to Soconusco and Suchitepec with 1,000 pesos' worth of "ropa de China y de la tierra" and use the profits to purchase cacao or indigo, which he would bring or send to Puebla within one year; they would divide the profits evenly. Four years previously Blas Carrillo himself had made the journey to Soconusco.[87]

Clearly members of the immigrant community who themselves never participated directly in this trade invested in it by backing others who did. In January 1594 Melchor Rodríguez, recently arrived in Puebla, wrote to his brother Gaspar Rodríguez de Madrid in Fuentelencina that he was leaving in a week for "la provincia de Soconusco y los Susutepeques [sic]" with 3,000 pesos' worth of merchandise, having received credit from Pablo de Pastrana and Rodrigo García; "I'm told it's a trip one can make a living from."[88] He may well have traveled with Blas Carrillo, who also left Puebla for Guatemala in January 1594. In 1607 Melchor Rodríguez and Juan de Angulo[89] bought cacao from another vecino of Puebla, and in 1608 Rodríguez was an obraje owner. Rodríguez, then, almost perfectly exemplified a typical immigrant's career path; he initially obtained backing from established immigrants for a trading venture to Guatemala and later became involved in other commercial and industrial enterprises in Puebla, both in partnership and on his own. During those years he also sent for his family to join him.

Other briocenses continued to participate personally in the trade with the south for longer periods of time. In February 1592 Miguel Toribio stated that he had received merchandise "de la tierra y de Castilla y de la China," money, and three horses and a mule, worth 1,500 pesos altogether, from Bartolomé Tartajo to take to Soconusco and buy cacao, which he would send to Tartajo in Puebla in a year. In 1597 Toribio took 300 pesos to Suchitepec to invest for the briocense Antón Barbero in cacao, to be sent in seven months; Toribio called himself "tratante en la provincia de Soconusco y Suchitepeque." When his wife, María de Bonilla, made her will in 1614, their collective assets included 60 cargas de cacao and 26 pack mules, so clearly Toribio remained active in the cacao trade.[90] Toribio's brother Diego Toribio, who arrived in New Spain in 1602, also participated in the trade. In May 1612 Diego Toribio, "dueño de recua," said he had received from his nephew Pedro Toribio 1,604 pesos 3 tomines to take to Huehuetlán, in Soconusco, and give to the governor, Baltasar Muriel de Valdivieso, in payment for 40 cargas de cacao that he had sent to Pedro Toribio in Puebla to sell. He also took 1,538 pesos 5 tomines to Pedro de la Plaza, vecino of Huehuetlán, in payment for 38 cargas de cacao that he had sent to Pedro Toribio.[91]

The details of these transactions suggest that most of the briocenses who participated in this trade did not deal directly with indigenous producers of cacao but rather relied on Spanish traders and officials living in the region who acted as middlemen. Presumably it was these locally based individuals who dealt directly with the Indians who cultivated the cacao. Some of the immigrants who spent longer periods in Guatemala may have become involved in the trade at that level as well, and a few briocenses may have settled there. In Puebla in May 1606 Cristóbal García de Zúñiga gave his power of attorney to two vecinos of Brihuega to take possession of olive groves, vineyards, or other lands or houses that he had bought on behalf of Bartolomé Tartajo from a man named Martín Mateo. Mateo was a vecino of the pueblo of San Antonio in the province of Suchitepec and had inherited the properties from his parents in Brihuega.[92]

Bartolomé Tartajo was one of the most active figures in the trade with Guatemala; he traveled there several times and even lived there off and on. Tartajo was part of the large group that left Brihuega for New Spain in 1573. In Puebla in 1580 he married Catalina Ramírez, who brought a dowry of 1,200 pesos. When she died in 1590, Tartajo was in Guatemala; his first cousins Juan Carpintero and Juan Llorente acted on his behalf to settle the estate. In March 1590 Tartajo sent Llorente twelve cargas of cacao, two of which belonged to Llorente; in the same month Llorente sent a number of items, including a dozen quintales of wheat flour, biscuit, two small casks of wine, cheese, and two pounds of pickled carrots, to Tartajo in Huehuetlán with a muleteer from Tehuantepec.[93] Tartajo was back in Puebla in October of that year, when he sold "two pairs of houses" next to his own house to a vecino of Carrión (Atlixco). In December 1590 he made a will before departing again for Soconusco, but he had returned to Puebla by February 1591; in December of that year he purchased eight cargas of cacao from Sebastián Tomellín, an obraje owner who was the brother-in-law of the obrajero Juan de Ribas. At some time in the 1590s Francisco Carrillo's son Mateo accompanied Bartolomé Tartajo on a trip to Guatemala; Francisco Carrillo had given Tartajo 400 pesos to invest.[94]

Juan Llorente is a good example of someone who combined several fairly small-scale entrepreneurial activities, working closely with relatives, such as Bartolomé Tartajo and his son-in-law Esteban Carrillo. Born in 1550, he was already married when he arrived in Puebla around 1580, although he did not immediately bring his wife, María de Pastrana. She was the sister of the obrajero Juan de Pastrana, whose daughter Catalina de Pastrana married the obrajero and sometime regidor Alonso Gómez, but Llorente seems to have had little to do with his wife's family. He owned a bakery and wine shop but was never involved in clothmaking. In her will of 1590 María de Pastrana stated that their assets came to a modest 3,000 pesos, representing the value of their house and furnishings and "certain things my husband has sent to Soconusco."[95]

Tartajo was not the only man with whom Juan Llorente formed a part-

FIGURE 4. *Pastrana Family*

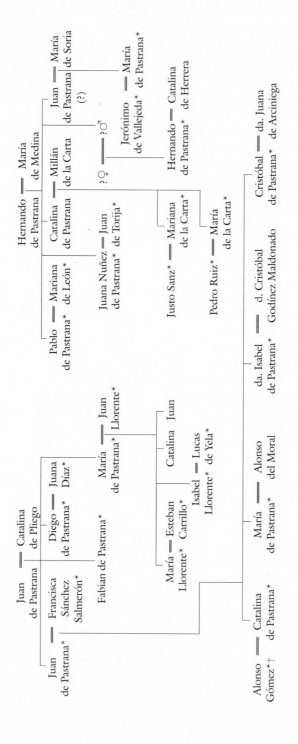

nership to work the trade with Soconusco; in February 1592 he invested around 1,500 pesos in a two-year partnership with a man named Juan Alonso Vivas, who was to travel to Soconusco to buy cacao, and in June of that year he sent nine arrobas of wine to Miguel Toribio, who probably was a cousin. His daughter Mariana de Pastrana married a carter from Brihuega named Esteban Carrillo in 1592,[96] and in the early years of the seventeenth century especially Llorente and Carrillo had extensive joint financial dealings, particularly in the purchase of silver. Llorente's brother Diego also was involved in the trade with Guatemala; in 1591 he invested 1,000 pesos in a partnership with a man named Martín de Alberto, who was to employ "his person and work" in the cacao trade in the province of Suchitepec for four years.[97]

Pablo de Pastrana, who went to Puebla to work for his first cousin Juan de Pastrana in 1573, was a key figure in the briocense commercial community. His interests were not exclusively mercantile, as he owned an obraje and a tannery, which he built with a license he received from the city council in October 1593,[98] in addition to his store and bodega. He was closely associated with his nephew Hernando de Pastrana for a number of years; the two had a retail store in the 1580s, selling 900 pesos' worth of merchandise, including locally manufactured cloth and cloth from Castile and China, to a man from Antequera in 1586. Juan de Pastrana in Mexico City also was his partner and acted as his supplier; Pablo gave him his power of attorney in January 1589 to buy merchandise "for the partnership that we have."[99] The next year he was selling wine from Jerez with his brother-in-law Juan de Torija. In December 1591 he bought 26 arrobas and 20 pounds of indigo from a vecino of Guatemala, perhaps for the obraje that he owned with Hernando de Pastrana but most likely for resale. In February 1593 he said he had sent 32 pounds of indigo to Spain in eight boxes marked with a double P, and a year later he and Hernando sold 238 pounds of indigo in Puebla.[100] Later in the same year he empowered Melchor de Pastrana, a vecino of Mexico City whom he called "my nephew," to buy merchandise and silver for him, and around the same time he authorized Hernando de Pastrana to purchase up to 6,000 pesos' worth of merchandise and silver. Pablo de Pastrana died by December 1604, leaving his family well off. In January 1607 his widow gave her power of attorney to a man named Mateo de Herrera to spend up to 10,000 pesos on silver, gold, cochineal, hides, wine, cacao, tools, and other merchandise. Five years later she owned a sugar estate near the pueblo of Chietla and sold the house and tannery her husband had built in Puebla for 1,200 pesos.[101]

Although the trade with Guatemala, in cacao and indigo, certainly seems to have been the principal mercantile activity of briocense entrepreneurs, they participated in other branches of commerce as well. Even people whose commercial dealings were fairly limited bought and sold wine. There are occasional references to investments in trade with the Philippines; Cristóbal de la Carrera gave his power of attorney to someone who was traveling to Acapulco in November 1612 to collect goods sent to him from the Philippines in which he had invested 1,300 pesos.[102] Briocenses exported indigo, cochineal, and hides to Castile, as investments or sometimes in lieu of remitting money to family members.[103] Juan de Brihuega sent 350 arrobas of cochineal to Castile in March 1580, apparently as a means of transferring his assets back to Brihuega, to which he subsequently returned, and Gabriel Caballero sent a box of indigo to his mother, Isabel de Brihuega, in Budía in 1607. Briocenses also participated in the lucrative regional trade in cochineal. In 1612 Juan García Barranco sold 40 arrobas of "grana" to a vecino of Mexico City for 5,600 pesos.[104]

Just as many briocenses had some commercial interests, a number of them also were involved to some degree in transport, which was, of course, closely connected with trade as well as stock raising. In January 1571 the briocense Diego del Río and several other vecinos of Puebla gave their power of attorney to Francisco García Ramiro to appear before the viceroy and other royal officials to request an extension until the end of March of the "service of the Indians who serve in the carts on the road to Veracruz." Alonso de Ribas, who owned estancias as well as an obraje, sold off four carts and 70 oxen in 1576 for 888 pesos.[105] Hernando de Pastrana, who in addition to his commercial enterprises owned estancias devoted primarily to stock raising, made a partnership agreement in December 1604 with a man named Juan Jaimes in a "cuadrilla de carros." Pastrana's investment of 6,097 pesos represented a cart, 238 oxen, 22 horses, 232 pesos in the debts of six Indian men and women, and 1,140 pesos in cash. Jaimes's contribution consisted of 55 oxen, 7 horses, 2 carts, and the debts of four Indian men and two women. Jaimes was to accompany the carts and cover his own expenses except when actually traveling. The partners agreed to divide the profits equally after recovering their investments.[106] The second-generation obrajero Andrés de la Fuente bought 30 mules for 1,305 pesos in December 1612. In 1618 Juan de Roa Anzures, who owned a bakery and estancias, hired a man named Juan López del Real to work with his pack train for three years at a salary of 125 pesos a year; Juan López had received an advance of 370 pesos, which Juan de Roa paid to get him out of jail.[107]

For men such as Hernando de Pastrana and Juan de Roa Anzures carting and pack trains doubtless represented an investment rather than an activity in which they participated directly; probably other briocenses were more closely involved in the transport business. In any case, transport seldom was the sole economic interest of the briocenses who were involved in it in one form or another, although certainly in some cases it could be a significant or even principal pursuit. The brothers Juan and Miguel de Angón, for example, both owned bakeries but were involved in carting over a long period of time. In November 1581 Juan de Angón sold a house in the barrio of San Francisco, 20 oxen, and two carts with "the service of certain Indian carters" to a man named Juan Domingo; in 1600 his brother Miguel, together with their fellow briocense Juan de Trixueque, sold 107 oxen, ten horses, and three carts plus the service of two Indians for 920 pesos. On August 25, 1609, Isabel de Cara, the widow of Miguel de Angón, in the name of her son Juan de Angón sold half of a *cuadrilla* that consisted of fourteen carts, 550 oxen and horses, and the contracts of seven Indian workers for 3,700 pesos. The buyer, a vecino of Puebla named Alonso Miguel, was to take possession of his half of the oxen and carts two weeks hence, when her son returned from a trip to Mexico City.[108]

Something of the nature of arrangements that might be made for local transport can be seen in a suit that Pedro de Angulo brought against his compatriot Miguel de Angón in 1587 over a debt of 50 pesos. According to Angón, Pedro de Angulo lent him 100 pesos, of which he repaid 50. The remainder Angulo said he could pay off by picking up 1,800 arrobas of wool at the estancia of Juan Blanco, for which he would pay Angón 9 pesos per 100 arrobas. Angulo claimed that he had gone to the estancia to await Angón, who failed to arrive. They subsequently went together to see the carts that Angón was supposed to use, only to find them in such disrepair as to be unusable; at that point Angulo canceled the deal. Cristóbal García de Zúñiga, a fairly distant relative of Miguel de Angón who was living with him at the time, testified that he had offered to help weigh the wool when Angulo and Angón made the agreement. He had gone to Juan Blanco's estancia with nine carts and spent ten days there, but Blanco did not want to hand over the wool until Angulo arrived. Angulo contended that Angón did not have any carts at the time but was supposed to buy some from Juan de Trixueque. Don Cristóbal Godínez, the son-in-law of Juan de Pastrana and himself an obrajero, testified that around the same time Angulo was supposed to pick up his wool, he had hired 40 mules to collect 200 arrobas of wool at the same estancia. Since he knew that Angulo also had bought wool there, he had suggested they go together and use any extra mules to carry part of Angulo's wool. Angulo, however, had explained that Miguel de Angón owed him money and was going pick up the wool in his carts. Godínez also testified that Angón's carts were in such poor condition that they could not be used.[109]

Carting must have been a difficult activity for some men to pursue part-time, since it required grazing land to maintain the livestock and experienced workers when a trip was to be undertaken. The connection between ranching and carting can be seen in the estate described in the 1614 will of Juan de Iñigo el mozo. He and his mother owned two estancias in Amalucan, one with seven caballerías of land that had a house built of stone, 110 "bueyes de carreta," 50 cows, 400 sheep, and pigs, mares, and horses, as well as four carts, twenty Indian workers described as "carreteros y carpinteros y gañanes," and a slave named Juan. The other estancia, with two caballerías of land, had 34 oxen and one cart, 15 mares, four Indian workers, and another slave named Juan and his four-year-old son.[110]

Rural Landownership

The briocenses who settled in Puebla acquired land in the countryside, particularly cattle ranches, from an early time. Cristóbal de Ribas bought 2,000 head of cattle in 1570 and in the same year formed a partnership with a man named Pedro Cano in a cattle ranch for six years. Cano invested 3,054 pesos in cows and mares and Ribas nearly 6,500 pesos; Cano was to live on the ranch for six months out of the year. Ribas, however, departed for Castile the following year, at which time he sold to his brother Alonso de Ribas two "sitios de estancias de ganado mayor con dos caballerías de tierra." The sale price of 5,400 pesos included the land, houses, corrals, sheep, and horses. He also sold his brother another caballería near Puebla in the Amalucan Valley.[111]

Although doubtless for most briocenses, at least of the first generation, keeping cattle and sheep was a secondary rather than a principal pursuit, some of them became prominent ranchers. Diego de Anzures, the obrajero and escribano who established himself in Puebla by 1560, together with his brother-in-law Alonso de Ribera bought two estancias and a third of another with 14,000 "cabezas de ganado ovejuno" as well as houses, a horse, shears, and the service of Indian workers for 10,500 pesos in October 1569.[112] In 1574 he sold calves to two fellow briocenses, Juan de Trixueque, called "estanciero," and Hernando Díaz. He was elected *alcalde de la mesta* (head of the stockmen's association) in 1576. When he returned to Castile in 1580,

Puebla's sheep raisers empowered him to represent their interests at court.[113] Diego's brother Pedro de Anzures served as alcalde de la mesta in 1585, the same year he sold an estancia with nearly 20,000 sheep to two vecinos of Tlaxcala for 14,490 pesos. Pedro bought another estancia near the pueblo of Mapaluca in 1591 for 6,000 pesos; the estate produced wheat, maize, and barley and had 40 plow oxen.[114]

Ownership of estancias and cattle afforded the means to provide dowries in other than cash. The bulk of the dowry of 6,000 pesos that Pedro de Anzures earmarked for his daughter doña Antonia de Anzures Guevara when she married Miguel García Calvo consisted of an estancia with eleven caballerías of land near the pueblo of Cuautinchan. The share of the dowry that the briocense Diego de Urgelos provided in 1598 for his niece doña Isabel de Parraga consisted of two years' rental of an estancia with four caballerías of land near Huejotzingo and the 50 plow oxen and 50 mares that Urgelos had on the estate.[115]

Some of the briocenses and their children became increasingly involved in stock raising and agriculture over time, a trend that seems to have affected many other members of Puebla's Spanish community as well in the late six-teenth and early seventeenth centuries.[116] Cristóbal de Beguillas "el mozo" bought an estancia and agricultural land from the briocense Pedro Cama-rillo near Cholula in 1609. The purchase price of 6,500 pesos included houses and corrals as well as 350 fanegas of maize, 36 pigs, 27 oxen, and the debts of fourteen "indios gañanes."[117] In 1618 Cristóbal de Ribas, probably the son of Alonso de Ribas, rented from don Carlos de Arellano an "hacienda de labor" in the valley of San Pablo near the pueblo of Acatzinco for three years. The rental included plows and other tools, two carts, maize and wheat, pigs, goats, plow mules, and twenty workers. Ribas was to sup-ply Arellano with 700 fanegas of wheat each year and also to pay 100 pesos to don Tomás Pérez and doña Magdalena de Tapia, "indios principales del pueblo de Acatzinco," which he owed them for some of the land of the hacienda.[118] Doña Teresa Caballero, whose parents, Lázaro Caballero and Mariana de Cifuentes, were from Brihuega and married in Puebla in 1620, bought an hacienda named Nuestra Señora de la Concepción in the juris-diction of Tlaxcala while she was married to her second husband, although she was sole owner.[119]

The acquisition or rental of farms and ranches may have resulted in a certain amount of movement out of Puebla, as people, especially in the sec-ond generation, took up residence near or even on their estates. Pedro del Río was a vecino of Tepeaca when he made his will in May 1631. He owned an "hacienda de labor" in Tepeaca's district with fourteen caballerías of land, 80 oxen and 40 mares, and fourteen "indios gañanes" in his service.[120] The briocense Pedro del Molino was a vecino of the Indian town of Totomehuacan in 1642 when he married Isabel de Merino, also a vecina of Totomehuacan, who was the daughter of the briocenses Martín Merino and Isabel de Angón.[121]

Probably the biggest first-generation landowner was Hernando de Pastrana, the nephew of Pablo de Pastrana, who also was one of the most commercially active of the briocense immigrants, at least in his younger years. He became involved in ranching and stock raising through his marriage to Catalina González de Herrera, whose father, Hernán García de Herrera, endowed her with fourteen "sitios de estancia" with 10,000 sheep when she married Pastrana.[122] The first mention found of Hernando de Pastrana, born around 1570, was in February 1586, when he sold some cloth with his uncle Pablo de Pastrana. In the 1590s the two men pursued various mercantile activities together and separately. In January 1593 Hernando de Pastrana and Melchor Caballero formed a partnership in an obraje with 60 Indian workers in the barrio of San Agustín, for which they paid 2,600 pesos and obligated themselves to pay a censo of 2,400 pesos.[123] Although he did not immediately give up his mercantile interests—in 1603 he still owned a store in Puebla[124]—from the time he married he was closely involved with his father-in-law's affairs. As the executor of the will of Hernán García de Herrera, who died in 1598, Pastrana administered the estates that his father-in-law left until a division of property was made between his wife, Catalina de Herrera, and her sister Isabel de Grajeda.[125]

In the early seventeenth century Pastrana devoted increasing attention to business related to his estates, although he often rented them out rather than operating them directly. In February 1600, for example, he and a man named Diego de Morales made an agreement for two years by which Pastrana rented an hacienda de labor near Tlaxcala with 24 oxen, 240 pigs, and plows; Morales was to plant wheat and maize. During the same month Pastrana bought an estancia for "ganado menor" (sheep) near Tlaxcala for 300 pesos and sold to his uncle Pablo de Pastrana 4,000 arrobas of wool for eleven reales per arroba. The wool, to be delivered in September, would come from one of his estates and one that was part of his father-in-law's legacy.[126] In April 1600 he rented an "hacienda de ovejas" with 21,500 head of sheep to a vecino of Puebla, Lorenzo Sánchez, for three years. Every year Sánchez was to give him 70 arrobas of wool for every 1,000 sheep; they apparently renewed the agreement for another three years in 1602. That year Pastrana was buying more cattle—in January, with his brother-in-law Pedro

González de Herrera, all the cattle and horses that Francisco Blas Ramírez had on an estancia in "tierra caliente," and in March 4,000 lambs with their wool from the same estancia. In 1606 he sold 4,500 lambs and bought 200 bulls. The following year he rented two haciendas de ovejas with 25,745 head of sheep and 35 "indios e indias pastores" to a vecino of Tecamachalco for three years.[127]

Together with his wife's brother-in-law, Pedro González de Herrera, Pastrana was expanding the scope of his operations. In January 1608 they stated that in November 1600 they had formed a partnership in cattle estancias in which each had invested 9,000 pesos. They had planned to divide the profits at the end of five years but instead decided to extend the partnership for as long as they both were willing. González de Herrera apparently managed the ranches; his contribution consisted of two estancias near Cosamaloapan. Pastrana had given him 2,000 pesos with which to buy calves; the other 7,000 went toward the joint purchase of two other nearby estancias for 26,000 pesos. Pastrana declared that he still had not paid off another 22,000 pesos for cattle that he bought in the years between 1604 and 1606. He also owed 2,300 pesos in tithes. Perhaps because of these debts, in January 1608 Pastrana, his wife, and her sister and her husband sold a censo for 6,000 pesos on two houses belonging to Pastrana on the calle de San Agustín in Puebla and an hacienda de labor with 28 caballerías near the pueblo of Huamantla.[128] Pastrana and his brother-in-law also jointly owned an hacienda called Mapachapan in the "provincia de Guazacualco."[129] They formed a partnership with a man named Pedro Díaz Matamoros, who was to administer the hacienda for two years. They gave him 2,450 pesos as well as cloth and other merchandise to sell. Pedro Díaz was to receive a fifth of the male cattle three years old and above, and if they made hides on the hacienda, he would get one-fifth of them as well; he was also to receive one-third of any profits from the money and merchandise they provided.[130]

Hernando de Pastrana also formed a partnership with a man named Alonso Rodríguez Mateos in July 1612 in which he invested 3,000 pesos, 1,478 of which represented a tannery near the pueblo of Orizaba "con un indio oficial" and the rest 21 mules and the service of two other Indian workers. Alonso Rodríguez, who invested 800 pesos, was to manage the tannery and pack train and work full-time. The following April, however, they terminated the partnership and Pastrana rented to Alonso Rodríguez an estancia with twenty horses and a slave for 500 pesos a year for four years and sold him the tannery for 1,478 pesos.[131] During these years most of the money that Pastrana did not invest in estates and cattle went for purchases of gold and silver. It appears that after his uncle Pablo de Pastrana died, Hernando more or less withdrew from mercantile activities. Having arrived in New Spain as a teenager, he made the transition from entrepreneur to landowner and stock raiser by the age of 40.

Cristóbal de Pastrana and his son Juan de Pastrana also moved away from trade and manufacturing into large-scale ownership of cattle ranches and sugar estates. Cristóbal went to New Spain in the early 1570s and settled in Mexico City as a merchant. Ordered by the Audiencia to return to Spain to live with his wife, Juana Gutiérrez, he instead sent her nephew Gaspar Gutiérrez to bring her and their children to join him.[132] Cristóbal and his son Juan owned an obraje near La Fresnada and acquired two sugar estates, one called San Bernardo, near the pueblo of Tochimilco, and the other San José, near Tepexoxuma. In 1609 Juan de Pastrana stated that his estate near Tepexoxuma consisted of seven caballerías of land, four of them irrigated, on which he had eight slaves. San Bernardo had twenty caballerías of land, some of it irrigated as well, and 60 slaves. There he planted wheat and maize as well as sugar. These properties were heavily encumbered by censos, which totaled more than 50,000 pesos when Juan de Pastrana sold the San José *ingenio* (sugar mill) in 1618. Probably because of his increasing involvement with the estates, Juan de Pastrana was living in Puebla rather than Mexico City in 1612, although he was called *residente* rather than vecino.[133]

Briocenses doubtless became involved in agriculture and stock raising for a variety of reasons. Obrajeros such as the Anzures brothers may have seen some advantage in being able to supply both themselves and other textile producers with wool, and they both formed close ties with Puebla's landowning group through marriage and officeholding. Land on which to breed and graze cattle was an important factor in maintaining a successful carting business. Some immigrants, such as Macario de Anzures's brother-in-law Francisco Barbero, were labradores rather than entrepreneurs by background. Cristóbal García de Zúñiga, who first worked with his relative Miguel de Angón, acquired an estate with eight suertes of irrigated land on the Atoyac River with a gristmill, mules, oxen, three slaves, and several married Indians who worked as carters. He sold the property for 12,000 pesos to his sister María García's second husband, Lorenzo de Pajares, and a canon of the cathedral, Alonso Hernández de Santiago, when he left for Castile in 1608. María García and her first husband, Antón de Bonilla, had gone to Puebla to join her brother, and Bonilla probably worked with him. She owned a bakery when she made her will in 1613, so probably they had operated the estate, mill, and bakery as one enterprise.[134] Yet while acquisition of farms and ranches was common, and some briocenses, such as Hernando de Pastrana, became substantial landowners, no wholesale movement to abandon their mainly commercial activities in favor of estate ownership took place within the briocense community in Puebla, at least during the first couple of generations.

Economic Achievements and Impact

Judged collectively and individually, the economic progress of the briocenses in Puebla was considerable. If relatively few immigrants achieved real wealth, evidence from wills, dowry agreements, and investments suggests that in Puebla most of them improved their economic circumstances. As we have seen, a number of immigrants stated that when they married in Brihuega they had little or nothing in the way of capital or goods; given that starting point, the advances many of them made were substantial, even if they achieved modest economic security rather than genuine wealth. In his will of 1598, for example, Pedro Camarillo stated that his first wife, Catalina de Atienza, brought a dowry of 100 ducados when they married in Brihuega, and "I had no goods whatsoever." When he married again in Puebla, his second wife, Mariana de Santiago, brought a dowry of 600 pesos, and his capital totaled 2,000 pesos—by no means impressive sums but still representing real improvement in his circumstances.[135]

Other immigrants did become quite wealthy. Both Diego and Pedro de Anzures established entails. Diego returned to Brihuega in 1580 to acquire *señorío* of the town of Romancos (which he held only a few years before the town purchased its independence) and marry his daughter, doña Catalina de Barrientos, to the *alcaide* (warden) of the fortress of Brihuega, don Francisco Pacheco, who belonged to a leading noble family of Guadalajara. Alonso Gómez left his heirs an estate in houses, obrajes, and batanes worth over 120,000 pesos, and Juan de Pastrana's sugar estate was worth 148,000 pesos when he sold it in 1618.[136] Wealth and marital connections enabled some of the briocense nouveaux riches to acquire such municipal offices as regidor, *alcalde ordinario*, and *alférez mayor*. Juan Barranco founded the convent of Jesús María with a *colegio* (school) for girls in Puebla, and his relative Juan García Barranco left money to establish a school in Brihuega.

The dowries that some of the briocense immigrants in Puebla provided for their daughters also reflected their economic progress. Francisca Sánchez Salmerón, wife of the obrajero Juan de Pastrana, stated in her will of 1591 that her dowry had been a very modest 12,000 maravedís (just over 30 ducados) and her husband had nothing when they married. Their success in Puebla enabled them to give their daughters handsome dowries: they gave

María 3,000 pesos when she married Alonso del Moral, Catalina 5,000 pesos when she married the obrajero Alonso Gómez, and doña Isabel a substantial 8,500 pesos when she married don Cristóbal Godínez Maldonado.[137] Pablo de Pastrana and his wife endowed their daughter Leonor with 12,000 pesos when she married Cristóbal de Mendizábal, an immigrant from Oñate whose arras was 2,000 pesos. That amount included 4,000 pesos in cash, seven bars of silver worth 1,500 pesos, jewelry worth 1,000 pesos, a house on half a lot valued at 3,000 pesos, two slaves (a man and woman), and other jewelry, clothes, and household furnishings.[138] Hernando de Pastrana and his wife provided a dowry of 10,000 pesos when their daughter María married Hernando de Carmona Tamariz.[139]

Relatively few briocenses became truly wealthy. In the agreement made between the mother and widow of Juan de Olivares regarding the settlement of his estate in 1602, his widow, María de Ochoa, declared that when they married, his capital totaled 1,500 pesos and she brought a dowry of 1,900 pesos, but the six years of their marriage had not resulted in any gains. When Olivares died, their assets consisted mainly of a small obraje with 30 Indian workers "inside the house" and a dozen more outside, three looms for coarse cloth and other equipment, wool, yarn, dyes, and some cloth, a small bakery, ten jugs of honey, María's clothes, and a sword, dagger, crossbow, and horse that belonged to Olivares.[140] Olivares died young; had he lived, perhaps in time he would have been successful. All the evidence suggests that in Puebla obraje ownership was considered to be a lucrative business. Juan de Ribas's wife, Beatriz Martínez, who was barely ten years old when they married in 1580, brought a dowry of 9,000 pesos. During the course of a lengthy suit in 1583–84 between Ribas and Pedro de Alcanadre over an obraje and batán that Ribas and his father, Alonso de Ribas, bought from Alcanadre, the value of Juan de Ribas's goods was declared to be 7,000 pesos.[141] Beatriz's substantial dowry and her young age suggest that her parents chose Ribas as her spouse more for his future earning potential than for his current worth.

The briocenses in Puebla to a great extent were able to use the experience and skills they brought with them.[142] Cloth shearers, fullers, farmers, merchants, and notaries all put their background to good use, although the nature and scale of the obrajes were such that people with a background in cloth manufacture did far more than simply practice their trades as they had done in Brihuega. Instead they embarked on an almost entirely new kind of enterprise that required at least as much skill in business and management as in the various stages of cloth manufacture.

The size and coherence of the immigrant group guaranteed multiple connections of kinship, compadrazgo, and friendship that helped new arrivals establish themselves. Although many families remained close to their commercial and working-class origins, immigrants were more than willing to involve themselves in a variety of enterprises. Economic success and advantageous marriages certainly could pave the way for upward mobility over generations. Among the children of Pedro de Anzures and his wife, doña Isabel de Vargas, for example, don Diego de Anzures eventually sat on the cabildo, Bach. Pedro de Anzures became an ordained priest, and Lic. don Josephe de Anzures, who died on the way to Spain in 1625, was a lawyer of the Audiencia and served as governor of Tlaxcala three times.[143] Their first cousin Gabriel de Anzures Guevara, son of the labrador Francisco Barbero, was an escribano and also served as *alguacil mayor* of Huejotzingo. All in all, immigrants' careers, activities, and marriages and the strength and duration of the connection between Brihuega and Puebla offer ample proof that they found a good life in New Spain.

They left their mark on Puebla as they pursued economic success. During the years they were settling in the city, San Francisco, officially an Indian barrio located northeast of the main plaza and going down to the San Francisco River, became highly commercialized. Briocenses owned and rented houses as well as obrajes, mills, tanneries, bakeries, and inns in that area. Between 1568 and 1575 the city council granted the obrajeros Andrés de Angulo, Alonso de Ribas, and Juan de Pastrana property near the river, where they built batanes. Juan de Pastrana owned an obraje on the street of the Hospital of San Pedro, and in 1608 his brother-in-law Juan Llorente rented a house next door to his for six years. Llorente's close associate Bartolomé Tartajo also owned houses in San Francisco, as did his brother Pedro Llorente and his wife and their daughter María Llorente and her husband. Miguel Toribio, another associate of Juan Llorente and Bartolomé Tartajo involved in trade and transport, owned a house in the same barrio. Isabel de Guadalajara owned a house and bakery in San Francisco, next to properties owned by Miguel de Angón, whose brother Juan de Angón also lived there. These are only some examples. This high concentration of both commercial activity and residential choice suggests that the briocenses played a major role in transforming San Francisco from a peripheral Indian barrio into a key commercial-industrial zone.

The expansion of the textile industry under the direction of the briocense immigrants certainly had an impact on the development of poblano society. The colonial obraje generally, and justifiably, has been portrayed in the historical literature as a highly exploitative institution where Indian workers were poorly fed, housed, clothed, and compensated and often were not at liberty to leave. The obraje, however, also brought representatives of different socioeconomic and ethnic groups into close contact. It served to integrate migrants into poblano society, whether they were artisans and entrepreneurs from Castile who managed and owned the textile shops or Indians from other towns of New Spain who came to Puebla looking for work. In the obrajes Indian workers and Africans and people of African descent, slave and free, learned skills and trades associated with Spanish textile production. While the exploitative, coercive aspect of colonial textile manufacturing is undeniable, viewed from a somewhat different perspective the obraje can also be understood as an institution that facilitated the integration of members of several groups into a new society and introduced them to a new form of productive enterprise.

The economic impact of the movement to New Spain on Brihuega is harder to gauge. Clearly the connection to Puebla afforded a very significant outlet for vecinos who found themselves in deteriorating or at least stagnant circumstances, and remittances and legacies from family members who had emigrated no doubt could be important even though, sporadic as they were, they hardly offered a long-term solution to economic difficulties. In many cases entire generations abandoned Brihuega for Puebla or elsewhere, a good indication that many families found little to keep them at home. Townspeople could hardly ignore the size and implications of the movement to America. In December 1583, for example, the town council discussed sending someone to court to argue that the town could not pay the alcabala "because the rich people are diminishing and have left and every day vecinos leave for the Indies and in the three years of the tax assessment it's expected that many more will go."[144] The very small number of returnees underscores how limited were the opportunities in Brihuega even for those who brought back some capital. Cristóbal de Ribas, who returned to Brihuega with his family in the 1570s, owned property and censos in the 1580s, but he departed again in 1593 accompanied by all his children, married and single, and some of their in-laws. The sons of the returnees Juan de Roa and Andrés de Angulo also all went back to Puebla to live. While visits and short-term returns to Brihuega were common, the attractions of Puebla clearly proved superior for those who had personal experience or connections there.

CHAPTER THREE

Politics and Public Life

In the second half of the sixteenth century, as seen, the possibility of relocating elsewhere began to exercise a powerful appeal for the people of Brihuega, taking perhaps a thousand or more of them to New Spain during the five decades from around 1570 to 1620 and leading another sizable contingent to settle in the Alpujarras in the early 1570s.[1] Brihuega was becoming impoverished, the number of villages in its jurisdiction dwindling and its textile industry fallen on hard times.[2] A crisis that began at the end of the 1570s compounded these difficulties and further burdened the town's diminishing resources. The crown removed the town from the archbishopric of Toledo and made it part of the royal domain, clearing the way for its sale to benefit the royal treasury. The crown found one and then another noble buyer. The town's citizens protested and attempted in vain to negotiate the change of jurisdiction. The municipality went heavily into debt to finance its self-purchase, a measure advocated by some vecinos and strongly opposed by others; this *tanteo* (matching bid) took effect in the mid-1580s. About twenty years later Brihuega arranged to return to the archbishop's jurisdiction.[3]

These events generated a great deal of fairly well documented activity: discussion among the town's officials and other vecinos regarding the possibility of preventing the transfer of jurisdiction and then the feasibility of self-purchase in preference to the appalling prospect of government by an unknown lord after centuries of residing cozily within the archbishopric; compilation of the only known detailed census of taxpayers for the period with each vecino's economic assets and tax liability noted;[4] disputes that erupted because some vecinos decided to pursue self-purchase and were accused by others of proceeding clandestinely and without the consent of all necessary parties; and negotiations to return to the archbishopric after twenty years of self-government had yielded political discontent and no means to retire the enormous debt the municipality assumed for the tanteo.

The existence of this and other kinds of documentation on Brihuega, together with evidence on the political activities of the immigrants in Puebla, affords an opportunity to examine and compare attitudes toward and participation in local government in the two places. Did political institutions and activity in Brihuega reflect or subsume social and economic conflict? Were those institutions restricted or relatively accessible to all, as is sometimes assumed to have been the case for smaller municipalities in Castile? When immigrants from Brihuega found themselves in the new political and social environment of Puebla, did they attempt to enter into, use, or oppose political institutions in ways familiar to them from home? Did returnees from New Spain have an impact on local politics in Brihuega? Discussion of these questions offers insight into how the meaning and function of local government and participation in public life changed in Spanish America in a case where a large and coherent group with a presumably shared political culture established itself in a single community.

Government and Politics in Brihuega

In her landmark study of the creation and self-purchase of municipalities in early modern Castile, Helen Nader discusses the tendency for municipal officials to proliferate; their numbers often were disproportionately large in relation to the local population.[5] Brihuega, officially a *villa*, certainly was no exception in this regard. The town's general council (*ayuntamiento general*) consisted of two councilmen or regidores, one representing the "estate" of hidalgos, the other representing the estate of taxpayers or pecheros; four representatives (*diputados*, also called *jurados*) of the hidalgo group; and four diputados who represented the town's four parishes. All served one-year terms. In addition a procurador general (general representative) was chosen, alternating annually between estates, as well as one magistrate (alcalde) for each of the two *hermandades* (leagues) of hidalgos and pecheros, and a *fiel* (inspector of weights and measures) for each estate, all also serving on a yearly basis. A corregidor appointed by the archbishop presided over the council except during the years in which the town was in the royal domain, when two alcaldes ordinarios (one from each estate) were elected annually. The council itself nominated candidates for all these offices, and the archbishop made the final choice; in the years when the town governed itself, hidalgos voted in all cases but commoners voted only for positions earmarked for pecheros. The council appointed other officials and at times met together with the representatives of the towns and villages in its jurisdiction (in 1580 there were eight, but their number decreased with sales and self-purchases).

The way nominations for seats on the general council were generated was a crucial determinant of the council's makeup. The system worked to ensure a high degree of continuity and redundancy, even though individuals did not succeed themselves in office. Lope de la Carrera was regidor de hidalgos in 1582, fiel de hidalgos in 1583, and procurador general in 1584; in 1586 he was regidor again. His brother Cristóbal de la Carrera was regidor de hidalgos in 1583 and fiel de hidalgos in 1584. They both went to Puebla in 1593 in the entourage of Cristóbal de Ribas, who had returned to Brihuega from Puebla around 1570.[6] There are many such cases. At least among the not very numerous hidalgos, repetition in and circulation among municipal offices was virtually the rule, since there were only six or eight hidalgo families in all. But repeated officeholding could be found among prominent pecheros as well, as in the case of Cristóbal de Ribas; he served as regidor de pecheros in 1582 and was chosen as the alcalde ordinario of pecheros in 1585 and again in 1589; his son Cristóbal de Ribas el mozo represented the parish of Santa María de la Peña as diputado in the council in 1583 and again in 1585. Rodrigo de Anzures, whose three brothers were among the most prominent and successful emigrants to Puebla, served in one capacity or another (including stints as *teniente de gobernador,* or deputy governor) during most of his adult life.

Despite its size and prerogatives, the general council hardly monopolized Brihuega's political life. There also existed an *ayuntamiento de pecheros* (commoners' council), a more shadowy institution since records of its proceedings, if maintained, have not survived.[7] This council consisted of eight diputados, presumably two from each parish, and had its own procurador general. Finally each parish had a council (*cabildo*) and officials, including two alcaldes and a procurador general. The parish priest played an active role in the political affairs of the parish but was not actually a member of the council. I have found no indication of how the pecheros' council was constituted or how those council members or officials of the individual parishes were chosen. The scanty evidence available, however, suggests that in these councils as well a fair amount of repetition was common, although the pecheros were so much more numerous than the hidalgos that the rep-

FIGURE 5. *Local Government in Brihuega*

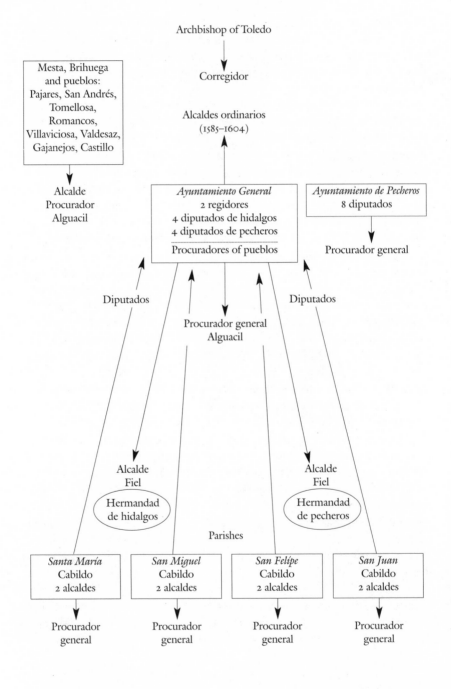

etition was not so pronounced. Furthermore, there seems to have been no clear distinction between the commoners who served on the general council and those who served on the pecheros' council. Martín Carrillo de Salcedo, for example, served as the general representative of the ayuntamiento de pecheros and as regidor de pecheros on the general council and in addition was a familiar of the Santo Oficio. In other words, he was well within the political and social mainstream. Melchor Carpintero, who was a representative on the ayuntamiento de pecheros, also served as a representative of the parish of San Felipe on the general council and as the parish's general representative. Alonso Gutiérrez, who went to Puebla in 1580, said that his father, Diego Gutiérrez ("el de San Juan"), was at one time or another jurado of the general council, procurador general de pecheros, and magistrate (alcalde) of the cabildo of San Miguel; his father's brother Alonso Gutiérrez served as regidor.[8] This institutional blurring, at least as regards personnel, certainly warns against any temptation to assume that the two town councils normally opposed rather than complemented each other.

Although information on the pecheros' council is scarce, it is clear that it functioned autonomously and that its fiscal affairs were separate from those of the general council. In 1572 a royal official sent to Brihuega to verify sales of *tierras baldías* (common or crown lands) confirmed the sale of a property consisting of 50 fanegas of agricultural land called Majadallana to the ayuntamiento de los pecheros.[9] In 1560 the "hombres pecheros" of Brihuega obtained a royal provision to collect 200 ducados and then another 800 in 1562 for the purpose of financing a suit against the town's hidalgos. Presumably it was the pecheros' council that requested the authorization and carried out the *reparto*, or assessment of each person's obligation.[10]

If the two town councils were not entirely distinct with regard to personnel, did representation by parish reflect distinct groupings or interests? A padrón of 1595, much less detailed than that of the previous decade, lists the town's vecinos by parish.[11] The most striking feature is a very strong tendency toward familial residential grouping, notable in all four parishes. Fifteen vecinos with the surname Alvarez lived in Santa María in 1595, for example, and not one Alvarez was listed in any other parish. This pattern was perhaps most pronounced in San Juan, the smallest parish and the most agriculturally oriented in respect to the vecinos' occupations; there were twenty listings (out of a total of 124 vecinos) for Cifuentes (3 other vecinos of that surname lived in San Felipe), thirteen for Corral, and eight for Trixueque; those three surnames alone accounted for one-third of the parish's vecinos. Although in the absence of a more detailed demographic study of the town one cannot be confident that all these families were related, it is safe to assume that for the most part they were, or thought they were, or had a common place of origin.[12]

Yet if parish residence was to a great extent based on kinship and place of origin, officeholding doubtless hinged more on economic position (and presumably social clout) than on a kin group's weight in numbers. Higher officials at least tended to be fairly substantial citizens, although I have found no indication of a property qualification for officeholding. A pattern of concentration in higher-level officeholding again seems clear, although possibly membership in the parish cabildos was more inclusive. Still, the same people who ran things at the municipal level seem to have played a similar role within their respective parishes. In a fight that took place in the Plaza del Coso, near the church of Santa María, in October 1584 over the issue of the tanteo, most of the participants—or at least those mentioned by name by witnesses—had held office at both the municipal and parish levels. Felipe de Peralta, who was fiel de pecheros in the 1580s, testified that "many people from the cabildo of Nuestra Señora [de Santa María]" were present, including the regidor (of the ayuntamiento general) Hernando Ruiz, Cristóbal de Ribas and his son of the same name (who, as seen, held offices in the 1580s), and Sancho de Urgelos (who also served at some time as a regidor as well as the procurador of the ayuntamiento de pecheros and a diputado on that council).[13] The incident illustrates, among other things, the concentration of officeholding at all levels in a relatively small number of individuals.

This pattern of multiple officeholding surely would have compromised the distinctiveness of the many political bodies that existed in the town and that might have functioned to reduce political conflict. By representing different estates and kin- or origin-based residential groupings, political institutions theoretically should have worked to channel conflict, but the concentration and overlapping of officeholding may have rendered them inadequate for the purpose. As a result, conflict tended to bypass or spill over from the institutional framework. Antagonism arose not between organized institutions but rather between political insiders and outsiders.

A dispute in 1589 over the admission of certain individuals to the cofradía of Nuestra Señora Santa María de la Misericordia y Remedio that reached the chancillería of Valladolid suggests some of the tensions in the town.[14] A group that included present and past members of the general council from both estates and the parish priest of San Juan sued for admission to the cofradía. The brotherhood was based in the parish church of San Felipe, although its members included residents of all the town's parishes, and they met once a year in each of the churches to celebrate mass and conduct a procession. The majority were labradores and rural workers, but certainly some artisans belonged as well.

Quite a few of the *hermanos* (brothers) agreed that the officials of the ayuntamiento were honorable people ("gente honrada") qualified to join the cofradía, but the perception of at least some members was that "oficiales" should be excluded. This term could, and in this case apparently did, refer to both officeholders and tradesmen (a telling linguistic ambiguity). The questions to be put to witnesses on behalf of the cofradía included whether they were aware that Jerónimo de Orozco (who was regidor de hidalgos) and others had stated publicly that "they will destroy the cofradía . . . and for this purpose they want to join it . . . to bring it to ruin." The escalating bad feeling was reflected in one witness's testimony that several members of the cofradía contended that "they shouldn't agree to admit any oficiales even if they waste their money on suits." He went on rather melodramatically to claim that from this conflict "there has resulted . . . in this town much slander and scandals so great that if his Majesty doesn't resolve the matter . . . men could die." Cofradía members described an incident that took place three years before during the cofradía's festival, held annually in September, in which someone—"one of the consorts of Benito Ruiz [the parish priest of San Juan] who are going around trying to destroy the cofradía"—had grabbed the brotherhood's banner. Martín Carrillo, one of the cofradía's alcaldes, alleged that one man seeking admission, a shoemaker named Pedro de Alcalá, had boasted that "whenever the cofradía takes its banner out they would tear it into pieces because there were a lot of young men on his side who were shoemakers and carders." Carrillo also thought that the people trying to gain admission planned to undermine the cofradía by putting a man in office who had been punished by the Inquisition.

Here are suggestions of the lines along which the town tended to divide, which were not those of estate, since the hidalgos were almost too few to carry much weight on their own (and for the most part they were not very wealthy), but more likely economic. Power lay with the hidalgos and their allies, the town's wealthy merchants and clothmakers who because of their economic activities often were associated in people's minds with conversos (hence the expressed fear that the people bringing suit for admission would "destroy" the cofradía from within by making a known converso an important official). The allegation of converso background surfaced so commonly in both personal and political disputes that it seems all but meaningless; it was, however, almost invariably directed toward people active in commerce and trades (especially clothmaking) and officeholders. In a complicated

Inquisition case of 1592 brought against a priest and commissioner (*comisario*) of the Santo Oficio in the town of Fuentelencina, a town with close ties to Brihuega, one witness made the surprising statement that "in this town when there weren't any hidalgos the offices were divided, and half of them the Old Christian farmers had and the other half the converso merchants and tradesmen," and everyone knew who was who.[15] The rhetoric employed in the suit over admission to the Cofradía del Remedio in Brihuega suggests that the assumption of a connection between commercial activity, officeholding, and converso background was common even if seldom articulated so concretely. Nor was the association between them baseless; but the passage of time, intermarriage, geographic mobility, and the presence of different families sharing the same surname all worked to render the identification of certain individuals or families as conversos increasingly questionable and probably for the majority of people irrelevant in any case. Whereas in the mid–sixteenth century many residents of small towns such as Brihuega and Fuentelencina probably still knew who the local converso families were, by the end of the century both interest and certainty had waned. Inquiries into an individual's descent usually yielded blanket affirmations of Old Christian background, or more infrequently an almost equally useless (because not specific) assertion that all the people with a particular surname were conversos.[16]

The lines along which the vecinos of Brihuega divided over the self-purchase further underscore the difficulty of differentiating contending factions by status, occupation, or office. In the late summer and fall of 1584 the general council first sent Cristóbal de Ribas el mozo (then the diputado from Santa María) and then the two regidores (Juan Matallana and Hernando Ruiz el mozo) to court to try to persuade the crown not to sell the town to a new lord. These initiatives failing, in October the council summoned a dozen leading citizens (and frequent officeholders), including Rodrigo de Anzures and his returnee brother Diego de Anzures and the returnee Cristóbal de Ribas (el viejo), to meet with the ayuntamiento. The parties present agreed to send two more representatives—Rodrigo de Anzures and Lic. Cervantes (who at the time was one of the diputados de hidalgos)—to court to make the same request; this time, however, they further empowered them to negotiate with the king for the town's self-purchase. By the spring of 1585 the negotiations for the sale had concluded.[17]

If the officials of the general council and their close associates concurred on the plan, who opposed it? Doubt arose regarding exactly who had made the decision to send Cervantes and Anzures to court to initiate the process of self-purchase. The procuradores of all four parishes, in the name of their respective cabildos, opposed the purchase on the grounds that the town lacked the resources (*propios*) to finance it. They said the decision to send the representatives to court had been made secretly at night and asked that an open meeting where all could speak and vote ("concejo abierto . . . y todos voten y sean oidos dello") be held. Dr. Urgelos, the town's lawyer, signed the petition.[18] The town's general representative, Pedro de la Carrera, alleged that the decision to send representatives to court had not been made by the general council as a whole; rather certain members, acting as private individuals and contrary to the will of the council and the procuradores of the parishes, had carried the tanteo through, to the detriment ("en perjuicio") of the town and its vecinos. The petition, presented on October 25 before the *teniente de corregidor*, Diego Gutiérrez, included the names of two diputados of the ayuntamiento general, the magistrate of the league of commoners, and the constable. They too claimed that "certain private citizens" ("ciertos vecinos particulares") had empowered the representatives to proceed without summoning an open council or ascertaining the opinion of the rest of the vecinos. The petitioners repudiated their action "and said that this town doesn't have the means [*propios*] to purchase itself and if it had . . . they would be happy" to do it, "but from their possessions they do not . . . want to buy the town because they are poor people and the land is needy." Two diputados of the ayuntamiento de pecheros said that their council had not been consulted, as it generally had been regarding serious matters affecting the town "since ancient times."[19] The commoners' council authorized the two diputados to repudiate the self-purchase.

In this crucial episode in the town's history, then, the vecinos used the institutional framework and legal means at their disposal to try to assert themselves in opposition to a decision that at first glance seemed to have been taken by the general council but in fact proved largely to be the work of the town's most powerful inner circle. That group included past and present members of the ayuntamiento general but was not synonymous with the council itself; hidalgos, priests, and several returnees from New Spain figured prominently. The protesters, with the single known exception of Pedro de la Carrera (described in the tax list as "hidalgo pobre"), were pecheros, although their numbers included officeholders as well as some well-to-do individuals. Juan de Brihuega, who was involved in the dispute among the members of the cabildo of Santa María mentioned earlier (his son Francisco de Brihuega got into a physical fight with Cristóbal de Ribas el mozo in the presence of both their fathers), stated that he opposed the tanteo because people of means like himself would be expected to contribute disproportionately to the costs. The final outcome of events demonstrated that real political power in the town resided not in any institution or office but rather in a less easily defined grouping of families who participated in local government but did not confine their exercise of political power to its institutions.

When the possibility of returning to the archbishopric arose twenty years later, some of the same individuals who had been instrumental in effecting the tanteo played an active part in negotiations for this second change of jurisdiction: the wealthy returnee Diego de Anzures (who by 1604 was fray Diego de Anzures de Guevara of the order of San Juan) and his brother Rodrigo de Anzures (both in their 70s by then) and the frequent regidor and wealthy cloth merchant Hernando Ruiz.[20] Many who opposed the town's self-purchase naturally supported the return to the archbishopric, and greater consensus characterized this second round of negotiations over the town's jurisdictional status.

During all these years of political uneasiness and jurisdictional change, people were departing for New Spain in numbers that could not fail to come to the attention of the town council. In June 1582 at the time of the annual election council members noted that Hernán Pérez de Parraga, who had been elected diputado the previous year, had "gone to the Indies and taken his wife and children and sold his estate." In 1583 the council wanted to send someone to court to explain that the town could not make the customary alcabala payment "because rich people are diminishing [in number] and have left and every day vecinos go to the Indies and in the three years of the assessment [of the alcabala] it's expected that many more will go." Perhaps the sheer volume of the movement accounts for the ease with which a small number of returnees blended into local society; the Indies—specifically the city of Puebla—had all but taken Brihuega over. Hence not only did people such as Diego de Anzures and Cristóbal de Ribas participate prominently in local affairs and officeholding, but their status as returnees was almost never noted. The part that they and other subsequent emigrants (such as Lope and Cristóbal de la Carrera) played in local politics and the connections that other emigrants had with officeholding in Brihuega provide a starting point from which to consider the briocense emigrants' political experience in Puebla.

Politics and Local Government in Puebla

The governing structure of Puebla de los Angeles stood in sharp contrast to that of Brihuega. Local government in Puebla was simple and monolithic. Participation was restricted to the privileged few, although despite the power and pretensions of the city's elite, the old hidalgo-commoner distinction in officeholding that prevailed in much of Castile did not exist as such in Puebla. The city council consisted of the regidores, whose positions could be passed along or sold and whose terms were indefinite; an alférez mayor, who also had a vote as a regidor; an alguacil mayor (chief constable); and two alcaldes ordinarios named annually by the regidores.[21] An alcalde mayor appointed by the viceroy presided. Although there were alcaldes for the Indian barrios, the city's Spanish vecinos had no governing bodies or representation other than the cabildo.

Notwithstanding the idealized vision of those who conceived its founding in the 1530s, and despite its role as a lively center for commerce, agriculture, and, increasingly, industry, Puebla in the second half of the sixteenth century was in some ways an aristocratic city. The leading families who claimed descent from conquistadores and held encomiendas dominated the city council, although their hold was loosening as individuals with overt commercial connections began to take their place on it.[22] As relative latecomers who were active in the commercial sector, the Brihuega immigrants were unlikely candidates for high office in Puebla, although clearly a precedent for the acceptance (however grudging) of people of entrepreneurial background already existed. Nonetheless, individuals who had enjoyed broad political experience in Brihuega generally found themselves excluded in the much more restrictive political and social atmosphere of Puebla; for the most part the offices and honors open to them were minor ones that could be purchased or positions in neighboring towns. Cristóbal de Ribas, who served so frequently in office in Brihuega, was *veedor de paños* (cloth inspector) in Puebla and either captain or *sargento mayor* of an infantry company on one occasion when the English threatened the port of San Juan de Ulúa. Francisco Barbero, who had been an alcalde ordinario in Brihuega, also served as a captain of infantry in New Spain in 1612. The brothers Gabriel, Gaspar, and Melchor Caballero (who were from Budía but were related to a number of the Brihuega emigrants and closely connected with them) served in a variety of offices but mainly outside Puebla itself: Gabriel was treasurer of the sales of *cruzadas* (indulgences) for the bishopric of Tlaxcala for one year; Gaspar was corregidor of the pueblo of Quimistlán and alguacil mayor of Huejotzingo and Carrión (in Atlixco); Melchor for six years was regidor of Veracruz and later alcalde ordinario of Carrión and alguacil of Huejotzingo.[23]

Three men from Brihuega—Alonso Gómez, Rodrigo García, and Gabriel de Angulo—became regidores of the city council in the 1590s, probably largely as a result of their marital ties with families that customarily held seats on the council. They had to overcome considerable opposition from members of the council, however. All three owned obrajes (as did Juan García Barranco, who became alférez mayor) and thus in theory were ineligible to be regidores. Ordered to divest themselves of their textile shops, they arranged sales that clearly were fictive. In his report on Puebla's obrajes in 1595 Dr. Santiago del Riego stated that the alférez Juan García Barranco owned two obrajes, Rodrigo García one, and Alonso Gómez two, one of them located in his own house, "on the pretense that they belong to his sons, who are still under his paternal authority."[24]

Of these first briocenses who acquired *regimientos* (seats), only one, Rodrigo García, had a son, Juan García del Castillo, who later sat on the council. This suggests that the briocense community in Puebla, even its more influential members, on the whole did not stake a very solid claim to presence on the council. Nonetheless, briocenses continued to figure among the regidores throughout the seventeenth century. The son of Pedro de Anzures, don Diego de Anzures, served as regidor in the 1630s, and a grandson of Alonso Gómez and Catalina de Pastrana, Capt. don Juan de Carmona Tamariz, was regidor in the 1660s. A briocense immigrant named Juan Bautista de Salaíces served as regidor from 1673 to 1694 in a seat vacated by Rodrigo del Castillo Villegas, probably a descendant of Rodrigo García.[25]

The one position the briocenses were able to retain for much of the period was that of alférez mayor, which ironically carried considerable prestige (its price was almost double that of a regimiento) and conferred the vote of a regidor on the holder. The position was first held in Puebla by Diego de Anzures, who went to Puebla in the 1550s and held a series of offices (escribano del cabildo, escribano de la grana, alcalde de la mesta, alcalde ordinario) before purchasing the title of alférez mayor in 1576. Although Anzures passed along this position to a relative of his wife when he left for Brihuega in 1579, subsequently two other men from Brihuega— Juan García Barranco and later his brother-in-law Lope de la Carrera—held the office for many years. Like the three briocenses who served as regidores around the turn of the century, they were also obraje owners; Lope de la Carrera, it will be recalled, had served in many offices in Brihuega. In the 1650s don Jerónimo Carrillo, the son and grandson of immigrants from Brihuega, was alférez in Puebla.[26] The briocenses' claim on this office doubtless hinged on the fact that Diego de Anzures had in effect created it, and so could designate his successor.

On the whole the briocenses failed to establish a substantial presence on the city council in the late sixteenth and early seventeenth centuries. They did achieve a lasting connection with it, however, particularly when their larger circle of associates and relatives by marriage is taken into account. In a dispute of 1627 between Dr. don Antonio de Cervantes Carvajal, a canon of the cathedral and comisario of the Santo Oficio, and the city council, don Antonio referred to Juan García del Castillo, together with another regidor and the alguacil mayor, as "individuals who lead the rest of the secular cabildo." The canon, at least, was well aware of Juan García del Castillo's origins, calling him "a very ordinary man of very humble background, and it's well known that his parents were from Brihuega in Castile, textile manufacturers, which at present he is, he and his mother, and that's an occupation of low and humble men and . . . all the other regidores are of similarly humble origins . . . without a single man among them of even middling quality."[27] The implication of this tirade is not that Juan García del Castillo was odd man out on the council but instead (and regrettably) a key and representative member. In view of the fact that at the time Juan García Barranco was still alférez mayor, Juan de Carmona Tamariz (the son-in-law of the former regidor Alonso Gómez) was *depositario general* (general trustee), and Marcos Rodríguez Zapata, a longtime close associate of the briocense obrajeros and merchants, was the notary of the city council, his judgment seems to have reflected the reality of local government at the time.

The briocenses' strength in the notarial profession also gave them an entrée into local politics, although here again, in the absence of personal connections, this kind of background would not necessarily have brought them much closer to the real center of power and influence. In this arena of officeholding as well Diego de Anzures led the way. Son of a man who was both a textile manufacturer and notary in Brihuega, Anzures obtained appointment as notary of the city council in 1566, a position he subsequently passed on to his younger brother Pedro de Anzures, who assumed office in 1570.[28] Their nephew Gabriel de Anzures Guevara also was an escribano (although not of the cabildo) in Puebla, as were at least three other briocenses in the early seventeenth century.[29] Briocenses also established close ties with other notaries, such as the influential Marcos Rodríguez Zapata,[30] longtime notary of the city council and accountant, and Juan de la Parra. Apparently the latter was at one time the subject of an investigation by the Inquisition during the course of which one briocense, Francisco el Rojo, not only testified against him but openly discussed his testimony, an indiscretion that brought an Inquisition charge against him in 1602. Pablo de Pastrana, for many years a key figure in the briocense commercial community, testified that Rojo had said that Juan de la Parra "has done more harm to those of our country [tierra] than anyone else in this city." According to Pastrana's compadre Marcos Rodriguez Zapata, Pastrana was very upset about Rojo's testimony because Juan de la Parra was such a good friend and was worried that "this man has destroyed everyone from our tierra by showing hatred and enmity toward Juan de la Parra."[31]

Well-to-do and well-connected briocenses in Puebla, then, did gain some access to political power and influence through both formal and informal channels, notwithstanding the limited institutional framework of local government and the lingering suspicion of their background that persisted despite economic success, intermarriage, and, over generations, increasing respectability. The sons of doña Agustina Gómez and her husband, Juan de Carmona Tamariz, provide a case in point. By the 1660s Dr. don Joseph de Carmona Tamariz was prebendary (racionero) of the cathedral, Capt. don Juan de Tamariz was a regidor and depositario general, don Antonio de Carmona Tamariz a priest, and fray Pedro de Carmona Tamariz a member of the Dominican order. When the first three tried to get appointments as familiares of the Inquisition in the 1660s (their paternal grandfather, Diego de Carmona, had been a familiar), the question of the converso origins of their maternal grandparents, Alonso Gómez and Catalina de Pastrana, arose during the inquiry into their limpieza de sangre. The lengthy investigation into the Gómez and Pastrana families carried out in Brihuega and other towns revealed absolutely nothing that might substantiate suspicions regarding their background.[32]

Regardless of the success of what really was no more than a handful of individuals and families who through marital ties, economic clout, and sometimes education achieved some influence in poblano politics and society, the great majority of the briocenses who moved to Puebla lacked any voice or opportunity for political participation. In January 1582 two residents of Puebla, Lic. Salmerón, a lawyer of the Real Audiencia in Mexico City,[33] and Diego Cortés obtained a royal provision for the election of "procuradores del común," who could bring suits against the cabildo resulting from complaints by the city's vecinos. Salmerón claimed that "the council has been divided into two groups of relatives [parentelas], and the alcaldes whom they have elected and elect have been and are relatives and kinsmen of the cabildo members . . . and for this reason justice and its execution goes always by bias in favor of their relatives, and there has not been nor is there any justice other than what the regidores want."[34] Lic. Salmerón and a vecino from Brihuega named Francisco del Castillo presented to one of the city's notaries the provision authorizing the convening of a "concejo abierto" (open council) to deliberate on this election. The meeting took place at the church of Vera Cruz one afternoon in early January 1582. Of the 86 vecinos who attended, 17—around a fifth—were certainly briocenses.[35]

All of them were merchants, obrajeros, and tradesmen; only one (Alonso Gómez) eventually achieved office, although others were closely associated with men who did (Martín de Viñuelas was the compadre and brother-in-law of Rodrigo García; Pablo de Pastrana, as mentioned, was the compadre of Marcos Rodríguez Zapata). The participation of so many economically very active but for the most part thoroughly working-class immigrants from Brihuega in this episode suggests real frustration with the limited and exclusive nature of Puebla's politics and governing structure.

Briocenses and doubtless other immigrants as well had been shaped by a political tradition that reflected in its institutions the assumption that people of different estates would have distinct outlooks and concerns. This tradition also held that people excluded from the highest circle of local political power should have some recourse available to them and that government should incorporate a representative element (as seen in the presence of diputados or jurados on town councils). Surely these ideas contributed to the convening of the "concejo abierto" in 1582, in which many briocenses participated. Consideration of how Brihuega's political institutions responded to situations of conflict and crisis has shown that the high degree of concentration of officeholding in the hands of relatively few, mostly well-to-do individuals limited the independence and effectiveness of political bodies representing different constituencies (the pecheros, the parishes). Nevertheless, they could provide a forum for the expression of differing points of view and objectives and confine at least some disputes to legal channels. Certainly it was customary practice to convene open meetings at the parish level to discuss and vote on important issues. When the question of returning to the archbishopric arose in 1604, for example, 48 vecinos of the parish of Santa María, 40 from San Miguel, 31 from San Felipe, and 27 from San Juan conferred their collective power of attorney to vote in favor of the proposal.[36]

Puebla's elitist politics must have seemed strange to the immigrants, at least initially. Puebla was a new world indeed, offering a variety of economic opportunities but nothing comparable to Brihuega's lively politics, with its many institutions and officials and sometimes raucous debates and disputes. In Puebla the political sphere was closed and exclusive, the province of the wealthy and well connected. Certainly disagreement, antagonism, and even violence characterized poblano society and even the city council itself at times. The circumscribed institutional structure of local government, however, meant that factionalism and competition were more likely to manifest themselves outside the formal political arena than within it. With the great majority of vecinos in effect excluded from officeholding, people sought other avenues to influence and favor—joint economic ventures, compadrazgo, marital alliances with officeholding families. Yet even these options were available to relatively few. In Brihuega the large number of political offices and institutions may have enhanced the usefulness of economic, social, and kinship ties to persons in and out of office alike; the political sphere in Puebla was so small that forging similar ties with key officials lay beyond the realistic aspirations of most vecinos. The result may have been to heighten the economic and social distance between political insiders and outsiders within Spanish poblano society—not to mention, of course, the far more politically and socially marginalized indigenous, African, and mixed residents of the city.

The immigrants from Brihuega must have recognized the differences in the politics of the two places, but there is no way to know if it was a matter of much concern to them. Nearly all of the emigrants from Brihuega remained in Puebla, where they formed a fairly coherent community, united by long-standing ties of acquaintance, kinship, common economic interest, and a significant degree of endogamy.[37] A few returned to Brihuega, but some who did so later left again. Cristóbal de Ribas lived more than twenty years in Brihuega after his first sojourn in New Spain. As we have seen, he and his son of the same name were quite active in Brihuega's political affairs after their return; yet their local prominence did not persuade them to stay. When Ribas and his family went back to New Spain in 1593, their entourage included three siblings in the hidalgo Carrera family, who similarly had been active politically. The rewards of political participation were clearly insufficient to keep this extended family at home.

Once in Puebla, a few briocenses did enter local government. They succeeded most notably, however, when they were able to carve out their own particular niche, such as the office of alférez mayor. But the addition of this office and later that of depositario general changed neither the basic structure nor the function of the city council.[38] Despite the size of the briocense immigrant community and its economic importance, the newcomers had little influence on the nature of politics. Their political traditions of representation and annual rotation in office, and of parish cabildos that provided forums for what technically may have been residential units but were, in effect, kinship or origin-based groupings, had no impact on government and politics in Puebla. Puebla's council, along with virtually all other Spanish city and town councils in the Indies, may be seen as the final phase in the transition from the medieval participatory institution to the revamped early modern version, which lacked any vestige of the old representative principle and looked to the crown for confirmation (meaning sale) of its appointments. Brihuega's complex local government fell somewhere along the evolutionary spectrum from the old to the new model. Still incorporating many of the old elements of representation, yearly rotation in office, and division of offices between estates, the system of officeholding in Brihuega nonetheless had become fairly exclusive by the latter part of the sixteenth century. The immigrants who left that old political world for the new one of Puebla experienced an abrupt transition from one phase to another of a historical process in the evolution of Castilian municipalities that in Castile affected different areas with varying pace and intensity.[39] Brihuega's politics and government themselves doubtless had changed from the Middle Ages to the sixteenth century, and changed to some degree in the direction of the new style of municipal government that the crown was able to impose wholesale on the cities and towns of Spanish America; but they had not reached the level of elitism and reductionism that the Brihuega migrants encountered when they moved to Puebla.

Public Life

Discussion thus far has focused mainly on political officeholding and formal institutions, but participation in civic public life was not limited to government. In both Castile and New Spain there were other outlets for men who wished to gain honor and demonstrate largesse. Processions and festivities especially afforded opportunities for public display of status and financial wherewithal,[40] as did military rank in militia companies. Playing a major part in events such as those organized to welcome high-ranking visitors probably was a great deal more fulfilling emotionally than the humdrum activities associated with officeholding, even though that kind of participation did not provide the pragmatic or long-term advantages of political office. Unquestionably such occasions could be memorable, as suggested by one in which Gabriel de Angulo literally played the leading role.

Gabriel de Angulo, born in 1553, was the son of Andrés de Angulo, who had gone to New Spain and returned early to Brihuega, taking his wife, Isabel de Ribas, and children back to Puebla with him. Gabriel accompanied his parents when they went to live again in Brihuega in the late 1570s. A few years later, however, he and his brother Pedro de Angulo petitioned for a license to go back to Puebla, stating that their parents had left "certain goods and property and we need to go collect them." The license, issued in April 1582, included Pedro's wife, Inés de Ochoa, whom he had married during the years they were in Brihuega. Both brothers stayed on in Puebla, where they owned obrajes, and Gabriel married doña María de Hurtado, member of a prominent local family.[41]

In 1587 in Puebla Gabriel de Angulo prepared a deposition as part of a petition to be recognized as having the right to use the title of captain.[42] The document conceding him that rank, he alleged, was among a number of other papers and clothes in a box that had been stolen. Gabriel's claim to the title stemmed from his appointment by the town council of Brihuega to serve for two days as "captain of the people and soldiers" who welcomed the empress, sister of King Philip, when she arrived in the town. One witness, Diego Tomellosa, who was from Yunquera in the tierra of Guadalajara, said that a few years before he had seen and participated in the "celebrations and displays of soldiers" when the empress came. Tomellosa testified that Angulo had been in command; "with a single voice they all called him captain." Tall and handsome, well dressed and wearing a gold chain around his neck, Angulo must have cut a striking figure. When he went up alongside the litter in which the empress rode and knelt to pay his respects, she was heard to declare, "Rise up, captain, you have done very well." These words quickly circulated among the men he led, who, according to the witnesses, praised Angulo and held him in much esteem for the favor he had received.[43]

Although Brihuega's reception of the empress doubtless was carefully orchestrated, such planning did not preclude spontaneous gestures such as the commendation that Angulo received, which seems to have been a genuine expression of appreciation on the part of the visiting dignitary. This royal recognition probably marked the high point of Gabriel's young life; one wonders if he ever again experienced anything like the thrill of that occasion, when he was singled out for distinction simultaneously by the people who governed the town (who appointed him captain), the men he led (who supported him enthusiastically), and the empress herself, who showed him her favor. In Puebla he led an active life in both public and private sectors, using the title of captain fairly consistently by the early seventeenth century, but his activities suggest a certain restlessness or discontent. In an investigation into charges of mistreatment of Indian workers brought against his brother Pedro de Angulo in 1584, it was Gabriel who was accused of the most extreme conduct, reportedly hanging one worker by his feet over a fire of burning chili peppers. Pedro denied that Gabriel was either his mayordomo or partner in the obraje.[44] The testimony suggests that in contrast to his brother, who owned an obraje within a year of their return to

Puebla, Gabriel did not immediately settle down to work on either his own behalf or his brother's; perhaps initially his aspirations were higher.

Gabriel was far more intent on achieving public distinction than his brother Pedro, who apparently never served in any civil or military office, and highly conscious of what he felt to be his privileges and prerogatives.[45] The petitions that Gabriel prepared in the years 1587–90 concerned in part the question of *hidalguía*, claim to which his father apparently was litigating when he died. When Gabriel de Angulo was imprisoned in January 1588 for having fought with Juan Rodríguez Navarrete, he protested not his arrest but rather his incarceration in the public jail, since as a "caballero hijodalgo" he should have been imprisoned "according to the quality of my person" (his antagonist was confined to the more honorable quarters of the city hall).[46] Gabriel was the treasurer for the sales of the Santa Cruzada in the bishopric of Tlaxcala in 1587 and again in 1592 and 1593. At the beginning of 1593, as discussed, he also became a regidor of the city council; that December he received a response to his petition in the form of a royal instruction to the viceroy, don Luis de Velasco, that vaguely stipulated that Angulo should be granted a suitable office.[47] By 1600 Angulo already had requested a license to renounce his regimiento, although he was still pursuing litigation "sobre mi hidalguía" in the chancillería of Valladolid.[48] The rapidity with which he lost interest in public office suggests that, once achieved, it actually yielded little in the way of rewards or satisfaction.

Puebla of course offered many opportunities to participate in ceremonies and celebrations, and by virtue of their positions or influence some briocenses played prominent roles in their observance. In 1567, for example, Diego de Anzures, as the escribano del cabildo, declared that his predecessors in the office had always carried a "vara del palio del Santísimo Sacramento" (staff of the canopy of the Most Holy Sacrament), as did the city's regidores. He noted that he should enjoy the same prerogative, and the council members agreed.[49] The city's wealth, size, and influence, as well as its location on the road connecting Veracruz and Jalapa to Mexico City, meant not only that ceremonial occasions arose frequently but that the municipality would take quite seriously its obligation to observe them with pomp and considerable expenditure of funds. In 1589 the city staged a mock battle for the reception of the viceroy, and the council named Alonso Gómez the "gran turco" (great Turk) for the Turkish side, authorizing him to appoint whatever people he needed and earmarking 350 pesos from municipal funds for the construction of the castle and for gunpowder.[50] Altogether the city council planned to spend some 6,000 pesos. For the anticipated arrival of the new viceroy, the conde de Monterrey, in September 1595 the city council agreed to send two of the regidores to Jalapa to greet him. To celebrate his entrance into the city there would be bulls and a jousting match with twelve teams, six representing the cabildo and six the citizens, all dressed in colorful Moorish-style costumes paid for by the city. The council named the alférez mayor Juan García Barranco (from Brihuega) as captain general of the infantry that would meet the viceroy and noted that Francisco Rodríguez, probably also a briocense, had offered to play the role of the great Turk. Fireworks, rockets, and bugles would provide the background for what must have been a raucous and extravagant fiesta.[51]

Ceremonial occasions, although often characterized by great formality, could give rise to conflict if individuals disagreed over precedence or repudiated their assigned rank or function, revealing tensions over the terms by which public life was conducted.[52] The account of the dispute that resulted in the tirade by the canon of the cathedral, Dr. don Antonio de Cervantes Carvajal, against Juan García del Castillo and other members of the city council mentioned earlier demonstrates how political and social tensions could sabotage ritual and ceremony. The episode suggests that however outwardly formal such events appeared, they depended for their success on the willing collaboration of all the parties involved.

The dispute hinged on a procession that was supposed to take place at the end of February 1627. The officials of the city were to accompany the comisario (commissioner) of the Inquisition—Dr. Cervantes Carvajal, the canon of the cathedral—to the cathedral for the proclamation of the edict of faith. According to Dr. Bartolomé González, the prosecutor (*promotor fiscal*) of the Holy Office, it had been the "custom of many years" that when the commissioner of the Holy Office pronounced the edict of faith and "letter of anathema" in Puebla, the city's alcalde mayor, alcaldes ordinarios, and regidores would accompany him from his house to the cathedral on horseback. The alcalde mayor rode on the comisario's left side. The more senior of the alcaldes ordinarios rode on his right side and the other on the alcalde mayor's left, "in such fashion that the said comisario always goes in the superior place." Ahead of them went the familiar who acted as the tribunal's alguacil mayor, riding between the Holy Office's notary and another familiar, and in front of them the other officers and regidores rode intermingled. Upon reaching the cathedral they would conduct the canon to his place, which was at the level of the high altar and next to the Evangelio (Gospel), where the commissioner, "representing the Holy Tribunal," sat on a chair with a velvet cushion positioned on a small rug. Right behind him sat the other officers on two covered benches. All the municipal officials attended, and once the publication of the edict was celebrated, they would accompany the commissioner in the same order back to his house.

A few days before this ceremony was to take place the canon, Dr. Cervantes Carvajal, went to confer with the alcalde mayor, the *mariscal* (marshal) don Carlos de Luna y Arellano,[53] showing him a letter from the viceroy containing instructions regarding the reading of the edict, an apparent confirmation of a royal *cédula* (decree) of 1570 that had stipulated that municipal officials would accompany the Holy Office. Again according to the prosecutor, Dr. González, the alcalde mayor agreed to accompany the commissioner and said he would discuss the matter with the members of the city council. Allegedly the councillors refused to comply and agreed only to wait for the commissioner to arrive at the door of the cathedral and to accompany him from there. Furthermore, the alcalde mayor did not inform the canon of this decision until the evening of February 27, the eve of the scheduled proclamation, leaving the commissioner no time to arrange some alternative. When he sent a message to Pedro de Uribe, the most senior of the regidores, via the familiar Hernando de Carmona, Uribe replied that the councillors had already discussed the action they would take: they would meet him at the "Puerta del Perdón" (Door of Forgiveness) of the cathedral and from there accompany him "as private individuals" ("como particulares del pueblo").

In April of that year Juan Bautista de Villadiego, secretary of the Inquisition of Seville, arrived to investigate the matter and ordered the notary of the cabildo, Marcos Rodríguez Zapata, and his deputy, Nicolás Hernández de la Fuente, to hand over all the council records of the last fifteen years for his review. Some of the testimony suggested that, notwithstanding the prosecutor's statement that the protocol had long been observed in Puebla, either the practice of accompanying the commissioner had lapsed or it had never been adopted in the first place. The commissioner testified that the alcalde mayor, don Carlos de Luna, had little fondness for the Holy Office or even for the church itself, having been accused of witchcraft and sorcery by the bishop of Yucatán while he was governor of that province. He said he had spoken personally to Pedro de Uribe, to Juan García del Castillo (son of the briocense Rodrigo García, who had also been regidor), and to Miguel Rodríguez Guevara, the alguacil mayor, "as persons who carry behind them the rest of the secular cabildo," making to them the same request he had made to the alcalde mayor. They had assured him they would participate.

On Saturday evening, February 27, the comisario was visiting don Pedro Manrique, a canon who was gravely ill (he died two days later). A brother-in-law of the alcalde mayor arrived to tell him that the latter had said that although he personally would have been happy to accompany him, the regidores had refused. The following day the alguacil mayor, one regidor, and one of the alcaldes ordinarios did go to the commissioner's house; he thanked them but said that without the alcalde mayor and the other regidores he would not go. The officials claimed that the alcalde mayor had never shown them the letter from the viceroy. It is clear that no procession took place that morning, and the commissioner did not state whether, or how, he carried out the proclamation.

The commissioner was convinced that the alcalde mayor was primarily responsible for inciting the other officials to abstain from participation, although he also blamed the mediocre character of the regidores, as exemplified by Juan García del Castillo. Several other witnesses, however, insisted that Juan de Carmona Tamariz, the depositario general, particularly disliked the Inquisition, notwithstanding that his father, Diego de Carmona, had been a familiar as well as a regidor. Bernardino de Urrutia, the secretary of the tribunal of the Santa Cruzada, suggested that the origins of "this extraordinary hatred and passion" lay in Carmona's marriage to doña Agustina Gómez, the daughter of the briocense immigrant and wealthy obrajero Alonso Gómez, who also had been a regidor. Carmona had once served as the notary of the Holy Office, but soon after his marriage "he left off serving such an honorable office." Urrutia suggested that he may have been "disqualified" by questions related to his wife's background and claimed that he had always heard in Puebla that her lineage was of "defective reputation." Ostensibly this suspicion directed toward his wife fueled Carmona's resentment, compromising as it did his own reputation. As we saw earlier, the rumors about his wife's antecedents in Brihuega never were substantiated, even when a lengthy inquiry was conducted in Brihuega at the time his sons solicited offices with the Inquisition 40 years later. It is a significant indication of the continuing uncertainty of the briocenses' position in poblano society and of their qualified acceptance into its highest circles that some degree of responsibility for the conflict with the comisario seemed to attach to the briocenses in high office and their associates. The alcalde mayor's antagonism toward the Holy Office probably lay at the core of the dispute and the commissioner's resulting humiliation, but some observers found it more comfortable, more plausible, or both to blame persons who by their background and activities (Diego de Carmona, a native of Granada, and his sons, who, like the briocenses Alonso Gómez and Rodrigo García and their sons, were involved in the textile industry) continued to be viewed as outsiders in the realm of politics and public life.

Understanding Puebla's place in the viceroyalty perhaps illuminates the position of the briocenses who sought high social and political distinction in the city. Puebla itself aspired both to rival and to emulate Mexico City. Recognized by both contemporaries and historians as the second-ranking city of New Spain, at least during the sixteenth and seventeenth centuries, from early on Puebla tried to compete with the viceregal capital for position and preeminence. Despite its prosperity, however, Puebla was far outranked by Mexico City in both size and political importance. Criticism of and disputes over the quality of city councillors and even the continued high level of interest in officeholding among members of the city's leading families may well have reflected a more general concern with upholding Puebla's pretensions to near-equal status with the capital. Under the circumstances, it is somewhat ironic that the briocenses' principal collective contribution to Puebla was to make it the leading textile producer of New Spain. If the visibility of the entrepreneurs from Brihuega failed to enhance the city's social standing, they did make Puebla first in New Spain in one realm, at least.

CHAPTER FOUR

The Religious Realm

L ike many other aspects of the emigrants' lives, their relationship to the religious and spiritual realm reflected both their
background and experiences at home and their aspiration to integrate into
a new society. Their contributions to and participation in the religious life
of both Brihuega and Puebla demonstrated this dual influence, which was
exemplified by the charitable foundations sponsored by two briocense
emigrants.

Two Charitable Bequests

At the end of the sixteenth century a man named Juan Barranco set aside a
considerable portion of his assets in real property and rents to establish in
Puebla a colegio for girls to be associated with a new convent and known
as Jesús María. Born in Brihuega in the early 1540s, Barranco arrived in
Puebla in the 1560s and by 1570 owned an obraje and some rental properties in the city. When his compatriot Cristóbal de Ribas left Puebla in the
early 1570s, Barranco purchased his obraje, fulling mill, and other properties. According to Ribas, the properties were worth 17,000 or 18,000 pesos,
and Barranco took some time to pay off the debt.[1] A prominent figure in
the commercial circles of the briocense community in Puebla, Juan Barranco
apparently never married. He did have relatives in Puebla, however, including a sister and brother-in-law for whom he sent in 1573 and his brother
Cristóbal García, a priest.

Although the convent and colegio were founded in 1593, a year before Barranco's death, he had begun making plans for the school nearly a decade earlier. In August 1590 he stated that in July 1585 "I made a donation for a girls' school that I want to create"; the 20,000 pesos he donated was to be invested in rents, and the income would support the school. He also had donated the house in which he lived to serve as the school building. Subsequently he decided to substitute another house he purchased near the hospital of Nuestra Señora de la Limpia Concepción; it had belonged to the archdeacon don Francisco Pacheco, and Barranco noted that it was "of better work and construction than the house in which I live and it has a garden and there is more space and comfort."[2]

According to the official bull issued in Rome in February 1597, the convent was to be under the order of San Jerónimo.[3] Six nuns from the Jeronimite convent in Mexico City would form part of an initial group of 12; it was planned that eventually 44 nuns would reside there. Three of the nuns, chosen by the patron, were to live in the colegio "for the government and good instruction of the girls," who would be taught reading, writing, singing, and needlework.[4] If necessary another nun would live at the school, and "secular matrons of known virtue, reputation and maturity who are at least 40 years of age" also could be hired to help. The colegio was to provide the convent 1,500 pesos a year to help support the nuns. Although it was anticipated that in time the school would have 24 students, the number was limited to 15 during the first eight years. Six members of this start-up group were expected to profess as nuns in the convent and the other nine to marry. Any students who were related to Juan Barranco would receive preference if they wished to profess in the convent, and subsequent consideration was to be accorded to young women from Barranco's tierra. The same stipulations would govern admissions to the school and convent.

In his will of July 14, 1594, Barranco made the colegio his universal heir (that is, it would receive any and all of the estate not otherwise earmarked for particular donations) and named the bishop of Tlaxcala to succeed him as patron; previously he had designated the city council as the school's patron. In a codicil made the following month Barranco directed that two daughters of his fellow briocense Alonso Gómez were to be admitted as well as any of Gómez's other daughters who so wished, favoring them over his own female relatives. In addition, Barranco stipulated that the school's patron could choose one-quarter of the students and nuns from among the daughters of Puebla's vecinos or at least girls who were born in the bishopric. The students were to be "poor young women and orphans"[5] and could be Spanish, mestiza, or mulata. The school would admit girls between the ages of ten and fourteen. After eight years at the colegio, each young woman would receive a dowry of 400 pesos, which could be used to marry or to enter a convent.[6] In addition, provisions were made to accept paying students, who would be housed separately from the others, with a nun designated as their chaperon.

Juan Barranco explained that he wished to establish the school because he had "earned the greater part of his fortune in this city and to demonstrate his gratitude to it."[7] Nothing in his life up to that point indicated a strong religious inclination, and his own stated reasons for wanting to found the school hardly suggest that religious considerations were paramount. The colegio would provide a respectable position for his much younger brother, Cristóbal García, at least until the young priest could find a more prestigious or lucrative place.[8] After Barranco died, his brother was to serve as the colegio's chaplain and receive 1,600 pesos in rents each year, the money to go after Cristóbal's death to pay the dowries of four graduates of the school. Should the crown favor Cristóbal with an appointment as canon of the cathedral of Puebla or Mexico City, however, he would no longer receive the annual rent.[9] The provisions for his brother, together with the stipulations about preferences to be given to Barranco's kin and fellow briocenses, suggest that Barranco's concerns were as much social as religious. Yet one can hardly discount the nature of this foundation, which after all was to be a spiritual memorial to the founder. Nor should it be ignored that, although he assigned privilege of place in the colegio to his kinfolk and compatriots, Barranco made the colegio and convent, rather than any of his relatives, his universal heir.[10] Barranco's donation and legacy, then, demonstrate the complex intermingling of spiritual and social preoccupations and aspirations that characterized much of the religious life of both laity and clergy in the period. The terms by which he established the colegio also suggest that the immigrant community's distinctive sense of identity perhaps in some degree was rooted in the briocenses' individual and collective religious life in both Brihuega and Puebla. Thus, for example, while it is not known why Juan Barranco chose the Jeronimite order for the convent, it may be significant that when he left his hometown, Brihuega's only convent, San Ildefonso, was Jeronimite. Hence he may have been trying to foster a sense of continuity or connection between the religious life of the two places.[11]

The impression that preoccupation with place of origin and kin affected the conduct and nature of religious life, just as spiritual concerns colored social ones, is strengthened by another charitable foundation, this time in

FIGURE 6. *García Barranco and Carrera Families*

*Went to New Spain.
†Went to New Spain, returned to Brihuega.
‡See Figure 8.

§Born in New Spain, went to Brihuega, returned to New Spain. See Figure 3.

Brihuega, conceived by Juan Barranco's nephew Juan García Barranco some twenty years later and nearly parallel to the one realized by Juan Barranco. Born in Brihuega in 1565, Juan García Barranco became a highly successful obrajero and active entrepreneur in Puebla. He purchased the office of alférez mayor for 10,000 pesos in 1593 and retained that position until his death in 1619, in which year he also served as alcalde ordinario.[12] In the 1590s he witnessed some of the donations and other acts related to the founding of the colegio of Jesús María by Juan Barranco. Juan García Barranco associated closely with his brother-in-law Lope de la Carrera, who succeeded him as alférez in 1619 and was one of the executors of his will.

Like his uncle Juan Barranco, Juan García Barranco apparently never married and had no acknowledged children. In his will he asked to be buried in the monastery of Nuestra Señora del Carmen, to which he left 600 pesos, and requested that his executors provide for 2,000 masses in the churches and monasteries of Puebla, half of them for his soul and 500 each for the souls of his parents and those of "my slaves and the Indians in my service who died in it."[13] He also designated 500 pesos for the church of Nuestra Señora de la Peña in Brihuega. Again like his uncle, Juan García Barranco had begun making plans for the disposition of the major part of his fortune well before his death. In 1605 he had arranged to donate 36,000 pesos to establish a colegio for boys in Brihuega for "students [who are] my relatives and of my lineage and in the absence of those, the citizens and natives of the said town of Brihuega, where they would be taught doctrine, good breeding and the Trinity and virtue."[14] He also had set aside 16,000 pesos for "una memoria y obra pía" (pious work, or charitable foundation) to help young women who were his relatives to marry. In his will, however, he increased those donations, designating 50,000 pesos to be used to buy rents to support the colegio, an additional 4,000 for the purchase of a building, and 20,000 pesos for the charity to help pay the dowries of young women. He also specified that 5,000 pesos were to be used to establish a chaplaincy in the colegio for a mass to be recited daily for his soul. He made his uncle Bach. Cristóbal García (the brother of Juan Barranco) the chaplain, to be succeeded by "the first son of my sister María García, the wife of Lope de la Carrera, who is a priest, or the sons of my sister Ana García, the wife of Juan de Anzures Guevara," or if not them, then the closest relative who was a priest. The recipients of the dowries were to be his relatives within the fourth degree. Each of his sisters' daughters, if she married, would receive 1,000 pesos, representing the income from the principal for a year; otherwise two other young women would be endowed with 500 pesos. He had named Benito Ruiz, the cura of San Juan in Brihuega, as the first patron of both the colegio and the endowment for girls, but Ruiz having died, he named instead his brother-in-law Lope de la Carrera "if he goes to Spain." If he did not, his uncle Cristóbal García would take his place, but if he too failed to return to Spain, then Juan Ruiz, who lived in Brihuega, or one of his sons would succeed in the patronage.[15]

Unlike his uncle, Juan García Barranco made his sisters his heirs, although how substantial their inheritance was compared to the amounts earmarked for their brother's charitable foundations is not known. The money for the colegio and obra pía was to be sent to Spain in three shipments, and much of it seems to have arrived in a timely manner, beginning with the sum of 27,000 pesos that one of the patrons in Brihuega, Antonio Ruiz de Valdivieso, declared he had received in December 1619. Other amounts arrived the following year and apparently again in 1625, much of it converted into *juros*. The colegio did indeed come into existence in 1619, as did the endowment to help poor young women marry. Located near the Franciscan convent and known as La Encarnación or Jesús y María, the colegio apparently had two Latin instructors in the seventeenth century.[16]

The two foundations established in Puebla and Brihuega by uncle and nephew twenty years apart exhibit a symmetry that surely was not accidental. Juan García Barranco must have had his uncle's example in mind when he conceived his own charitable plans. He had quite direct ties with the convent and colegio that Juan Barranco founded in Puebla: in his will he donated a little slave girl named María, the daughter of two of his African slaves, to his two nieces, the daughters of Lope de la Carrera, who were nuns in "el convento de Jesús María y San Jerónimo." He stipulated that his heirs should give María 25 pesos a year for her clothing and other necessities. He donated another slave, named Domingo, to the convent, stipulating that the nuns could not sell him and that if they wished to do so they would have to free him. He also placed in the convent "a girl named María whom I have raised in my house, daughter of María, Indian, and Hernando, my black slave," who would receive 50 pesos a year throughout her lifetime.[17]

Any information on the religious life or activities of Juan Barranco apart from the foundation of the colegio and convent is lacking; in regard to his nephew, in contrast, there is evidence of a zealous religiosity. In 1599 Juan García Barranco denounced his slave Juan Carrasco to the Inquisition for having denied God while being beaten by another slave at his orders. García Barranco struck Juan Carrasco in the face and ordered him untied while he sent one of his criados to inform the comisario of the Santo Oficio of what had occurred. According to a carpenter named Alonso Hernández, who had witnessed the scene, García Barranco called Carrasco "traitorous dog" and declared, "I will make you burn."[18] Carrasco testified that while he was being whipped, some Spaniards who were there had asked García Barranco "for the love of God to stop it," but his master had refused. The Inquisition sentenced Carrasco to receive 200 lashes in Mexico City and another 200 in Puebla and then to work in his master's obraje for two years in chains.

In addition to the congruity of the founding of the colegios in Brihuega and Puebla, the active participation in both of Cristóbal García—brother of one founder and uncle of the other—provided another connection between the two, as he was chaplain of both colegios. In October 1606 the "dean and chapter" of Puebla's cathedral appointed Bach. Cristóbal Garcia Barranco mayordomo of the Colegio de Jesús María and convent of San Jerónimo; his nephew Juan Garcia Barranco served as his bondsman.[19] Around the same time, when his nephew was making plans to establish the colegio in Brihuega, Cristóbal García was also pursuing his options back home. In September 1605 he stated that his mother's brother, Antón Ruiz, clérigo presbítero, at the time of his death had entailed his property to found a chaplaincy in the church of San Juan in Brihuega for masses to be said for his soul, to be served by his closest relative. The first chaplain was Andrés Bautista, clérigo presbítero, and now he, Bach. Cristóbal García, as the closest relative who was a priest, should be the next to succeed. He authorized Bernabé García and the notary Pedro de la Carrera, both vecinos of Brihuega, to take possession of the entail in his name.[20] Although he continued to be economically active in Puebla during the years his nephew Juan

García Barranco was alive, buying a fulling mill on the Atoyac River in 1608 for 2,800 pesos, by December 1619 he had returned to Brihuega, where he was called one of the "patrones de las buenas memorias y obras pías que instituyó . . . Juan García Barranco" and as such was working to retrieve the money his nephew had ordered to be sent back to Brihuega.[21]

Little is known about the colegio in Brihuega, but the school and convent Juan Barranco founded in Puebla certainly attracted the support of the briocense community. In addition to Barranco's nieces, who entered the convent in 1604, two daughters of Francisco Alvarez and María de Ortega; a daughter of Cristóbal de Guadalajara and his wife, Catalina de Anzures; and two daughters of Antón del Río and María de Cifuentes all professed in the same year. In 1608 Catalina de la Fuente, the daughter of Isabel Bautista and Martín de la Fuente, refused to marry the mayordomo of her mother's obraje and entered the convent. Another daughter of Cristóbal de Guadalajara entered in 1612 and two daughters of Francisco Barbero and María Caballero at some time before 1616. One of Catalina de la Fuente's sisters also had entered Jesús María by 1611.[22] Thus when it came to placing their daughters, briocenses showed some preference for the convent founded by their compatriot, but not an overwhelming one. Three other daughters of Isabel Bautista and Martín de la Fuente entered the convent of Santa Catarina, for example, and another was a nun in the convent of the Limpia Concepción; and two daughters of Cristóbal de Beguillas entered the convent of Santa Clara in 1608.[23] The discernible yet far from unanimous support by the briocense community of the convent founded by Barranco reflects the number and variety of religious organizations (and options) that a thriving city like Puebla, seat of a bishopric, could offer compared to a Castilian town of modest size like Brihuega. It also suggests that the collective religious focus of the briocenses broadened and loosened as a consequence of the new circumstances in which they found themselves and the opportunities their new situation offered.

Religious Life in Brihuega

A consideration of Brihuega's religious life provides a basis for comparison with the briocense immigrants' experiences in Puebla. Lying within the Alcarria and New Castile, Brihuega can be assumed to have shared many of the practices and beliefs that William Christian has identified in that region. Unfortunately, the town was not included in the "relaciones geográficas" commissioned by Philip II, analysis of which forms the core of Christian's discussion and conclusions.[24] Existing evidence, however, suggests that Bri-

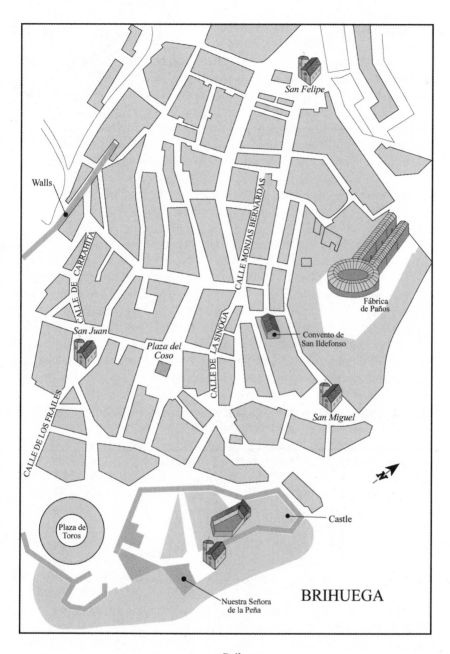

Walls

CALLE DE CARRAHITA

CALLE MONJAS BERNARDAS

CALLE DE LA SINOGA

San Felipe

Fábrica
de Paños

San Juan

Plaza del
Coso

Convento de
San Ildefonso

CALLE DE LOS FRAILES

San Miguel

Plaza de
Toros

Castle

Nuestra Señora
de la Peña

BRIHUEGA

MAP 5. *Brihuega*

huega's religious life resembled that of neighboring towns and villages, with cofradías and chapels dedicated to particular devotions, such as those of Our Lady of Hope (Esperanza) in the parish church of San Miguel, Our Lady of Succor (Remedios) in San Felipe, and the Virgin of Sorrows (Dolores) in San Juan. In San Juan they also venerated the Virgen de la Zarza. In 1403 the townspeople vowed to make an annual visit to Nuestra Señora de Sopetrán with three tapers.[25] The town also apparently instituted a vow commemorating an episode in which it was besieged by the troops of the "king" of Navarre in 1445. The vow took the form of a series of nine acts celebrated between Pentecost and the day of the Holy Trinity called "las salves del cerco."[26]

In the sixteenth century Brihuega had four parishes—Santa María de la Peña (the church was often referred to as "Nuestra Señora"), San Miguel, San Felipe, and San Juan. At some point San Felipe absorbed the parish of San Pedro, located in what had been the old Mozarab neighborhood.[27] The Jeronimite convent of San Ildefonso existed in the sixteenth century; a second convent, the Recoletos de San Bernardo, was established in 1615. Its devotion was to Santa Ana, and the convent possessed a "precious relic," the arm of San Fulgencio.[28] Both convents held land and censos. In the sixteenth and seventeenth centuries remittances from relatives in the Indies no doubt helped local women to profess. In 1635 Mari Rojo y Soria, a nun in San Ildefonso, declared that her cleric uncle Lic. Gabriel de Soria, who lived in New Spain, had provided the 950 ducados for her dowry. A list of the 35 women who received Mari Rojo as a nun in San Ildefonso in 1630 included 3 with the last name Anzures and 9 whose surname was Ruiz.[29] Both surnames were prominent in Brihuega as well as in Puebla's briocense community. In 1662 Juana Díaz de Pastrana, who was 60 years of age, was vicaress ("vicaria") of the convent. She stated that her father, Diego de Pastrana, had lived in Puebla.[30]

Brihuega also at one time had a Carmelite monastery. In June 1590 the town council decided to write to the provincial of the order of the Discalced Carmelites "that he should come with friars . . . to this town to settle the monastery that is abandoned," but apparently nothing came of this effort.[31] The proximity of the large and well-endowed Jeronimite monastery of San Blas in Villaviciosa may have discouraged the founding of monasteries in Brihuega itself, but the lack of such an institution clearly was a cause for concern in the town. In November 1581 the council decided to ask the guardian of the Franciscan monastery in Cifuentes to send a preacher to Brihuega. A solution finally presented itself in the early seventeenth century, when the man credited with having established the convent of San

Bernardo, a native of Brihuega named Juan de Molina, who was *refitolero* (person in charge of the rectory) of the cathedral of Toledo, founded a Franciscan monastery in the town.[32]

Like many other towns and villages of the region, Brihuega had its own legends and traditions. Fray Benito de Jesús María Trixueque y Carpintero, the labrador son of two parishioners of San Juan, had incurred a serious injury while chopping wood and entered the monastery in Brihuega. From there he moved to the Carmelite monastery in Pastrana, where he died in 1614 "en olor de santidad."[33] Capt. don Francisco de Torija, who was born in 1637 and went to Puebla, where he became a regidor and applied for the position of familiar of the Inquisition in 1694, had an ancestor whose tomb had been opened 36 years after his death. The body, found intact and uncorrupted, had been placed in the church of Santa María in a tomb with a blue stone.[34] The townspeople credited miracles to Nuestra Señora de la Peña. In October 1582 the town council charged its procurador general, Juan de Gamboa, to "try to confirm the miracles that Nuestra Señora de la Peña of this town has seen fit to perform by means of her divine majesty."[35]

As Christian suggests was the case throughout the region and as Sara Nalle has demonstrated for Cuenca, Brihuega's religious life was undergoing changes in the late sixteenth and early seventeenth centuries, as seen in the establishment of a new convent for women and the new Franciscan monastery. These changes probably responded to both internal and external pressures. A festival was added to the annual calendar in May 1604 when the agreement was made with the archbishop, don Bernardo de Sandoval y Rojas, for the town to return to the archbishop's jurisdiction. It provided for the observance of a fiesta "with its vespers and high mass, with a sermon in demonstration of thanks for this good event, going in a circle through the parishes of the town, beginning with the church of Santa María and then San Miguel and then San Felipe and then San Juan. . . . The abbot and council of priests and the council and officials of the town . . . will participate." The town and the clergy jointly would cover the costs.[36]

Lay religious organizations—cofradías—played an important role in the religious and social life of the towns of the Alcarria, as they did throughout the Iberian world. Doubtless there were (or had been) older cofradías in the town, but the ones identified during the second half of the sixteenth century probably were relatively recent creations.[37] They included the cofradías of the Santísimo Sacramento (Most Holy Sacrament), the Vera Cruz (True Cross), and Blessed Souls of Purgatory, all of which became prominent in the region in the second half of the sixteenth century.[38] The cofradía of Nuestra Señora Santa María de la Misericordia y Remedio (Our

Lady of Mercy and Succor, popularly known as the Cofradía del Remedio), founded in 1575, became the focus of much controversy in the 1580s, as seen in Chapter 3. This cofradía had a chapel in the parish church of San Felipe with a large, carved wooden statue of Mary that was carried in the brotherhood's processions. On the eve of the festival of Mary's birth a candlelight procession would conduct the image from San Felipe to the church of Santa María. Every three months, on the first Sunday of the month, the members met, alternating among the parish churches, for a high mass preceded by the ringing of bells and a procession around the church.[39] The cofradía's ordinances provided for services for sick or dying members. If a member were seriously ill, the mayordomos would visit and see that a will was prepared and that the last rites were administered, if necessary; cofradía funds would be used to pay for medical treatment. If the sick person had no one to care for him, members of the brotherhood would do so; they also participated in the funerals of members or their families. The cofradía maintained a storehouse for wheat that could be lent to members if they had none to plant, and the *cofrades* were obligated to assist in harvesting the crop of a sick member in return for fair payment. They also collected and distributed alms for the poor every two months.

The ordinances stated that any vecino and native of Brihuega could "freely enter" on payment of six reales with the approval of the majority of the members, but the controversy that erupted in the 1580s demonstrates that interpretation of the ordinance varied considerably. In November 1585 the parish priest of San Felipe, Esteban Carrillo, together with two other men donated some land and a grove of olive trees to the cofradía on the condition (to which the brotherhood's council apparently agreed) that only Old Christians would be admitted. Although the ordinances did not stipulate that the members must be male, apparently all of them were.[40] And although the cofradía drew its members from all the town's parishes and ostensibly was open to all vecinos, the ordinances suggest a strong orientation toward the labrador group.

Perhaps because of the town's fairly modest size and its proximity to other towns and villages, all religious festivities were occasions for general public participation. A description of the annual festival of the Cofradía del Remedio noted that "most of the people of the town of Brihuega and a great number of outsiders from the surrounding towns . . . had come to see the festivities." The crosses and banners of the four parish churches as well as of the cofradías of the True Cross and the Holy Sacrament all were brought to the church of San Felipe, where the image of Nuestra Señora del Remedio normally was kept.[41] Such festivities in one town or village were likely to attract people from other communities. An Inquisition case brought against a man named Hernando de Sahelices, a converso who was a vecino of Romancos but originally from Brihuega, hinged on a statement Sahelices had made while attending a fiesta in the town of Retuerta. Some vecinos from Romancos had participated in a religious tableau, nine or ten of them playing parts such as San Juan, San Pedro, Santiago, Mary, and Jesus. A man named Alonso García, who had been an angel, testified that at the end of the fiesta townspeople invited the participants, "each one who had friends [in the town]," to their homes to eat. When no one invited the man who had played Jesus, Sahelices allegedly suggested that "the devil can take Christ."[42]

Representatives of the formally organized church—parish priests and others who held benefices, friars and nuns, lay and clerical officials of the Holy Office of the Inquisition—maintained an active and visible presence in Brihuega, participating at all levels in the town's religious as well as social and political life, none of which can be easily separated. Their positions ensured a substantial degree of influence in areas where they did not exercise direct authority, as seen in the conditions attached to the donation of property by the priest Esteban Carrillo to the Cofradía del Remedio and the active role played by the parish priest Benito Ruiz, cura of San Juan, in the campaign to have certain officials admitted to the same brotherhood. Certain families seem to have been closely associated with the ecclesiastical establishment, with one or more men entering the priesthood each generation, just as other families participated consistently in politics. The surnames of priests point to such familial traditions. In 1518 Miguel Sánchez was the cura of San Miguel, and Benito Sánchez was cura of San Felipe, and there also was a young priest named Miguel Sánchez del Castillo. Early in the sixteenth century Francisco Ruiz was cura of San Juan, and Benito Ruiz was cura of the same parish in 1589, at which time there was also a priest named Antón Ruiz. In 1604 Lic. Benito Ruiz was cura of San Juan, and Lic. Alonso Ruiz was cura of Santa María. In 1584 Juan Bautista and Andrés Bautista were both priests in Brihuega, and in 1623 Andrés Bautista Sanz was *beneficiado* of San Felipe.

The testimony compiled by prospective emigrants frequently included references to kinsmen who were priests or who held positions with the Inquisition as evidence of a family's prominence and respectability, just as they often mentioned relatives who held public office. Witnesses for Cebrián Barragán in 1601 named three of his relatives whom they called "clérigos principales" and another who was a familiar of the Inquisition. Lázaro Bautista Sanz, who emigrated in 1621 with his wife and three children, had two brothers who were priests, and relatives of Alonso Bermejo, who went to New Spain in 1623 with his wife, included a man who had been a familiar and Lic. Gregorio Sanz, then deceased, who had been "vicario de Brihuega y su vicaría."[43] Simón del Campo, who had been born in Oaxaca but whose widowed mother had returned with him to Brihuega, in 1599 executed a deposition in which witnesses stated that Campo's uncle (his father's brother) had been a famous preacher and the prior of the monastery at Villaviciosa. He also apparently had been associated with San Jerónimo el Real in the Escorial and with monasteries in Madrid and Córdoba.[44] In a probanza of 1616 (made in Puebla) Francisco Barbero claimed that his brother Marcos Barbero was the cura of Santa María and that his mother's brother, Antón Ruiz, was the cura of San Juan. Francisco's brother Justo Barbero in 1608 had mentioned a cousin who was abbot of Santa Coloma, "dignidad en la Santa Iglesia de Sigüenza."[45]

In general the standards for clerical behavior and training rose toward the end of the sixteenth century. During the Inquisition trial of Juan Beltrán, which took place between 1516 and 1521, Beltrán's son, Francisco Beltrán, claimed that the priest Francisco Ruiz was his father's enemy "because an inspector for the cardinal came to the town of Brihuega and stayed in Juan Beltrán's house, which inspector found the said priest cohabiting with a woman [*amancebado*]."[46] When Gabriel de Trixueque, a "labrador rico," applied for the position of familiar of the Holy Office in Brihuega in 1614, much of the testimony centered on his maternal grandfather, a priest named Benito Sanz Carpintero, from Brihuega, who had a benefice in the town of Mesones.[47] There he met a woman named Francisca Ortiz, who worked as his housekeeper and, according to one witness, they fell in love. Around 1565 he brought her to Brihuega, where she lived first in his house and then in a separate one next door. Before they moved to Brihuega, Benito Sanz and Francisca Ortiz had had two daughters, one of whom was Lucía la Carpintera, the mother of Gabriel de Trixueque. They also had a son who drowned in a well. After his death and because of the gossip circulating about them, the priest had sent Francisca Ortiz to live in Casar de Talamanca (apparently her hometown); one of their daughters accompanied her and the other stayed with her father. On one occasion when Benito Sanz visited Francisca in Casar, one of her relatives, angry about the illicit relationship, threw a rock at him and broke his leg. At that point the couple and their children went to live in Brihuega. In his will Benito Sanz left his estate to another priest, Antón Ruiz, clearly with the intention that Ruiz would arrange to pass it on to Lucía's husband, Juan de Trixueque, and their children (apparently her sister never married). Because of a successful suit by a man named Andrés de la Torre, however, they received only part of the priest's legacy.[48] One witness, Juan de Trixueque's neighbor, said that when Trixueque married Lucía, Benito Sanz Carpintero "as her father" gave them a house.

No doubt later in the sixteenth century ecclesiastical authorities were less likely to tolerate such relationships, although the lifestyle of Gabriel de Trixueque's clerical antecedent in no way appears to have prejudiced his aspirations to serve the Holy Office; he did become a familiar. Reforms of the late sixteenth century that placed greater emphasis on higher education for the clergy did have an impact on the town's priesthood. In 1604 all four parish priests held the *licenciado* degree, whereas none of the town's clergy did in the sixteenth century. Holding the licentiate clearly became the norm for the clergy in the seventeenth century, although it was not invariable.[49]

The Inquisition was active in Brihuega, perhaps particularly so because the town came under the jurisdiction of the archbishop of Toledo, and Toledo was the site of one of the major tribunals. As elsewhere, the Holy Office both regulated aspects of the town's religious life and provided offices for those who sought that kind of distinction.[50] As was true generally in Castile, Inquisition cases early in the sixteenth century principally involved accusations of Judaizing, whereas by midcentury the focus had shifted to such concerns as blasphemy, "scandalous words," and bigamy. Inquisition records provide ample evidence that many converted Jews and their descendants remained in Brihuega and the region, although adjusting to their transformed circumstances cannot always have been easy. In 1492 a man named Diego Sánchez Rojo testified that he had become a Christian when he was twelve years old, at which time he "left the authority of my Jewish parents." By his own statement, however, he continued to have close relations not only with them but with other Jews as well. As a very young convert who still belonged mainly to the Jewish and converso community, he must have been in an awkward position. Some converts did not hesitate to express their bitterness. A former corregidor of Brihuega claimed that a shoemaker named Hernando el Rojo, at some time "reconciled" by the Inquisition, many times had said, "Please God that what you Christians wish for us should come to you."[51]

Even for those who apparently tried sincerely to fulfill the obligation to convert, the transition from being known as Jews to acceptance as bona fide Christians could be rocky. The example of Juan Beltrán (who was tried by the Holy Office around 1520) is a good case in point. Beltrán had gone to some lengths to integrate himself and his family into the Christian community. A parishioner of San Miguel, he belonged to the parish's cofradía and had placed his two young sons in school "so that they would learn the things of our holy Catholic faith."[52] He was known for his generosity in times of need.[53] Friars from the monastery in Cifuentes had stayed at his house, and he had good relations with several priests in Brihuega. Nonetheless, when, several years before the trial, members of the parish council of San Miguel wanted to choose Beltrán as one of the council's jurados, a man named Juan García Crespo objected that Beltrán had not been properly baptized. Beltrán had been involved in disputes with Juan García Crespo over payment for cloth that Beltrán had sold him and because of lies that Juan García allegedly told regarding rights to water. Juan García's accusations led to a bitter fight in the church "and later around midday in the plaza regarding the same there was a great scandal and disturbance in the town." The corregidor had to intervene. He imprisoned Juan García and fined a number of other people.[54]

Notwithstanding the support of many well-placed individuals, including the corregidor and the parish priests of San Miguel and San Felipe, Beltrán's insistence to the end that he was a good practicing Christian, and the flimsiness of the evidence (mainly relating to dietary preferences) and the questionable veracity of the main witness against him, Beltrán was "relaxed" by the Inquisition officials. Given the substantial presence of conversos in Brihuega at the time—many of the witnesses in the case were called converso or "nuevo cristiano de judío"—the execution of Beltrán to some degree might have been intended to be exemplary. There apparently were few cases involving Judaizing after the 1520s, although suspicions about Jewish practices and accusations continued into the 1550s. Whatever distinctive practices and beliefs conversos maintained seem mainly to have manifested themselves in individual behavior (especially diet) or as familial traditions kept alive in the household.

The persistence of an acknowledged collective identity may have sustained some communal (if clandestine) observances as well. In 1553 a man named Juan Cano testified regarding a scene he had witnessed in September of the previous year in the garden of the archbishop, along the bank of the Tajuña River.[55] A number of conversos, men and women, had congregated there. Cano said that someone else told him that he had passed by the same place and seen a bower ("enramada") that he thought they must have made. Given the description and the time of year, the gathering sounds like the traditional observance of the Jewish autumn festival of Sukkoth, in which people build a hut, covered by branches but open to the sky, where they eat their meals and spend time for a period of eight days. At this remove and with only an excerpt from the original Inquisition case available, however, it is impossible to reach a firm conclusion regarding the veracity of the allegation.

By the early seventeenth century the Inquisition seems to have become a factor in briocense life mainly as a source of prestigious positions. In this period there normally were five or six familiares of the Holy Office at any one time. Affiliation with the Holy Office seems to have been a tradition in some families. In 1616 Alonso Cubero, a 24-year-old labrador, hoped to replace his father, Bartolomé Cubero, who had died recently, as familiar in Brihuega.[56] Pablo Carpintero, a vecino of Tlaxcala who in 1633 aspired to be a familiar in New Spain, had a first cousin, Lic. Gregorio de la Fuente, who was comisario of the Inquisition. A brother of this cousin, Andrés de Pedroviejo, was a familiar, and another relative, Eugenio Bueno, was a censor of the Holy Office in the Indies.[57]

Religious Life in Puebla

Puebla was a leading ecclesiastical center in New Spain; in the religious realm, at least, Puebla achieved a prominence nearly equal to that of the capital.[58] In the 1540s the city became the official seat of the diocese of Tlaxcala, and thus the headquarters for a bishopric that, because of the region's agricultural productivity, would be much wealthier than the archbishopric of Mexico City.[59] By the mid–seventeenth century, and probably well before, Puebla's ecclesiastical establishment rivaled that of the capital in size and complexity.[60] Construction of Puebla's cathedral began earlier in the sixteenth century than that of Mexico City and actually was completed sooner. Under the aegis of Bishop Palafox, Puebla's cathedral was consecrated in April 1649 with several days of festivities.[61] Religious houses proliferated in the city during the latter part of the sixteenth century and early years of the seventeenth, the period during which briocenses were arriving in growing numbers and becoming increasingly prosperous. Juan Barranco's endowment of the convent and colegio of Jesús María must be considered in the context of a notable trend for leading families in the city to establish new convents. Barranco's colegio in a sense both symbolized and institutionalized the briocenses' new wealth and their contributions to the city's economic and social, and now its religious, life. The scale and variety of Puebla's ecclesiastical institutions and religious life provided numerous opportunities for the briocenses to participate.

The religious activities and involvements of the briocenses living in Puebla reflected their ties to the religious symbols and customs of Brihuega as well as their consciousness of a distinctive identity as immigrants. They sent home money for charitable purposes and offered assistance to new arrivals in the city. Juan García Barranco's establishment of the colegio for boys no doubt was the single largest charitable bequest to Brihuega made by any of the immigrants in Puebla. There were others as well, such as the *obra pía* founded by Francisco de Brihuega with 4,000 pesos, the income of which was to help poor young orphan women who were his relatives to marry.[62] Cristóbal de Salas established a *capellanía* in the church of San Miguel in Brihuega for his father, who had died in Peru.[63] Most known bequests to churches and charities back home were fairly modest. In 1640 Blas Carrillo willed 46 pesos to Nuestra Señora de la Peña "to be spent in the decoration of the sacred image" and two silver candlesticks for the chapel of Nuestra Señora de Remedios in the church of San Felipe.[64] Wills often included modest sums designated for churches or cofradías in Brihuega, although usually less than was earmarked for such legacies in Puebla.[65]

Immigrants in Puebla apparently collected and sent home charity for the poor in Brihuega, although how often they did so is not known. The briocense merchant Francisco Alvarez was responsible for sending a "box of alms for the poor . . . that is collected in this city" in 1606.[66] Apparently Alvarez's wife, María de Ortega, would receive poor travelers arriving from Spain and offer them accommodations until they could find lodging on their own.[67] Pablo de Pastrana also was involved in providing assistance to poor immigrants. Both he and Juan de Pastrana donated property to the Hospital de Convalescientes, later known as San Roque, which sheltered newly arrived travelers from Spain.[68] Presumably their immigrant compatriots from Brihuega and its region were the main intended recipients of this kind of aid.

Notwithstanding these charitable efforts geared toward their hometown and compatriots, it was in the religious arena that briocenses on individual and familial bases participated most fully in the opportunities afforded by their new home. They joined the city's many cofradías, forged relationships with members of the secular and regular clerical establishments, made charitable contributions and established capellanías, and sent their daughters (as seen) to virtually all the city's convents and their sons into the priesthood or regular orders. A few were renowned for their spiritual qualities. Arguably the briocenses became poblanos most rapidly with respect to their religious life. Their choices of marriage partners, godparents, and business associates all reflected a continuing strong preference for staying within the bounds of the immigrant community; in the religious realm, however, that orientation toward the group seems to have been less significant in shaping their behavior.

A number of young men from immigrant families in Puebla entered religious orders: two sons of Francisco Barbero and his wife, María Caballero, two sons of Juana de Pastrana and Juan de Torija, two sons of Alonso de Ribas and María de Pastrana, and others. Matías de Viñuelas, the son of Mariana García and Martín de Viñuelas, belonged to the Augustinian order, and his brother Martín de Viñuelas was the rector of the Jesuit colegio in Michoacán in the 1640s.[69] Some friars were themselves immigrants and acted much as did their compatriots, returning to Spain and bringing relatives in Brihuega back with them to New Spain. Fray Alonso de Vera Cruz, a member of the Augustinian order, returned to Spain and was in Madrid in the early 1570s. He took his nephew Juan de Cifuentes with him as his criado when he went back to New Spain in 1573. In 1577 Juan's brother Francisco de Cifuentes applied for a license to go join them.[70] Fray Juan de Cara, a Discalced Franciscan in Puebla, returned to Brihuega in 1604 for the express purpose of bringing his niece Mariana de Cara and her husband back with him. Fray Juan de Cara's sister, Isabel de Cara, and her husband were also in Puebla and had sent for them.[71]

An ecclesiastical career was a popular choice for the children of immigrants of both sexes. No doubt the number and variety of schools and religious houses that existed in Puebla or nearby offered many more opportunities for a religious life than existed in Brihuega. Many married couples in Puebla seem to have assumed that at least one son would enter the priesthood; the foundations of many capellanías stipulated that the chaplain would be whichever son became a priest. The economic gains made by immigrants helped to underwrite the social prestige that a family could attain by supporting a son in the priesthood and a daughter or two in a convent; at the same time, having children in religious life meant that economic assets would be concentrated in fewer hands. All six of the daughters of Isabel Bautista and Martín de la Fuente entered convents in Puebla, and their son Martín de la Fuente apparently studied for the priesthood, leaving only one son, Andrés de la Fuente, to inherit the family textile business. This pattern of ecclesiastical career choice (and consequent celibacy) for a number of children was notable among hidalgo families in sixteenth-century Castile.[72] Its appearance among the upwardly mobile briocense immigrants, who were mainly artisans and entrepreneurs, suggests that improved economic circumstances in New Spain offered many families new possibilities for achieving the prestige and influence to be gained by close association with the church. At the same time, they found themselves with new concerns about maintaining their recently acquired financial means.

Some second- and third-generation briocenses achieved a measure of distinction in ecclesiastical circles. Bach. Francisco de Brihuega Amarilla, the son of Cristóbal de Brihuega and his wife, Isabel Alvarez de Amarilla, was born in 1592. In 1633 he was the "cura beneficiado y vicario de la ciudad de la Nueva Veracruz" and aspired to be a comisario of the Holy Office.[73] Three grandsons of Alonso Gómez and Catalina de Pastrana pursued ecclesiastical careers. Dr. don Joseph de Carmona Tamariz, as seen, was a racionero of the cathedral in Puebla in the 1660s, and Bach. don Antonio de Carmona Tamariz was cura beneficiado of the "partido de Tetziutlan" in Puebla's bishopric.[74] Their brother fray Pedro de Carmona Tamariz was a member of the Dominican order.[75]

Many of the priests of the second generation seem to have been supported largely by chaplaincies established by parents or other relatives, at least during the early stages of their careers.[76] Lic. Pedro de Anzures Guevara, son of Pedro de Anzures and doña Isabel de Vargas, in 1608 was chaplain of capellanías founded for Josephe de Nava, who had been the husband of his cousin Catalina de Anzures, and his deceased brother-in-law Miguel García Calvo. His younger brother, Josephe de Anzures, was expected to succeed him as chaplain of Josephe de Nava's capellanía, so presumably he too was to enter the priesthood.[77] Bach. Francisco de Brihuega, son of Cristóbal de Brihuega, was only sixteen years old and a *clérigo de corona* (tonsured cleric) in 1608, when he was named the first chaplain of his uncle Francisco de Brihuega's capellanía. In the early seventeenth century Antón del Río and his wife, María de Cifuentes, planned to found a capellanía with 7,400 pesos "so that our son Bach. Francisco de los Ríos will have title of it if he is ordained as a priest."[78] Lic. Francisco del Río also served as the first chaplain of the capellanía that his uncle Diego del Río and his second wife, Beatriz García, established in 1607 with 5,600 pesos. The chaplaincy would underwrite four masses to be said each week in the monastery of Santa Catarina de Siena.[79] In her will of 1613 Mariana de la Torre, widow of the locksmith Juan Ponce, stated that in October of the previous year she had founded a "capellanía de misas rezadas" with a censo of 2,000 pesos on her house and named her son Pedro Ponce, "clérigo de menores órdenes," as chaplain. Since that time, however, she had found out that she could not place the censo on the house because it belonged to both her and her children. She hoped that Pedro Ponce would use his share of the inheritance to support the chaplaincy.[80]

The founding of capellanías points to the special relationships that some people may have formed with particular religious houses. Juan de Ortega Prieto and his wife, doña Jerónima del Aguila, in 1605 decided to found a capellanía for 75 masses each year, 25 of them chanted, with 1,400 pesos, which would provide an annual income of 100 pesos. They had spoken about it with fray Benito de Alarcón, who was prior of the Augustinian monastery in the pueblo of Acapiztlán, "en al marquesado del arzobispado de México." If that monastery were to be abandoned, then the chaplaincy would be transferred to the Augustinian house in Puebla.[81] The terms of wills regarding bequests and places of burial also suggest personal affiliations with specific houses. Pedro Barbero, who died in 1613, asked to be buried in San Francisco in the tomb where his father, Cristóbal Barbero, was interred.[82] María de Pastrana, the wife of Juan Llorente, in 1590 also asked to be buried in the monastery of San Francisco in Puebla, in the chapel of Nuestra Señora la Conquistadora, of whose cofradía she was a member. Another María de Pastrana, the wife of Jerónimo de Vallejeda, and María Díaz, the wife of Sebastián de Pliego, also asked to be buried there, in 1595 and 1612, respectively.[83]

The rather sparse evidence from wills shows that briocenses readily joined Puebla's many cofradías. In his will of 1603 Juan de Angón, who arrived in Puebla in the late 1570s, left three pesos to each of the cofradías "del Santísimo Sacramento y el Nombre de Jesús y la Soledad y la Santa Veracruz y Nuestra Señora del Rosario y Nuestra Señora de la Merced," to which he belonged. María García, who died in 1618, belonged to the cofradías of Nombre de Jesús and Nuestra Señora del Rosario, as did María de Pastrana, the widow of Jerónimo de Vallejeda.[84] Pablo de Pastrana was the diputado of the cofradía of Jesús Nazareno in 1595, and Sebastián de Pliego was the mayordomo of the Cofradía de la Conquistadora in 1598.[85]

The briocense immigrant community in Puebla produced individuals renowned for their devoutness and holiness. Among the holy people who have been identified for the seventeenth century, Cristóbal de Molina, a lay brother of the Augustinian order, probably was from Brihuega, and the Jesuit Nicolás de Guadalajara's father also probably was an immigrant from Brihuega.[86] Madre Isabel de la Encarnación was the daughter of the briocenses Melchor de Bonilla and Mariana de Piña.[87] She was born in November 1594 in the barrio of San Agustín and baptized in the church of Vera Cruz. According to her seventeenth-century biographer, Isabel grew up on her father's estate, not far from Puebla. She began to demonstrate her religious vocation before the age of ten, fasting and spending two or three hours at a time on her knees in prayer, constantly seeking solitude and tranquility and refusing to wear any finery.[88] At the age of nine she heard of the founding of the convent of Discalced Carmelites in Puebla and became determined to enter it. She did so ten years later, notwithstanding the objections of her parents and uncle, who, according to her biographer, hoped that she would marry "an honorable and rich man who asked for her, both for her virtue and spirituality and for her beauty and many natural graces."[89]

From the time she professed in 1613 until her death twenty years later, Isabel suffered almost constant illness and physical torments; at one point it was suspected that she was possessed, and an exorcism was attempted. In the end, however, the clergy concluded that her suffering, which she bore without complaint, was indeed caused by demons as a test of her faith. Her biographer did not credit her with any specific acts of healing or other miracles.[90] She was, however, known for her ecstasies and visions, which included a black bull that emitted fire from its mouth and lions roaming the city after violent deaths had taken place. The Virgin Mary appeared to her to promise that she would come for Isabel at the hour of her death and that she would not have to go to purgatory. When she died people reportedly came from all over the city to see her body and to demand relics. Her original physical beauty had been restored, despite the years of illness that had left her haggard and emaciated. She was buried in the Carmelite church in a special tomb covered with colored tiles.[91]

As in Brihuega, briocenses in New Spain became involved with the Inquisition in several ways—by seeking offices, denouncing others, or themselves becoming targets of investigation by the Holy Office. In 1603 the obrajero Alonso Gómez denounced his slave Baltasar de los Reyes for "having denied God, Our Lord, and his saints" while he was being punished by the mayordomo of Gómez's obraje, "the punishment being very moderate," according to Gómez.[92] In other cases involving slaves, the circumstances and responses were nearly identical. Gómez's son Pedro denounced a slave woman named Pascuala for the same reason in 1605; he also alleged that Pascuala had had dealings with a "black demon." In 1622 Pedro Gómez accused his mulatto slave Andrés Cetín of denying God when he was being beaten after having been found one night with a knife that he allegedly intended to use to kill Gómez, his mayordomo, and several other slaves in the obraje.[93] Juan García del Castillo, son of the regidor Rodrigo García, in 1605 claimed that on several occasions while watching a gardener named Diego de Arocha work in an orchard across the street from his father's house he had heard Arocha invoke Beelzebub and other demons.[94]

Accusations were not, of course, directed solely against members of the servile group. In April of the same year the briocense Catalina de Ayuso, the wife of Juan Díaz, stated that one morning about a month earlier a woman she called doña Mariana, who had been the wife of the barber Cristóbal López, came to her house "afflicted and in tears looking for a place to live." Catalina claimed that she had attempted to console her, telling her to be patient and to suffer these travails for the sake of God, but doña Mariana said she was "fed up with suffering for God." When Catalina asked for whom would she suffer if not for God, doña Mariana replied, "For the devil." She added that "if she were near England, she would go there."[95]

The accusations in these cases suggest that a quite orthodox notion of what constituted acceptable Christian belief and behavior prevailed. The few known Inquisition cases that directly involved briocenses, however, show that some cynicism about religious practices and institutions was hardly unusual. In 1596 Alonso Gómez was accused of speaking contemptuously about the sale of the *cruzada*. His fellow regidor Pedro Díaz de Aguilar stated that he had heard Gómez "talking about a certain person who was no more Christian than the great Turk. And this was at the time the Indians were going around excitedly in the city preparing the streets and plaza for the reception of the bull of the holy crusade, and seeing the excitement and hubbub of the Indians, Alonso Gómez regidor said, this seems to me to be like what the Moors do, that they give out some little papers and when they distribute them they say, take [them], with these you'll go to heaven." Apparently Pedro Díaz did not hear these words himself; they were repeated to him by his brother-in-law Hernando Díaz. Hernando Díaz noted that Gómez "was speaking freely as he is accustomed to do" and said that he also made a gesture "by way of making fun . . . with his arm and the thumb of his right hand."[96] As the record of the case is incomplete, it is not certain if the Inquisition officials pursued it, but it appears they did not.

A lengthy case in 1602 that did reach a conclusion involved a charge brought against Francisco el Rojo that he had discussed what had taken place when he and another man from Puebla testified before the Inquisition in Mexico City. Rojo apparently claimed that although the officials had cautioned him that the proceedings were secret, they had not threatened him with excommunication if he revealed anything about them, "instead only with two fingers of the hand, putting them to the mouth saying silence." In prison in the winter of 1602–3, Rojo admitted that he had made an error in talking about the case and begged for merciful treatment, asking the officials to take into consideration the four orphans he was raising. If he had repeated things, he said, "it was as an ignorant and ill-advised man little experienced in the style and affairs of the Holy Office, and he was deeply remorseful." The prosecuting attorney asked for the severest penalty, "bearing in mind the frequency of this crime and the freedom and daring with which they commonly discuss the affairs of the Holy Office . . . in the city of los Angeles so that the said Rojo should serve his punishment and [be] an example to others." In April 1603 Rojo received a sentence of two years' exile from Puebla (one of them voluntary) and a fine of 200 pesos, later reduced to one year of exile (half of it voluntary) and 100 pesos' fine. He probably paid the fine but was able to avoid even the reduced sentence of exile. Lic. Alonso de Peralta, one of the officials, said that it was lifted because they had taken into consideration "that he was a married man and what he had said about raising the orphans but had warned him that from today on he should keep secret the things that the Holy Office charged him with."[97]

The case brought against him may well have frightened Francisco el Rojo; he was said to have wept when he pleaded for mercy, and he marshaled a considerable number of his compatriots in Puebla to appear as character witnesses on his behalf. He got off quite lightly, however, especially in comparison with the accused slaves. Very likely he had not anticipated any truly serious repercussions. Rojo's claim of ignorance seems far from convincing, given his rather cynical explanation, repeated by more than one witness, for why he felt free to discuss what had taken place when he testified before the Inquisition—that is, that he had been told the proceedings were secret but not been warned that he could be excommunicated.

The prosecutor's statement about why he sought a severe exemplary sentence for Rojo is interesting as well, as it suggests the existence of a fairly widespread cynicism about the activities of the Inquisition or at least some lack of regard for the Holy Office among Puebla's vecinos. Men such as Alonso Gómez and Francisco el Rojo did not hesitate to avail themselves of the Holy Office's authority when it came to disciplining their slaves and others whom they saw as their social inferiors but perhaps did not feel that they should be held accountable in comparable fashion for their own actions and statements. Not two years after the charge was brought against Rojo he denounced a free black woman named Jerónima who had denied God during a fight with her husband, Francisco, a slave who belonged to the Jesuits.[98] The conflict in 1627 between the canon of the cathedral and the city's alcalde mayor and regidores over the procession to precede the declaration of the edict of faith, discussed in Chapter 3, certainly strengthens the impression that at least some people regarded the Holy Office less as a source of spiritual or religious authority than as an institution for social or political control that could be brought to bear on members of the humbler groups in society.[99]

Examination of the religious practices and attitudes of the briocenses both at home and in Puebla suggests considerable congruity in the religious life of the two places. Local cults flourished in the Hispanic world, as William Christian has shown in respect to New Castile, but the particular devotions and practices of different places were remarkably similar throughout the empire. Furthermore, the spread of new cofradías in the latter part of the sixteenth century would have further contributed to the sense of familiarity that briocenses probably felt upon entering into the religious life of their new home. Because of the close connection between cult and locality, affiliation with local devotions offered a readily accessible means for newcomers to play an active part in a sector of society that had considerable significance. By joining Puebla's cofradías and embracing its religious devotions and practices, the immigrants could take full advantage of an important avenue to social integration and acceptance without having to repudiate their attachment and loyalty to the religious traditions of home. Puebla indeed offered them expanded possibilities for participation in religious life, and the immigrants' improved economic situation provided the means to avail themselves of the new opportunities.

Ultimately, of course, personal choice determined where an individual's strongest loyalties lay. Bartolomé Tartajo, for example, although he provided generous bequests to many relatives in Brihuega in the will he made in Puebla in 1590, designated the "poor widows and orphaned young women in this city" as his universal heirs, each to receive between 25 and 100 pesos. Yet here again kinship concerns influenced charitable ones, and Tartajo stipulated that preference should go to his own relatives, young women to receive 200 pesos and widows 100 pesos each.[100]

In shifting the focus of their religious life from Brihuega to Puebla, immigrants necessarily had to adapt to the new situation in which they found themselves. With respect to religion as well as to politics, the briocenses in Puebla were newcomers who lacked any special connections either with the established hierarchy or with the city's traditions and practices. In both arenas they made the transition by participating in existing activities and becoming part of established institutions rather than attempting to carve a distinctive niche for themselves. Only after many years, at the very end of the sixteenth century and the beginning of the seventeenth, did the briocenses begin to exert some discernible influence over Puebla's religious life, as reflected in Juan Barranco's founding of the colegio of Jesús María, the Pastranas' support of the Hospital of Convalescents (later San Roque),[101] and the careers of some of the holy men and women who emerged from the immigrant community.

Settling in New Spain meant the virtual submersion of a distinctive religious identity rooted in Brihuega's cults and traditions, although a few remnants may have persisted, as seen in Juan Barranco's choice of the Jeronimite order for the convent and colegio he founded. For the most part, however, the strongest indications of any continuing orientation to Brihuega in the religious sphere were the charitable donations and foundations that immigrants made to people and institutions back home. Essentially, then, as the immigrants and their descendants gained prominence over time in Puebla's religious arena, they did so as poblanos rather than briocenses. Even their more ambitious activities did not reflect any obvious connections with Brihuega but instead were well in tune with the religious life of their new home.[102]

For both Brihuega and Puebla it is far easier to describe patterns of religious participation and behavior and how they reflected or dovetailed with social and even economic and political relations and concerns than it is to gain reliable insight into questions of individual faith. The sparse and often murky evidence on belief suggests that individuals, especially laypersons, who considered themselves to be orthodox Christians to some degree defined their faith, and hence their religious identity, in comparison with or opposition to the beliefs and practices of members of other ethnic groups whose Christianity was suspect—conversos and Moriscos in Castile, Africans and Indians in New Spain. This tendency may in some part account for the fervent but seemingly unreflecting religiosity that briocenses could demonstrate, since defining oneself in contradistinction to others involves an unambiguous assertion of faith that emphasizes differences from other (presumably opposing) models rather than focusing attention on more subtle and complex spiritual introspection. Hence in the area of belief as well as in practice, religion functioned to define and uphold the social order.

CHAPTER FIVE

Marriage and Family

C hapter 1 examined some aspects of marriage choices and family and kinship relations, particularly as they affected and in turn were shaped by factors related to geographical location and physical mobility. It showed that the maintenance and memory of familial and kinship ties helped to preserve a collective sense of identity in the face of geographical separation and provided options and resources to individuals and families seeking to relocate. Mobility and migration could enhance the well-being and status of a family and its members but also at times resulted in considerable economic strain and probably emotional stress as well. The discussion of economic activity in Chapter 2 demonstrated the importance of marital and kinship ties in economic enterprises; family and kinship played a part in determining patterns of political participation as well. This chapter addresses other aspects of marriage and family life that influenced the personal choices and experiences of briocenses at home and in New Spain. It also attempts to assess the extent to which they conserved a distinctive collective identity in Puebla in this arena of their lives, as in others.

Marriage

In keeping with the pattern that prevailed throughout Castile, couples in Brihuega and the neighboring towns of the Alcarria tended to marry in their early to midtwenties, men somewhat later than women. Teenage marriages were not uncommon, however. When Lázaro Bautista Sanz and his wife,

Juana de Mena, went to New Spain in 1621, he was 36 and she 35 years old. Their three children ranged in age from two to seventeen, so Lázaro probably was eighteen or nineteen and his wife seventeen or eighteen when they married.[1] Simón del Campo, who was born in Oaxaca but went to live in Brihuega as a boy when his widowed mother returned there, was 33 years old in 1600 when he and his wife, Isabel del Olivar, decided to go to New Spain with their children. Isabel was eight years younger and would have been only sixteen when their daughter María was born. When they made their deposition they had three other children as well, the youngest only a month old.[2] Perhaps more typical, both in terms of the difference in age between spouses and the age at which they probably married, were Juan Acacio and Isabel Alvarez, who were 30 and 28 years old in 1583 and had a seven-year-old son named Juan.[3] Justo Barbero and María del Castillo also must have married in their twenties. When they went to New Spain in 1608 he was 37 and she three years younger. The oldest of their four children, Francisco, was eleven years old.[4]

While some of the ages at marriage seem young, by his mid- to late teens a young man could be earning his living. When Juan García del Castillo, the son of the emigrant Rodrigo García, was only fifteen years old, he already was co-owner of an obraje in Puebla. In November 1602, after a year of partnership, he bought out his partner.[5] Hernando de Pastrana formed a partnership with his uncle Pablo de Pastrana in Puebla when he was sixteen. These cases may be unusual. They do suggest, however, that at least in some instances an economically active, older family member could provide the guidance and backing that would allow a teenager to participate directly in business endeavors. By his late teens a young man could be well on his way to achieving financial independence.

Going to the Indies could delay marriage somewhat, especially for men, who usually needed a few years to establish themselves after emigrating. Juan de Angón, for example, went to New Spain in 1578 but did not marry until he had been there for ten years. When he made his will in 1603, his son Juan was only three years old.[6] Melchor de Alberto, born in 1587, accompanied Justo Barbero as his criado in 1608 but did not marry until 1617, at the age of 30.[7] Given that many of the single men who emigrated, often as criados, might still be in their teens when they left Brihuega, even putting off marriage for a decade or so did not necessarily mean they married especially late. Antón Barbero, for example, was sixteen years old when he went to New Spain in 1582 but still only 26 when he married María Briceño in Puebla.[8]

The relations between spouses probably comprised a mixture of affective ties and pragmatic concerns. There is little direct evidence that shows how people typically chose their marriage partners. It seems fair to infer, however, that for the most part in a town like Brihuega, which was of middling size and economically and socially fairly homogeneous, with few hidalgos or very wealthy people, young people had ample opportunity to meet and become acquainted with suitable prospective spouses. In most cases young men and women probably were directly involved in deciding on marriage partners. Juan de Campos wrote from Puebla to his brother Pedro de Campos in 1589 that he had heard that Pedro had married "a daughter of Juan de Durán, our neighbor."[9] Martín Hernández Cubero wrote to his nephew Pedro Hernández Cubero in Fuentelencina in 1572 that he had heard that his nephew was now married, "very much to your happiness, to Catalina, daughter of señor Alonso Gil, the youngest one, and that they gave you with her up to 300 ducados." He went on to point out that if his nephew had only followed the suggestion he had made in one of his letters and decided to come to New Spain while he was still single, he would have made sure "that your marriage would have been worth at least 15,000 pesos, because here they don't hold men who have your qualities in such low esteem."[10] Very likely, having already found the wife he wanted, Pedro Hernández was unswayed by the hypothetical financial gains that a marriage in New Spain might have brought him.

Parents of course could object to a child's choice of spouse, perhaps more easily or effectively in the case of a daughter, since her family usually provided the dowry and therefore could withhold it if they wished. In 1553 Esteban Cortés, a fuller (*batanero*) in Brihuega, ended up before the Inquisition accused of blasphemy, for which he received a penance. He had set out to confront one of his sons, who he claimed "had married without my permission" and had spoken insultingly to him. Armed with a dagger, the 65-year-old Cortés was looking for his son when the town's alguacil, Pedro de la Carrera, encountered him and tried to persuade him to pardon his disobedient son. When the constable tried to disarm him, Cortés replied to the effect that God was not strong enough to take the dagger from him, much less the constable.[11] As the case discussed in the next chapter suggests, flouting parental authority not uncommonly provoked a violent response.

Provisions in wills sometimes reflect the emotional ties that bound married couples. María de Bonilla, who died childless in Puebla in 1614, stated in her will that her husband, Miguel Toribio, had been a "good companion" who had cared for her in her illnesses. Although her mother was her heir, she designated 500 pesos as well as the "third remaining from the fifth" ("tercio remanente del quinto") for her husband. Mariana Carrillo, who had no children of her own when she died in 1600, left the "third and fifth" to her husband, Cristóbal García de Zúñiga.[12] Bartolomé Tartajo, who was a widower when he made his will in Puebla in 1590 before departing for Guatemala, made a number of bequests to his late wife's relatives as well as to his own, suggesting that he was close to her family.[13] Blas Carrillo, who died in Puebla in 1640 at the age of 46, made his wife, María Carrillo, his heir.[14]

Marriage also could have a darker side, especially when couples were separated. The absence of husbands and fathers almost invariably hurt women and children economically; in the 1585 vecindario of Brihuega, for example, all but one of the seven women whose husbands were listed as absent was described as poor. Separation could bring loneliness and anxiety as well. Antón Torijano, addressing his wife, Catalina Ponce, as "señora hermana" ("lady sister") in a 1581 letter from Puebla to Brihuega, wrote that his brothers had mentioned nothing about her in their letters. "Were I another man, or not having the trust I have in you, I would suspect something. And for this reason I beg you for the love of God to leave that country and come to this one."[15] Other men who found themselves on their own in the new country expressed their desire to reunite with their wives in more practical terms. In the deposition María Lagúnez prepared in 1584 to secure a license to join her husband, Cristóbal de Salas, in New Spain, she stated that he had written her letters in which "he says he wants to send for me because he can't live without me because of the great trouble and ill treatment done to men who live in those parts without a wife."[16] For that reason she had decided to join him. Alonso Alvarez, who returned to Brihuega to find his wife and six children living in poverty, does not seem to have tried to bring his family to join him. In 1590 he testified that "more than ten years ago I went to New Spain and all this time I have lived in Mexico [City] and as the officials there found out I was married and had a wife and children in Spain they arrested me and sent me in the fleet of [15]86 and did not give me a chance to take care of my estate."[17]

Some individuals, of course, neither married nor entered the church. Certainly this generally was an easier course for men to follow than for women, as men had many more possibilities for earning a good living on their own than did women. Juan Barranco, founder of the colegio of Jesús María in Puebla, apparently never married, nor did his relative Juan García Barranco, who founded the colegio in Brihuega. Their failure to marry obviously did not stand in the way of their accumulating considerable fortunes or achieving a solid position in local society. Given their prominence and success, it is regrettable that neither of these men left any explanation of his choice not to marry, since in remaining single they acted against the prevailing norms. Perhaps their reasons were as uncomplicated as those of the immigrant Martín Hernández Cubero, the man who expressed his disappointment at his nephew's choice of spouse. He wrote that he had put off marrying until he was too old to do so, "but with all that I live very much at my pleasure, without any of the vexation that others experience from children and wife."[18]

Women who failed to marry were much less likely to find themselves in a comfortable situation. Most of the fifteen women listed in the 1585 tax list for Brihuega who were single were described as poor. María de Arroyo was called a "poor beggar" ("pobre mendicante") and Inés Arias, who lived with her "companion Beatriz," also was "pobre." Not all the single women were poor, however. Some acquired or inherited property, or pursued a trade that afforded a decent living. The *beata* Catalina de Peregrina, for example, owned a house and harvested grapes and also baked bread for sale. Her tax assessment was twelve reales, which placed her well within the middle range of the town's taxpayers.

Even marriage, of course, afforded no lifelong guarantee of economic security for women. Of the 150 widows included in Brihuega's 1585 tax list, 70—close to half—were described as poor.[19] Catalina de Ciudad Real was a poor widow who lived off charity, and Alonso de Bonilla's widow, Catalina, was "very poor." The widow of Alonso Cuadrado was poor and said to have "many children." Some widows, however, seem to have been able to maintain themselves well enough. The widow of Juan Gutiérrez, for example, had two looms at which her daughters worked, and the widow Librada de Villarreal, whose tax assessment of 3,750 maravedís placed her among the better-off vecinos of Brihuega, owned an inn and also bought and sold olive oil. The widow of Pedro Valentín was a midwife. The grown children of widows might take care of them. The widow of Eugenio de Trixueque was said to "have given her estate to her children and they feed her." The widow Isabel Gutiérrez lived in the household of her son-in-law Juan Llano. Widowers could end up in a similar situation. Juan de Brihuega, "el licenciado," was "old and poor, he's in the house of his son who feeds him."

Most of the married emigrants who left Brihuega had chosen their spouses from within their own community. In nearly 95 percent of the married couples (123 of 130) who are known to have emigrated, both spouses were from Brihuega. Not surprisingly, the proportion of endogamous marriages within the briocense community in Puebla was not nearly so high, but it was substantial nonetheless. In 27 marriages in Puebla involving briocenses, both spouses were immigrants from Brihuega, and in another 37 cases the man was from Brihuega and the woman was born in New Spain into a briocense family. In 6 other cases the reverse was true—a man born in New Spain to a briocense family married a woman who had emigrated from Brihuega. Altogether, then, 70 marriages of briocenses in Puebla from around 1570 to 1620 could be considered endogamous. During the same period 50 men from Brihuega married women who were not briocenses by birth or parentage, 8 women from Brihuega married men who were not briocenses, and 3 men and 13 women who were born into the briocense community in Puebla chose spouses from outside the community. Thus of 144 marriages of briocenses that have been documented in Puebla, nearly half were endogamous. If we also take into account the 123 emigrant couples in which both spouses were from Brihuega, we find that the great majority of married couples who formed part of the briocense community in Puebla in the last third of the sixteenth century and first decade or two of the seventeenth had married endogamously. There is evidence that the pattern of a daughter whose family had connections to Brihuega marrying an immigrant from the town continued into the third generation as well.[20] It is no wonder that the briocense community managed to retain its cohesiveness and visibility for some time.

Many second marriages also took place within the briocense community. In 1591 the immigrant Pedro del Amo married Isabel del Río, the widow of Andrés Alvarez, with whom she had left Brihuega for New Spain.[21] The second husband of María García, the widow of Antón de Bonilla, with whom she had emigrated to Puebla, also was a briocense immigrant. In 1623 Cristóbal de Cifuentes married Inés de Machuca, widow of the briocense Juan Caballero; she would have been in her mid- to late 30s at the time of her second marriage.[22] Even women who had married into the briocense community showed some preference for remarrying within it. Catalina de Vergara, who does not seem to have been a briocense, married the immigrant Juan de Atienza in 1589 and then Alonso de Pastrana in 1596.[23] The second husband of doña Ursula de Barrientos, the widow of Cristóbal Barbero, was another briocense immigrant, Juan Crespo Carrillo.[24] In 1625 the immigrant Juan de Guadalajara married María de Alcanadre, who was the widow of Pedro Gómez, the obrajero son of the immigrants Alonso Gómez and Catalina de Pastrana. She probably was the daughter of the obrajero Pedro de Alcanadre, who was not from Brihuega.[25]

Children

With fairly early marriages and the likelihood of remarriage when a husband or wife died, especially if the surviving spouse were still young, family sizes could be large, although high levels of mortality kept many families much smaller than otherwise might have been the case. By the time Andrés de Angulo took his family to New Spain in 1565, when he was 35 and his wife 33 years old, they already had eight children. Isabel de Ribas had probably married Angulo in her late teens.[26] Another large emigrant family was the product of two marriages. Francisco de Medina was 50 years old when he went to New Spain in 1608 with his second wife, Mariana de Torija, twenty years his junior. They took with them five children from Medina's first marriage, three boys and two girls who ranged in age from eleven-year-old Diego to 23-year-old María, and a boy and girl from his second marriage.[27]

Since many couples left Brihuega while fairly young, their growing families often included children born on both sides of the Atlantic. Juan Ponce and his wife, Mariana de la Torre, for example, went to New Spain in 1573 with their three children, Alonso, Mariana, and Quitería. Another son named Alonso was baptized in Puebla in 1575, so most likely the first Alonso had died. Bartolomé, Leonor, and Pedro were baptized in 1579, 1581, and 1582. In her will of 1613 Mariana de la Torre listed her heirs as Alonso, Mariana, Bartolomé, Isabel, Pedro, and María Ponce.[28] María Díaz, the woman who was living in Mecina de Buen Varón when her husband, Sebastián de Pliego, sent for her, requested a license to go to New Spain to join him with her five daughters, Ana María, Magdalena, Gracia, Angela, and Isabel. She and her husband baptized a son, Sebastián, in Puebla in January 1585 and another daughter, María, in July 1587. In her will of 1612 María Díaz named seven children as her heirs: María, Magdalena, Isabel, Francisco, Ana, Mariana, and Sebastián.[29]

The main factors limiting family size were age at marriage (which of course helped determine how many years a woman would be able to continue to conceive and bear children), mortality rates, the degree of fertility of both spouses, and separations, which could affect emigrant families if the husband went first on his own and later sent or returned for his family. Alonso Alvarez, who returned to Brihuega in 1586 after several years in New Spain, for example, admitted that he had left his wife with their three sons and three daughters "very poor." Doubtless the family would have been larger still had he remained in Brihuega during those years.[30] Illness could wreak havoc on families. In April 1571 Diego de Pastrana wrote to his uncle

Juan Díaz in Fuentelencina about the loss of his children Miguel and Mariana, who had died within five weeks of each other. His wife, Juana Díaz, had given birth to two other children since they had settled in Puebla, neither of whom survived. They subsequently had four more children, born between 1575 and 1586.[31] Diego de Anzures and his wife, María de Montoya, apparently had several daughters, only one of whom survived to adulthood.

Apart from these constant if mostly random factors that limited family size, the normally fairly short intervals between births, usually between one and two years, did make large families common if not exactly the rule. In May 1573, when Macario de Anzures wrote to his brother-in-law Francisco Barbero asking him to come to Puebla with his family and to bring his son-in-law Juan de Iñigo, his desire to have them join him hinged to some extent on his disappointment at having no children of his own. The following year, in August 1574, however, he and his wife, Isabel de Oliveros, baptized their first child, a daughter named Juana, and seven more children were born between then and January 1587; some of the intervals between births were as short as thirteen or fourteen months. Doubtless not all of these children survived; their first son, Diego, was baptized in March 1577, and another Diego was baptized in November 1581.[32]

There seems little doubt that for most briocenses, as for their contemporaries in Castile and New Spain, bearing and raising children and heirs constituted the central, essential purpose of marriage. Referring to the deaths of his two oldest children, Diego de Pastrana wrote that "since we lost them there is nothing in this life that gives us contentment or happiness, and since this [happened] my wife has never again been happy." Pastrana's wife, Juana Díaz, was extremely fond of her aunt Damiana Gil in Fuentelencina and missed her dreadfully. "Before with the children," he wrote, "she didn't miss that country so much."[33] Although granted that Pastrana, like others, also expressed his sorrow over the loss of his children in terms of his regret at not having heirs who would benefit from his economic success, the deaths of children and the prospect of an empty home clearly took an emotional toll on married couples. Even older couples whose children were grown and living on their own had difficulty adjusting to a childless household. Diego de Pastrana, who was supposed to bring the children of his brother-in-law Juan García Rodrigo with him to New Spain, was unable to persuade his parents, García de Pastrana and Elvira Lagúnez, to allow him to take their eight-year-old granddaughter, Isabel, with him. They argued that she was "sickly and delicate" and would not be able to withstand the journey. Pastrana suggested that they wanted to keep her because they were lonely now that all their children had left the household. His parents said they had great love for Isabel because they had raised her from birth and had no other children.[34]

For most people, then, the essence of married life was having and raising children. Children provided an important outlet for the expression of love and affection; in some senses the love of parent for child may have served as the ideal for affective relations. Diego de Anzures wrote to his cousin Andrés de Ortega in 1571 to "please do me the favor of bringing with you Antoñico, the son of Juan de Pastrana, and bring him well outfitted, as if he were your son."[35] Some parents tried to reunite with children they left behind. In April 1602 Juan Pérez de Angulo arranged for Cristóbal de Ribas (el mozo), who was on his way to Castile, to bring his ten-year-old son, Francisco de Angulo, his child with his first wife, back with him to Puebla. He told Ribas that his son was "in the house and [under the] authority of my cousin Diego de Angulo, regidor of Talavera de la Reina," and promised to pay him 300 pesos to cover his costs and give him nine yards of cloth for a suit of clothes when his son arrived. He agreed to pay Ribas in full even if his son died on the journey.[36] Juan Pérez de Angulo had remarried two years before. Some parents, however, showed little apparent concern for the children they had left behind. Jerónima Hernández, who obtained a license to go to New Spain with her husband, Juan Crespo, in 1590, stated that her parents had been living in Puebla for more than 28 years and had left her with an uncle.[37] Pedro Camarillo, who had been married in Brihuega to Catalina de Atienza, left a son and daughter there when he went to New Spain, where he remarried in 1593. In 1598 he stated that he had sent 500 pesos in the form of 100 hides as a dowry for his daughter María Camarillo, but the hides were lost and he had not sent anything else. By then he had three children with his second wife. He did specifically name all his children, including the two in Brihuega, as his heirs.[38]

Childless couples might adopt children, at least informally.[39] In pleading mitigating circumstances in hopes of reducing the sentence he received from the Inquisition in 1602, as seen earlier, Francisco el Rojo stated that he had no children of his own but was raising four orphans.[40] Cristóbal de Ribas (el mozo) and his wife, who were childless, must have been about 50 years old when they adopted a girl named Juana, whom they took with them to Brihuega around 1618 and then back to New Spain a few years later.[41] Many people raised children other than their legitimate offspring. Often these children were the products of nonmarital relations between the head or some other member of the household and a woman who most likely was not Spanish. When Francisca Sánchez Salmerón, the wife of Juan de Pastrana, died in April 1591, she left 100 pesos each to Francisco and Juan, "boys of around four or five years old whom I have raised in my house and it is said they are the sons of my son Cristóbal de Pastrana." She asked her husband to keep the boys in the household. The father-in-law of Hernando de Pastrana, Hernán García de Herrera, in his will of 1598 left 1,000 pesos each to two children who were his "hijos naturales." He said he had raised Leonor, who at the time he made his will was living with his son-in-law Hernando de Pastrana; his four-year-old son Hernando lived at his ranch. Hernando de Pastrana was to hold their legacies until they came of age and to send Hernando to school; in a codicil, however, he reduced the bequest to 800 pesos each.[42]

In other cases the relationship between a child who had been incorporated into a household and the head of the household was never made explicit. Rodrigo García, for example, in a will he made in 1591, provided that each of two girls he had raised, María and Isabel, would receive 300 pesos when she married, stipulating that the girls would not receive the money if they married against the wishes of his wife, Ana del Castillo, his compadre and brother-in-law Martín de Viñuelas, or his brother Juan García Carrillo. If his wife died before the girls married, Viñuelas would be responsible for them. In the will he made much later, in 1616, Rodrigo García stated that he had provided dowries of 600 and 500 pesos for María Lagúnez and Isabel Carrillo. Their surnames suggest that they were his daughters, but he never stated so.[43] Mariana Carrillo, the wife of Cristóbal García de Zúñiga, who made her will in 1600, left 100 pesos each to an orphan named María Sanudo, "a girl I have raised in my house," and a boy named Tomás García, whom she also raised, "for the love and good will I have for him."[44] Bartolomé Tartajo, who had no children from his marriage, left 200 pesos for a boy named Bartolomé whom he had raised and another 100 for his servant Juan Vivero, "mulato libre," when Juan reached the age of sixteen. María García, the widow of Lorenzo de Pajares, said that she had raised a mestiza girl named Catalina Sánchez at the request of Pedro Sánchez, and that he had left the girl 300 pesos for her marriage in his will. At the time María García made her will in 1613, Catalina had left her house and she did not know where she was; but in a codicil of September 1613 she said that Catalina had married and she had paid her and her husband the 300 pesos.[45]

Doubtless Catalina Sánchez was Pedro Sánchez's daughter, and when faced with the prospect of his own death, he put her in the care of a friend. María García found herself in a similar quandary in 1613. She was then twice widowed and still had young children. Her nephew Juan Alonso had been living with her for some time. She had hoped that he would remain in the house, run the bakery, and care for her children for six years, but instead he decided to enter a religious order. She then appointed her compadre Juan Díaz Trixueque as the children's guardian, but in a codicil to her will she stated that he had too many children and obligations of his own and was getting old. In his place she named the briocense Andrés Pérez de Angulo, who also owned a bakery. She made a special bequest of 300 pesos to her daughter, Jacinta, saying that the other children, "being men, can work."[46]

Children in turn showed their love and concern for parents in letters and bequests in wills. In his will of 1597 Martín de la Fuente left his father (of the same name) 150 pesos to go to Castile if he wanted or to do whatever he wished. He also renounced any legacy that might have been due to him from his mother and ordered that no accounts be made with his father or anything taken from him.[47] María García's first husband, Antón de Bonilla, made his father his heir; if he were dead, then María García and his two brothers in Brihuega would inherit equally. Isabel de Morales made her grandmother Isabel de Brihuega her universal heir.[48]

Children embodied their parents' hopes for an economically secure and stable future that could be attained through marital alliances and family-based economic enterprises. As we have seen, some of the most effective and durable business partnerships formed in the briocense community in New Spain were between fathers and sons, such as Cristóbal and Juan de Pastrana, who jointly owned an obraje and sugar estates, or between men and their sons-in-law, such as the baker and merchant Juan Llorente and his carter son-in-law Esteban Carrillo, or between uncles and their nephews.

In their careers and economic activities the children of the briocense immigrants often followed closely in their parents' footsteps. Both sons of the obrajero Alonso Gómez became obrajeros, as did the two sons of the obrajero Rodrigo García, one of whom also succeeded his father as regidor. Alonso de Ribas's sons Juan and Lucas de Ribas also both owned obrajes; Alonso de Ribas and his son Juan jointly purchased an obraje. In successful families children of the second generation might pursue diverse careers and move into different economic activities, as seen in the family of Pedro de Anzures and his wife, doña Isabel de Vargas. In 1597 their daughter doña Antonia married Miguel García Calvo, the parents providing a dowry of 6,000 pesos, 5,000 of which represented the value of a cattle ranch with more than eleven caballerías of land. Pedro de Anzures's new son-in-law was still a minor, and Anzures acted as his tutor for some time.[49] Their daughters Isabel de la Encarnación and Juana de San Pedro entered the convent of Santa Catarina in 1590 and 1606, respectively. Their son don Diego de Anzures Guevara served as regidor in Puebla, and Lic. don Josephe de

Anzures y Guevara was a lawyer for the Audiencia in Mexico City; he died en route to Spain in 1626.[50] A third son, Bach. Pedro de Anzures Guevara, became an ordained priest. When children had accompanied their parents from Brihuega and so were themselves first-generation immigrants, sons were much more likely to go into business rather than the church or professions and daughters more likely to marry rather than enter convents.

The strong bond that connected siblings often encouraged them to emigrate to Puebla together, or to follow one another there, so that at times they created substantial nuclei of families even in the absence of their parents. As seen, Diego de Anzures was joined by his brothers Alonso, Pedro, and Macario and their sisters Francisca and Isabel (with their husbands). Juan, Pedro, Francisco, Cristóbal, and Leonor de Brihuega also all went to Puebla. They were joined by their nephews Gabriel, Gaspar, Melchor, and Josephe Caballero and their niece Ana Caballero, children of their sister Isabel de Brihuega, who married in Budía, and their nieces María and Isabel de Cifuentes, the daughters of their sister María de Brihuega. No doubt the decision of one sibling to emigrate often persuaded others to go as well, particularly when the first person to go was successful, as in the case of Diego de Anzures. Nonetheless, in a number of instances several siblings emigrated together or followed one another after only very short intervals. Pedro, Gabriel, and Andrés de Angulo went back to Puebla together after their parents returned with the family to Brihuega. Alonso, Lope, and Cristóbal de la Carrera all emigrated in 1593 in the entourage of Alonso's father-in-law, Cristóbal de Ribas. Catalina de Pareja went to New Spain with her husband, Melchor Caballero, in 1594. In 1601 both her sister María de Pareja with her husband, Juan Carrasco, and their five children and their brother Jerónimo de Pareja with his wife and children also went.[51] There are many other such examples.

These familial clusters underscore the strength of the tie between siblings, who frequently looked after one another, especially if parents were absent or dead. Macario de Anzures said that his oldest brother, Rodrigo de Anzures, had been like a father to him and his other brothers. He wrote to Rodrigo from Puebla in 1576 that they "would like to have in this country someone of yours for whom they could do something for what they owe you and have received from you as a father."[52] Their own father had died some twenty years earlier. Brothers concerned themselves with the well-being of younger orphaned siblings and of unmarried sisters. Gabriel de Anzures Guevara, son of the immigrants Francisco Barbero and Isabel de Anzures, in 1605 donated his inheritance from his father (who died in 1598)

FIGURE 7. *Brihuega Family*

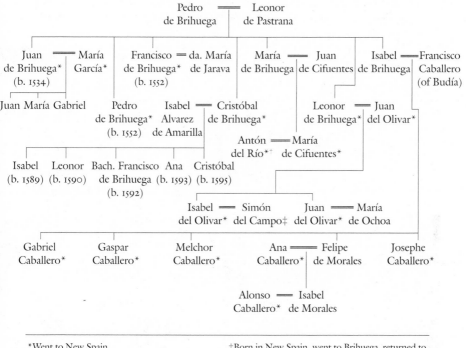

*Went to New Spain.   ‡Born in New Spain, went to Brihuega, returned to
†See Figure 9.   New Spain.

together with whatever legacy he would inherit from his mother to his "her-manas doncellas" (maiden sisters), Juana and Ana.[53]

The importance of the connection between siblings often extended to the next generation as well. The relationship between Juana Díaz and her aunt Damiana Gil in Fuentelencina is captured poignantly in the letter Juana's husband, Diego de Pastrana, wrote to his uncle: "My wife is forever mentioning her aunt Damiana Gil. The love she has for her is really great, because she says she will never be able to repay the great debt she owes her in this lifetime, that she never would be a woman if it were not for her." Damiana Gil had been seriously ill, and Juana Díaz sent medicinal herbs for her with Juan de Pastrana, who was returning to Castile to visit.[54]

Immigrants in New Spain sent for their nieces and nephews and remembered them, as well as their siblings, in their wills. Juan de Angón left 100 pesos each to two sons of his deceased brother, Andrés de Angón, in Bri-

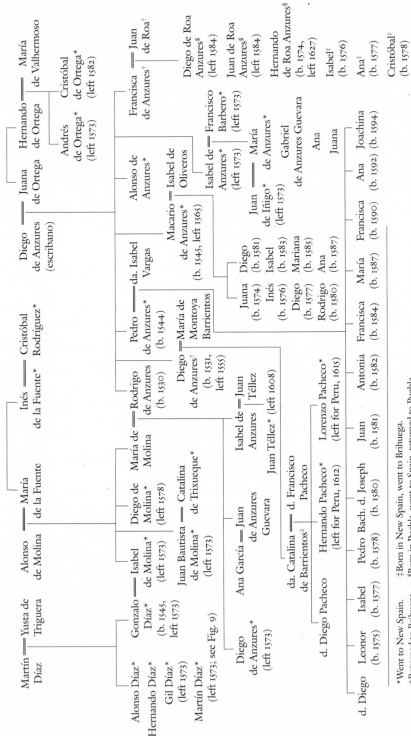

FIGURE 8. *Anzures Family*

huega "because they are my nephews and orphans." If either had died, the money was to go to pay for masses for his parents.[55] Bartolomé Tartajo willed 1,000 pesos to his brother Eugenio Tartajo in Brihuega, "in reales and cochineal." If Eugenio had died, then any children he had would inherit, and if there were no children, the money would be used to provide dowries for orphans chosen by Tartajo's uncle Diego Toribio and cousin Juan Tartajo in Brihuega. He left his sister Lucía's daughter, María la Tartaja, 300 pesos toward her dowry. He also left a few hundred pesos each to his deceased wife's nieces.[56] In her will of 1599 Juana de Pastrana, the wife of Juan de Torija and sister of Pablo de Pastrana, left 200 pesos to her niece Isabel de Vallejeda, "whom I have raised in my house."[57] Blas Carrillo made his will in Puebla in January 1640 leaving 500 pesos to the daughter of his sister Catalina Carrillo, the bequest to be divided equally between his sisters Sebastiana and María Carrillo in Brihuega if his niece had died. He also left each of his sisters 100 pesos but increased this amount considerably, to 1,000 pesos each, in a codicil of 1641.[58]

Kinship and Compadrazgo

Brihuega's modest size and relatively stable population fostered the development of a dense matrix of kinship relations that bound the town's vecinos and emigrants to one another. It would distort reality to imply that nearly everyone in the town was related to everyone else in some degree, although at first glance—and even more strongly if one sketches out family trees over a couple of generations—that may appear to be the case. The kinship and marital ties that connected some families seem to become progressively more inclusive the further one traces them.

This phenomenon can be observed clearly in the case of some of the emigrant families that left Brihuega in the 1570s and 1580s. The extended network of kinship and marital ties that branched off from the Anzures family offers one of the best documented examples. Six children of Diego de Anzures and his wife, Juana de Ortega, left Brihuega for Puebla: Diego, Pedro, Macario, Alonso, Isabel with her husband, Francisco Barbero, and Francisca with her husband, Juan de Roa.[59] The oldest son, Rodrigo de Anzures, who remained in Brihuega, was married to María de Molina. Three of her siblings—Isabel, Juan Bautista, and Diego de Molina—went to Puebla. Juan Bautista de Molina emigrated in 1573 with his wife, Catalina de Trixueque, whose brother Juan de Trixueque was already in Puebla. Catalina and Juan de Trixueque claimed to be first cousins of Juan Barranco (the founder of the colegio of Jesús María in Puebla), although the actual relationship between them is not known. Diego de Molina emigrated in 1578 with his nephew Diego de Anzures, the son of Rodrigo de Anzures and María de Molina; Diego de Molina had been living with Diego de Anzures. Another son of Rodrigo de Anzures, Juan de Anzures Guevara, who stayed in Brihuega, married Ana García, sister of the emigrant Juan García Barranco, who founded the colegio in Brihuega. Juan de Anzures Guevara's sister-in-law, María García, accompanied her husband, Lope de la Carrera, to New Spain in 1593 in the entourage of Cristóbal de Ribas (whose daughter Ana de Ribas was married to Lope de la Carrera's brother Alonso).

Isabel de Molina's husband was Gonzalo Díaz. They left Brihuega for New Spain in 1573 at the same time as her brother Juan Bautista de Molina, taking with them Gonzalo Díaz's younger brother Gil Díaz. Gonzalo Díaz had two other brothers already in Puebla, Hernando and Alonso Díaz. Another brother, Martín Díaz, also emigrated with his wife in 1573. His wife's sister, María de Atienza, and her husband, Felipe del Río, went to New Spain in the same year. Thus the Anzures family was connected through marriage to the Molinas, the Molinas to the Díazes, Trixueques, and Barrancos, and the Díazes to the Ríos. The Río family sent quite a few emigrants to Puebla. In addition to Felipe del Río's brother Sebastián, his nephews Antón and Diego and nieces Isabel and Catalina, the children of Felipe del Río's brother Pedro, all went to Puebla. Their first cousin on their mother's side, Isabel Alvarez, the wife of Juan Acacio, left Brihuega for New Spain with her husband in 1583, the same year that Antón del Río went with his wife, María de Cifuentes. Her sister Isabel de Cifuentes also emigrated, with her husband, Gaspar de Mena. María and Isabel de Cifuentes were the granddaughters through their mother of Pedro de Brihuega and Leonor de Pastrana, whose children Cristóbal, Juan, Francisco, Pedro, and Leonor de Brihuega all went to Puebla. Their nephews Melchor, Gaspar, Gabriel, Josephe, and Ana Caballero, the children of Isabel de Brihuega (daughter of Pedro de Brihuega and Leonor de Pastrana) and Francisco Caballero of Budía, also all went to Puebla.

The immigrants in Puebla actively maintained these relationships. Macario de Anzures, for example, mentioned his brother Rodrigo's sister-in-law Isabel de Molina and her husband in his letter of 1576; Diego de Anzures and his wife were the godparents for their daughter who was born in May 1575.[60] In May 1607 Cristóbal de Brihuega, together with his niece's husband Antón del Rio, his nephews Gaspar and Gabriel Caballero, and another man named Pedro de Aviles, all of them obraje owners, authorized a merchant and vecino of Seville, Cristobal Gutiérrez Rojo, to pay up to

1,000 pesos to a maestro Gabriel de Brihuega, a vecino of Alcalá de Henares and probably a relative, who was doing some business for them.[61]

Following the relationships of the Anzures family in another direction, we find that their first cousins on the maternal side, Andrés and Cristóbal de Ortega, emigrated from Brihuega to Puebla. In 1573 Francisco Barbero departed Brihuega with his wife, Isabel de Anzures, taking as his criado his "nephew" Francisco de Viñuelas, whose wife, also named Isabel de Anzures, probably was the daughter of one of Barbero's wife's siblings. The brothers Alonso and Martín de Viñuelas also were in Puebla. Although they apparently were not siblings of Francisco de Viñuelas, they probably were closely related to him. In November 1581 Juan de Iñigo and Maria de Anzures, the daughter of Francisco Barbero and Isabel de Anzures, were the padrinos for Juana, the daughter of Martín de Viñuelas and Mariana García. In March 1592 Francisco de Viñuelas and his wife became the godparents for Matías, another child of Martín and Mariana. Martín de Viñuelas also was the compadre and brother-in-law of the obrajero and regidor Rodrigo García; he was married to Rodrigo's sister Mariana García Carrillo. Rodrigo García was the nephew of Diego de Pastrana. Martín de Viñuelas and his brother Alonso had a cousin named Andrés del Condado who in the 1580s owned a store where he sold cloth in Puebla. In 1584 their relatives Miguel Relaño and Antón López, who were vecinos of Algecilla, near Brihuega, and Gil Alonso, who was from Fuentes, another nearby town, all called labradores, secured a license to go join them in New Spain.[62]

The strong preference for marrying within the immigrant community meant that in Puebla multiple ties would continue to proliferate. Isabel del Río, the niece of Felipe del Río and sister of Antón and Diego del Río, went to New Spain with her husband, Andrés Alvarez. After his death she married Pedro del Amo, and their son Pedro was born in 1593. Cristóbal de Brihuega, who was the uncle of Isabel del Río's sister-in-law María de Cifuentes, was a witness at the wedding as well as the godfather for their son Pedro. Antón de Bonilla, the first husband of María García, called Pedro del Amo his cousin. He left 100 pesos to Pedro del Amo's daughter María in his will of 1599.[63]

Godparenthood both extended and reinforced kinship and marital ties. People often chose parents, siblings, and other close relatives as well as in-laws to be their children's godparents. Juan de Pastrana and his wife, Francisca Sánchez Salmerón, were godparents for their granddaughter Francisca, the child of their daughter doña Isabel de Pastrana and her husband, don Cristóbal Godínez, in January 1585, and in April 1590 for María, the daughter of their son Cristóbal de Pastrana and his wife, doña Juana de Arciniega. Juan de Pastrana and his wife had also been the godparents in 1585 for Pedro,

FIGURE 9. *Río-Alvarez Family*

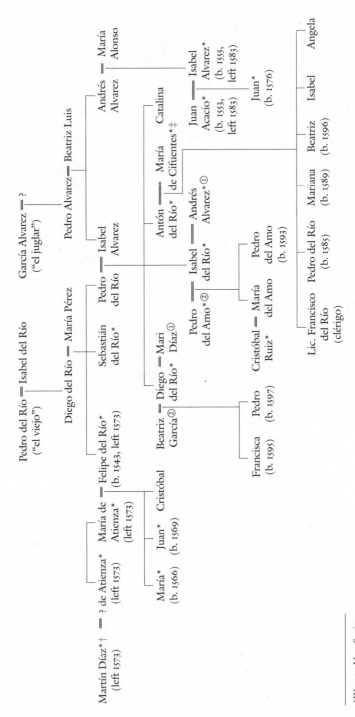

the son of their daughter Catalina de Pastrana and her husband, Alonso Gómez. In February 1584 Pedro and Agustina Gómez, the children of Catalina and Alonso, who must have been quite young themselves, were the godparents for their sister Juana.[64] In many instances, then, the choice of godparents reinforced existing familial relationships.

As was the case with marriage partners, there were plenty of candidates within the briocense community from among whom the immigrants could choose their compadres and comadres, although they did not always limit themselves to that group. Prominent members of the briocense group served frequently as godparents for other friends and acquaintances as well as for their relatives and compatriots. In the years between 1561 and 1579, when they left Puebla to return to Brihuega, Diego de Anzures and his wife, María de Montoya, served as godparents at eleven baptisms performed in the cathedral, and Anzures and his daughter doña Catalina for one. Half of the godchildren's parents were briocenses, in four instances close relatives or in-laws. Macario de Anzures and his wife, Isabel de Oliveros, served as godparents at thirteen baptisms in the cathedral between 1575 and 1589, nine of which involved Macario's relatives or his in-laws or briocenses who were not related to him. Their choice of godparents for their own children followed a similar pattern, with four out of eight being relatives of either Macario or Isabel (who was not a briocense). Thus compadrazgo not only reflected existing kinship ties but also could strengthen the connections between briocenses and other poblanos with whom they associated. At the birth of their daughter Ana, for example, Macario and Isabel chose doña Ana de Ribera and her husband, Francisco de Torres, as godparents. Doña Ana was the niece of Macario's brother Diego's wife, María de Montoya. Diego de Pastrana and his wife, Juana Díaz, were godparents for twelve children born between 1578 and 1586. As Pastrana was originally from Brihuega but had become a vecino of Fuentelencina before leaving Castile for New Spain (Juana Díaz was from Fuentelencina), he had close ties with people from both towns. He and Juana were the padrinos for two sons, born in 1579 and 1586, of Gaspar Rodríguez de Madrid and his wife, María de Madrid, who doubtless were from Fuentelencina, and also for children born to the briocenses Juan Mateo and his wife, María la Carpintera, and Alonso Portugués and his wife, María de Burgos.

Naming Patterns

Naming patterns among the briocenses and their relatives and associates from other towns of the Alcarria suggest a kind of pragmatism that may have been rooted in a desire to facilitate recognition and maintenance of kinship ties, at least on the paternal side. In most Brihuega families, with very few exceptions, all the children took their father's surname. Daughters were much more likely to use a feminized version of the father's name (Tartaja for Tartajo, Caballera for Caballero, Barbera for Barbero) than their mother's apellido. Thus Isabel de Guadalajara's two sons and daughter by her first husband, Melchor de Pastrana, all used the surname Pastrana, and her three sons by her second husband, Juan de Ortega, all were named Ortega. Because of this pattern, which is rather different from the prevailing Castilian practice of taking surnames from both the paternal and maternal lines, over time kinship ties on the maternal side may have been less likely to be recalled and actively maintained. The pattern also helps to account for the rather large clusters of vecinos with the same surname in the tax lists for Brihuega; the exclusion of married women from the list of vecinos probably reduced the variability in surnames. Because certain surnames were so common, on the tax lists a vecino sometimes would be identified as the son of a particular individual by the addition of his father's first and last names rather than the maternal surname. In the 1595 list, for example, Alonso de Campos is distinguished from Alonso de Martín de Campos, and Juan de Campos from Juan de Martín de Campos.

Certainly there was variation. Some people did combine their maternal and paternal surnames. The sons of Pedro García and María la Barranca were known as Juan García Barranco and Bartolomé García Barranco; both of them lived and owned obrajes in Puebla. Given the prominence in Puebla of their uncle Juan Barranco, their preference for the maternal surname is not surprising.[65] In the family of Mancio Alonso de Piña and his wife, María de Urgelos Lagúnez, who are discussed in the following section, the prestige associated with the maternal line was such that three of the children—Sancho de Urgelos, Francisco Lagúnez, and María Lagúnez—took a surname from their mother. Juana de Durango, the daughter of the immigrants Martín de Viñuelas and Mariana García Carrillo, was named after Viñuelas's mother.[66] Variations in the naming pattern in Brihuega that placed heavy emphasis on the paternal line probably appeared most frequently in upwardly mobile families and among briocenses who settled in New Spain. Lic. Cristóbal de Soria y Velasco, who in 1662 was archpriest and vicar of Brihuega, was the son of Pedro de Soria and Isabel Gutiérrez de Velasco, who belonged to the family descended from Juan Gutiérrez "el bueno" (discussed in Chapter 1). Some people decided to add substance to their rather modest surnames once they had achieved a measure of success. Juan Ponce, the locksmith who emigrated to Puebla, at some point began to call himself Ponce de Torralba, and by the late sixteenth century most members of the Anzures family, both in Brihuega and in Puebla, had added Guevara to their surname, although the source of this name is a mystery. The only surviving daughter of the returnee Diego de Anzures (y Guevara) and his wife, María de Montoya, was doña Catalina de Anzures y Barrientos, the latter a surname from her mother's family. Most often she was called doña Catalina de Barrientos. She married the noble don Francisco Pacheco, and as would be expected, her sons all used the surname Pacheco.

The use of don and doña marked an elevation in status that was rarely achieved by members of these working-class families, even with the wealth acquired in New Spain. Diego de Anzures's daughter was called doña Catalina before her marriage to don Francisco Pacheco, probably because her father had created an entail and briefly was a "señor de vasallos" after the family returned to Brihuega and he purchased the town of Romancos. Generally the only women in briocense families who used the honorific were younger or youngest daughters (doña Catalina was an only child) who, by virtue of the wealth that accrued to their parents over time, were able to marry men a cut above them socially. Agustina Gómez, daughter of the wealthy obrajero Alonso Gómez and his wife, Catalina de Pastrana, never was called doña until after her marriage to Juan de Carmona Tamariz, and then only erratically. Catalina de Pastrana's younger sister "doña" Isabel de Pastrana married don Cristóbal Godínez Maldonado. The daughter of Alonso de Ribas and María de Pastrana, María de Ribas, was called doña when she married Pedro Calderón Vargas. Although her husband lacked the honorific don, his sisters were doñas (his mother, however, was plain Inés de Vega). The daughter of Mariana García and Martín de Viñuelas was called Juana de Durango in 1599 when she married the immigrant Jorge de la Hoz, but she became doña Juana with her second marriage, to Hernando de Aranda Saavedra.[67]

In their strong preference for the use of paternal surnames the people of Brihuega do seem to have deviated somewhat from the practices that were traditional elsewhere in Castile. Many Castilian hidalgo families in particular used names to emphasize an individual's connection to the lineage (usually but not invariably the male line), and they perpetuated the memory of prominent antecedents over generations by repeating particular combinations of first and last names.[68] The custom of drawing on the same pool of given names generation after generation was in fact common in all social classes, and the briocenses followed it as well. Emigration and the achievement of a degree of wealth and status in Puebla apparently affected naming practices among the briocenses in the period under consideration here, but they did not result in the complete elimination of the older pattern. Since almost all children continued to take the father's name, certain surnames remained common among the immigrants in Puebla. Thus the briocense naming pattern helps to convey a notion of just how substantial the community had become by the end of the sixteenth century. By the late sixteenth and early seventeenth centuries probably nearly all vecinos of Puebla named Carrillo, Pastrana, Merino, Barbero, and Ribas were immigrants from Brihuega or their descendants, although they cannot all be documented as such.[69]

Separating and Reuniting

Emigration and relocation, as seen, affected families in a number of ways, creating new opportunities and new problems as well. The complicated mechanics of the move from Brihuega to Puebla of a man named Mancio Alonso de Piña and his wife and children illustrate how a family could carry out a long-term plan to relocate. Mancio Alonso's parents lived in the town of Villada, where he probably was born, but he was a longtime vecino of Brihuega and had served as diputado on the general town council there. Two of his brothers were vecinos of Ríoseco and said to be prominent and very wealthy. The father of his wife, María de Urgelos, was Sancho de Urgelos, who had been regidor in Brihuega and served in other posts as well. She also had an uncle, Lic. Urgelos, who was a lawyer said to be living in Mexico.[70] Mancio Alonso's tax assessment in Brihuega in the 1580s was a middling 1,800 maravedís, although he had already left Brihuega by the time the 1585 vecindario was compiled; in his absence his wife was called "poor." Hence the family appears to have been fairly comfortable and well placed in Brihuega, yet the attractions of New Spain eclipsed whatever advantages their position in Brihuega offered, as it did for other comparably situated families.

The first family member to go to New Spain was their son Juan de Piña, who departed in 1577 when he was twenty years old. He was a notary, although when he actually secured an official position is not known. In 1590 he left Puebla to return to Castile. Two years later, however, he asked permission to go back to New Spain with his wife and four criados, saying that he had come on business but was "very poor" because the English had robbed him on the trip. He received a license to go back with his wife and a criado and criada.[71] Juan de Piña's father was already living in Puebla by this time, as were his sister María Lagúnez and her husband, the briocense Cristóbal de Salas. Both his father and his brother-in-law gave Juan de Piña their power of attorney to sell their properties in Brihuega. Cristóbal de

FIGURE 10. *Family of Mancio Alonso de Piña and María de Urgelos Lagúnez*

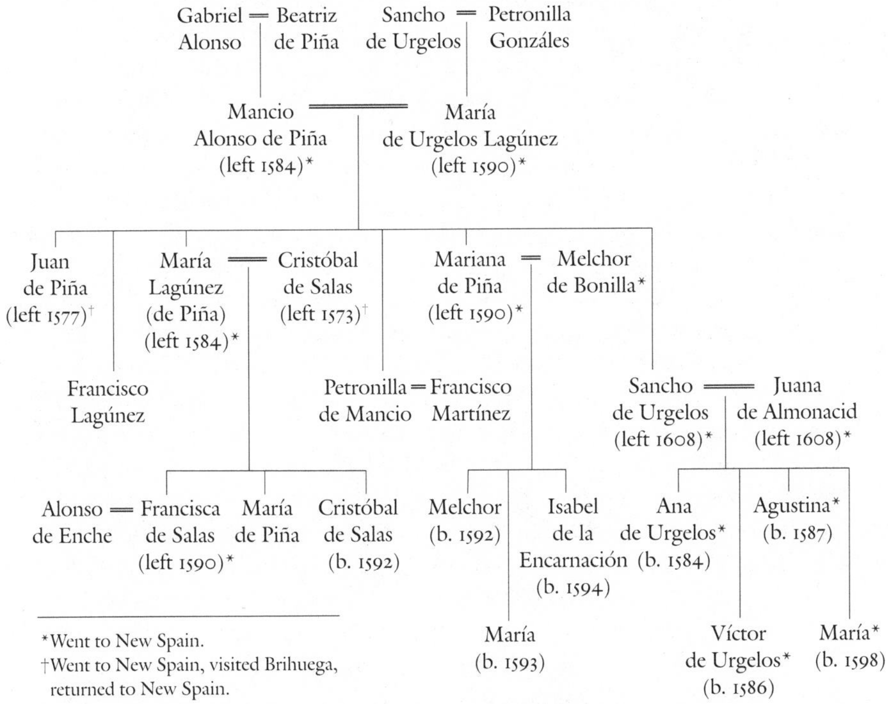

Gabriel ═ Beatriz Sancho ═ Petronilla
Alonso de Piña de Urgelos Gonzáles

Mancio ═══════ María
Alonso de Piña de Urgelos Lagúnez
(left 1584)* (left 1590)*

Juan María ═══ Cristóbal Mariana ═ Melchor
de Piña Lagúnez de Salas de Piña de Bonilla*
(left 1577)† (de Piña) (left 1573)† (left 1590)*
  (left 1584)*

Francisco Petronilla ═ Francisco Sancho ═══════ Juana
Lagúnez de Mancio Martínez de Urgelos de Almonacid
   (left 1608)* (left 1608)*

Alonso ═ Francisca María Cristóbal Melchor Isabel Ana Agustina*
de Enche de Salas de Piña de Salas (b. 1592) de la de Urgelos* (b. 1587)
 (left 1590)* (b. 1592) Encarnación (b. 1584)
     (b. 1594)

Went to New Spain.   María Víctor María
†Went to New Spain, visited Brihuega, (b. 1593) de Urgelos* (b. 1598)
 returned to New Spain.   (b. 1586)

Salas and his wife authorized him to sell their home in Brihuega, which backed on the yard of Mancio Alonso's house, as well as a wine cellar ("una bodega y cueva") that they owned.[72]

Juan de Piña's father, Mancio Alonso, joined him in New Spain seven years after he went there, probably accompanied by Juan's sister María Lagúnez. María was already married to Cristóbal de Salas, and they had a daughter, Francisca, who remained in Brihuega with her grandmother María de Urgelos. Salas first went to New Spain in 1573 but had returned to marry María Lagúnez, probably around 1580.[73] In Puebla, Salas and his wife lived in the San Agustín neighborhood and owned property there as well as in the Indian barrio of San Sebastián. Their daughter María de Piña married a *briocense* immigrant named Alonso de Enche.

Still living in Brihuega in 1590, in that year María de Urgelos petitioned for permission to join her husband in New Spain, saying that he had sent money for her passage and for that of their children, including her daughter Petronilla de Mancio; Petronilla's husband, Francisco Martínez; and their three small children. María de Urgelos took her daughter Mariana de Piña with her to Puebla and presumably her granddaughter Francisca de Salas as well, but apparently Petronilla de Mancio and her family remained in Brihuega. In June 1591 Mariana de Piña married a briocense immigrant named Melchor de Bonilla in Puebla.[74] They became the parents of the holy woman Isabel de la Encarnación. When María de Urgelos was getting ready to depart from Brihuega in 1590, her husband sent her his power of attorney to sell whatever "houses, vineyards, lands and other goods" he owned in Brihuega. In 1602, when she was living in Puebla, she donated houses she had inherited from her parents to her son and daughter in Brihuega, Sancho de Urgelos and Petronilla de Mancio.[75] By this time her husband had died.

Another son, Francisco Lagúnez, also apparently remained in Brihuega.[76] Sancho de Urgelos eventually joined his family in New Spain in 1608, taking with him his wife, Juana de Almonacid, and their three daughters and son, who ranged in age from 10 to 24 years. Thus he, like his parents, emigrated when he and his wife must have been in their 40s and his children of an age to marry, although they were all still single. Unlike his parents, and doubtless aided by the presence of siblings who had long since established themselves in Puebla, Sancho de Urgelos and his wife relocated as a family rather than stretching the move out over many years, as his parents and other siblings had done. Still the parallel is interesting, as both Sancho de Urgelos and his wife and Sancho's parents made the decision to leave Brihuega for Puebla when they were already middle-aged, suggesting that Puebla's appeal remained strong and Brihuega's attractions uncertain, even for families that were well connected and influential.

Women and Emigration

The situation of María de Urgelos, described as poor in the 1585 tax list in the absence of her husband, and of other women whose husbands had emigrated to the Indies raises the question of the extent to which husbands and wives jointly made decisions about relocating. The evidence suggests that women who were left on their own in Brihuega generally did not do well economically; they were usually described as impoverished. Women no doubt would be more positively disposed toward the possibility of accompanying or joining emigrant husbands when they faced little more than poverty and privation if they decided to stay at home.[77] There is no reason to assume, however, that men always initiated and carried out plans to relocate, thus forcing their wives to decide to either go with them or remain at home on their own. Isabel de Guadalajara, for example, declared in her will of 1595 that when she and her second husband, Juan de Ortega, left Brihuega for New Spain, she sold a house and tannery that she had from her first marriage so they could make the journey. Juan de Ortega had brought nothing to their marriage. The sale of her property suggests that the move may have been principally her idea. In Puebla, Isabel de Guadalajara owned a bakery; she was an independent businesswoman, hardly a person one would expect to acquiesce passively in the sacrifice of her property in Brihuega for an undertaking imposed on her by her husband.

Examples in which women clearly appear to have taken the initiative in decisions about emigration are rare, but at the same time there is no evidence that their participation in the movement was essentially passive. True, if husbands were determined to go to the Indies, the options available to their wives in Brihuega—to either accompany them or stay behind in what probably would be insecure and deteriorating economic circumstances—were not very attractive. Still, there is no real proof that decisions to emigrate originated primarily with men or that men were always the chief advocates of such undertakings. Couples who went to New Spain were as likely to be attracted by the presence of relatives on the wife's side as on the husband's, and in the majority of cases both partners were first-time emigrants. These factors suggest a strong likelihood that women participated actively in decisions regarding emigration and underscore the importance of kinship ties on both sides. The collaborative nature of decision making about emigration surely arose from and reflected a general perception of marriage as a partnership in which the wishes and contributions of both spouses figured significantly.

Furthermore, from the early 1570s onward the briocense emigrants enjoyed advantages that few other Castilian emigrants could claim, and these might have been especially important and attractive for women. Rather than leaving friends and family behind to accompany or join a husband, father, or brother in a place where there were perhaps a handful of relatives and fellow townspeople they scarcely knew, the briocense women who left home in the years between 1570 and 1620 went to join a large, close-knit immigrant community in which they most likely had many ties of kinship, compadrazgo, and long-standing acquaintance. The size of the immigrant community in Puebla afforded briocense women both in Spain and in New Spain a degree of familiarity and security that few other women touched by the Indies enterprise enjoyed. Despite the crown's efforts to restrict the emigration of married men without their spouses, if a woman failed to accompany her husband to America, his absence often meant the effective end of the marriage. Although women left behind in Brihuega suffered economically, and not all men returned or sent for their wives, the density of the network of ties between Brihuega and Puebla and the quantity of information that circulated via letters and word of mouth virtually guaranteed that the briocense men who went to New Spain were unlikely to disappear from sight or to remarry. Briocense women on both sides of the Atlantic could feel fairly confident that they would know what their husbands were doing, however distant and long the separation.

Generalizations about family life and relations are difficult to formulate, as nearly any observable pattern points to some counterexample. Family members and kin for the most part cooperated and supported one another in a range of situations, from collaborating on business endeavors to helping one another financially, remembering one another in wills, and aiding one another in disputes to serving as godparents and looking after children whose parents were absent or deceased. When Gabriel de Anzures Guevara purchased the office of alguacil mayor in Huejotzingo in 1607, for example, his bondsmen included his uncle Pedro de Anzures, his first cousin Juan de Roa Anzures, and his nephew Juan de Iñigo.[78] The documents contain scores of such examples of relatives working together to advance the interests of one or more of their number, as it was assumed that individual successes benefited the collective familial or kin unit.

Yet conflict certainly was not unknown. In contrast to Juan de Iñigo, who stated in his will of 1615 that he and his mother had never bothered to make a formal division of his father's estate after he died and jointly owned two estancias, Alonso Gómez sued his mother and siblings over the partition of his father's estate, claiming that he had not received sufficient compensation for the work he had performed in his father's obraje after his death. Andrés de la Fuente also disputed the settlement of his father's estate with his mother, Isabel Bautista, and her second husband and actively took his sister Catalina's side against his mother when she refused to marry and wanted to enter a convent. In 1587 Alonso Díaz sued his daughter and son-in-law when they would not relinquish the obraje that he had transferred to his daughter and her first husband in a fictitious sale for less than a third of its value when he went to Castile. He claimed that in addition to retaining the obraje, they had run up debts that had resulted in the confiscation of two of his slaves.[79] The outcome of this suit is not known. Problems within families could affect people outside the familial circle as well, as will be seen in Chapter 6.

Furthermore, while in theory the customs and laws that shaped the institutions of marriage and family should have guaranteed some degree of security and protection for all members, at times they failed to do so. Widows were left poor, and young people could find themselves on their own with no one to help them. The 1585 vecindario of Brihuega included a Mari López who "died and left three poor daughters." María and Juan de León stated in a deposition in Brihuega in 1592 that their mother had died eight years before and their father had gone to Zacatecas in New Spain and was living in "las minas del Fresnillo." They claimed that their tutor, Jerónimo Martínez, wanted to send them to their father "because they are very poor and have nothing to sustain them in this country." One witness claimed that their father had sent for them, although there really is no evidence that he did, and in any case he certainly took his time doing so. They did not actually depart until 1594.[80] The collective obligation of family members to love, trust, and protect one another probably at this time provided the best possible guarantee of an individual's welfare and security, yet human frailty, especially when coupled with economic uncertainty, could leave people vulnerable and all too alone.

CHAPTER SIX

Social Relations

The topic of social relations is inextricably bound up with the other aspects of the briocenses' lives that have been addressed up to this point. Their choices about relocating and settling down, economic activities and decision making, patterns of and attitudes toward participation in political and public life, involvement in religious life, and marriage, family, and kinship relations not only reflected and shaped the nature and meaning of social ties, aspirations, and interactions; they were virtually inseparable from them. It is impossible to look at social relations outside of their economic, political, and cultural milieu. The purpose here is to examine in detail some aspects of social relations and interactions among individuals and groups that may shed light on how people conducted their economic, political, religious, and personal affairs. Such topics as relationships between friends and neighbors; how people socialized and where they chose to live; social background and aspirations; situations of conflict, confrontation, and social censure; and perceptions of other social and ethnic groups all define and reflect the nature of social relations. This chapter focuses on certain situations that may serve as windows through which to view and analyze some of the phenomena that shaped and colored both daily life and long-term life experience.

A Broken Engagement

An accusation of bigamy lodged against Diego de Anzures, the individual who probably played the most crucial role in initiating the movement of people from Brihuega to Puebla, affords insight into how social relations and concerns both in Brihuega and within the immigrant community in Puebla were tied to legal and familial issues, patterns of mobility and relocation, and collective perceptions of individual behavior. The testimony elicited in two Inquisition cases brought against Anzures twenty years apart, one in Spain and the other in New Spain, provides a wealth of detail that may be explored to reach some understanding of how people perceived and explained both their own actions and those of others in a situation of conflict.[1]

Diego de Anzures left Brihuega in 1555, when he was in his early twenties, to go to New Spain with a family friend from Brihuega, Cristóbal Escudero, who was more than ten years older and had been living in Seville for some years, working as a merchant.[2] After they arrived in New Spain, Escudero remained in Mexico City, while Anzures went to live in Puebla and, as we have seen, became a successful obrajero and stock raiser and ascended through a series of key offices to become Puebla's first alférez mayor. At the end of the 1570s he returned permanently with his family to Brihuega, where he lived into his 80s as a wealthy and influential vecino.[3]

While Diego de Anzures was still living in Puebla, in 1573, a woman named María de la Paz, a 33-year-old vecina of Puebla who was originally from Guadalajara in Castile, brought a charge of bigamy against him before a canon of the cathedral, Alonso Hernández de Santiago, and the archdeacon don Hernando Pacheco, who was comisario of the Holy Office in Puebla. Coincidentally, 1573 was the year in which the movement from Brihuega to Puebla really took off; the archdeacon later explained to Inquisition officials in Mexico City that he had delayed reporting María de la Paz's accusation for six months in part because potential additional witnesses "are coming now from Spain."[4]

The story that María de la Paz recounted went as follows. Around six years before (which would have been in 1567, while Anzures was still notary of the city council) she had been in the house of the briocense obrajero Andrés de Angulo in Puebla, talking with Angulo's wife, Isabel de Ribas. Isabel told her that Diego de Anzures's wife recently had given birth to a daughter and that Anzures was "very angry" because the child was a girl, "for which reason he went unwillingly to visit his wife."[5] His angry reaction to his daughter's birth apparently reminded Isabel de Ribas of Anzures's father's response when his own wife had given birth to yet another daughter. When asked on that occasion who would be the godfather, the elder Diego de Anzures had replied that they should name Satan. Isabel went on to call Diego de Anzures (the son) a "bad Christian" because before he left Castile he had promised to marry a young woman named María de Encinas who lived in the town of Cifuentes and then refused to do so.

María de la Paz, her curiosity about (or animosity toward) Anzures apparently piqued by this information, over time questioned other people about the episode. She testified that while visiting in her house Pedro de Anzures, Diego's younger brother, had confirmed the story. According to Pedro, she said, Diego had been ordered to marry the woman, and after a fight with his father, "he fled to these parts."[6] María also discussed the matter with another obrajero, Juan de Brihuega. She claimed he had told her that while attending mass one time in Brihuega he had witnessed Diego de Anzures's excommunication. María stated that Macario and Francisca de Anzures, two of Diego's other siblings who were in Puebla, also had confirmed the story, as did Juan de Brihuega's wife. When questioned directly by Inquisition officials, Juan de Brihuega at first was vague about the details but then admitted that long ago, as a boy in Brihuega, he had heard about the case and that Diego de Anzures had been excommunicated. Later, however, Diego's older brother Rodrigo de Anzures told him that the matter had been settled. Andrés de Angulo testified that he thought Diego had left Castile while an appeal was still pending. Angulo suspected that María de la Paz's denunciation stemmed from a falling out with Anzures ("cierto enojo que había habido con el dicho Diego de Anzures").

Whether or not malice prompted María de la Paz's accusation—and it is difficult to imagine what else could have done so—the testimony, although often reluctant, of other briocenses who were close to Anzures, as well as the statements Anzures himself eventually made, revealed that a fairly notorious episode involving a possibly broken engagement had occurred before Anzures left Castile. On hearing of the accusation made against him, Diego de Anzures undertook to talk to don Hernando Pacheco, the archdeacon and comisario of the Holy Office in Puebla. Pacheco later wrote that one day after sundown Anzures came to his lodging asking to speak to him, not so much to seek his advice as to unburden himself ("descargar el pecho"). The two men chatted while standing in the garden. The tone of Pacheco's statement and Anzures's decision to consult him voluntarily rather than await a summons suggest not only that Anzures was aware that the episode was too well known to be denied but also that he probably was on friendly terms with the archdeacon and anticipated a degree of leniency as a result.

To Pacheco, Anzures confided that for 23 years he had been the "most disconsolate man in the world" because as a youth still living in his parents' house in Brihuega "a certain young woman" alleged that he had promised to marry her, and he later had been ordered to do so. On hearing of the engagement, Diego de Anzures's father had angrily thrown him out of the house and hurled a lance at him; he missed his target.[7] Anzures told the archdeacon that he had not wanted to marry the young woman because "she was of low quality and worthless people" ("era de baja suerte y de ruín gente"). He had appealed the bishop's order to marry her and subsequently left for New Spain, although he said that before departing he had discussed the case with lawyers, and they assured him that he was free of any obligation to the woman. He reconciled with his father, who died three years after Diego left Castile, and several years after arriving in New Spain, Anzures married María de Montoya. Notwithstanding his claim to a troubled conscience, Anzures admitted to Pacheco that he had decided to come forward with his story only because he had been denounced. The archdeacon recommended that he go voluntarily before the Inquisition officials in Mexico City.

Not surprisingly, Diego de Anzures's account of events and the version offered by members of the girl's family in Cifuentes when officials made inquiries there directly contradicted each other in certain details. It seems likely that Diego de Anzures became infatuated with María de Encinas. Carried away by youthful passion, he may well have made rash promises that his father subsequently gave him cause to regret; hence his change of heart. The elder Diego de Anzures was known as a harsh, impetuous man ("recio") with an almost uncontrollable temper; he himself admitted that when angry he was "worse than drunk" and later could not remember things he had said.[8] Although a commoner, the senior Diego de Anzures was prominent in Brihuega, strongly conscious of his wealth and position. Several witnesses in the case brought against him for "scandalous words" in 1553 recalled that on more than one occasion Anzures had boasted, "I swear to God I'd rather be a sodomite than a pauper" ("Juro a Dios que más querría ser puto que pobre").

The younger Diego de Anzures appears to have inherited in good measure his father's arrogance as well as his temper. In a letter to Cristóbal Escudero in Mexico City in which he proposed to explain to his friend the events behind the Inquisition case of 1573, he wrote of an incident in Brihuega several years before he departed for New Spain. Anzures claimed to have angered people in Brihuega by bragging that "where my father was, Jews would not become regidores" ("donde mi padre estaba no habían de venir judíos por regidores"); as a result, some merchants ceased to visit the town and people complained about him.[9] Although, as we have seen, by the latter part of the sixteenth century merchants were no longer coming to Brihuega to buy cloth, it is doubtful that Diego's offensive remarks played a significant role in the deterioration of the town's position in the textile trade; but people may have thought they did.

Diego de Anzures came to the attention of the Inquisition in Spain in 1553, at the same time the case was brought against his father, because of statements he made about the woman who expected to marry him. Clearly the ostensible engagement was the subject of much rumor and speculation in Brihuega, and people questioned and teased Diego about it. He denied any betrothal or marriage, sometimes making light of the matter and at other moments responding angrily. A young man named Pedro Lagúnez testified that one day when several people were at a fulling mill near Brihuega he told Anzures that if he were obligated to marry the woman, he should marry her, and if not, then not. Anzures replied that he would not marry her even if he were bound to do so. Another man working at the mill asked him, What about the soul? Diego allegedly answered that "in these times there's neither soul nor devil" ("ni ánima ni diablo"); other witnesses also heard this statement. For his part, Anzures testified that one day he ran into several women who asked about the alleged marriage, and he repeatedly denied it, finally saying that "even if God and Saint Mary and all the saints were present he wouldn't marry her but instead would become a friar or go to the Indies."[10]

Although at some points it is hard to reconcile the different versions of events, they appear to have occurred as follows. After Diego de Anzures stirred up trouble in Brihuega with his offensive remark about Jews (presumably he had in mind conversos), his parents sent him to live with a relative in Cifuentes who lived next door to a man named Cristóbal de Encinas, whose daughter was María de Encinas. Most likely the Encinas family was of more humble status than the Anzureses, although the artisanal background of the Anzures family doubtless was known to all. It surely was with conscious intent that one of María de Encinas's brothers, a shoemaker, later referred to Diego de Anzures as a wool carder ("cardador y peinador").

As temporary neighbors, the two young people became acquainted, although Diego would later claim they had spoken only through the window. Neither party to the dispute ever maintained that sexual relations had taken place, although Maria's father seems to have thought that possibly they had. In any case, the fight between Diego and his father strongly suggests that young Diego made promises to María that his father violently disapproved and no doubt ordered his son to repudiate. The Encinas family took the case to the bishop's court in Sigüenza. When summoned, Diego failed to appear; he was excommunicated for disobeying the order. María won the case, and the court ordered Diego to marry her. The Anzures family then appealed the sentence to the vicar in Alcalá de Henares.

All the parties involved acknowledged the sequence of events up to that point. Anzures later claimed to have won the appeal and stated that at the time he left Spain, he was free to marry whomever he chose. He also said that his father had urged him to marry, but by that time he was eager to leave for America. His father may well have been feeling rather desperate to make a suitable match for his impetuous second son. Juan García Rodrigo, a briocense immigrant living in Puebla in the 1570s, testified that he recalled a somewhat veiled statement that Diego's father made hinting at another romantic entanglement of his son's that he had been forced to resolve as well.[11]

One of the most extensive accounts of the events came from Alonso de Ribas, another obrajero from Brihuega living in Puebla, who was slightly older than Diego de Anzures. He was the brother of Isabel de Ribas, María de la Paz's original source for the story of Anzures's alleged first marriage, and probably related to the Encinas family in Cifuentes.[12] At the time the conflict over Anzures's engagement to María de Encinas erupted, people on both sides had called upon Alonso de Ribas to act as mediator. When María de Encinas's brother arrived in Brihuega with the order for Anzures to appear before the bishop, he sought out Ribas, and after his excommunication Diego de Anzures asked Ribas to intercede with the Encinas family on his behalf. Alonso de Ribas did go to Cifuentes to talk to María's father. According to him, Cristóbal de Encinas said he would be willing to drop the suit, regardless of what had happened between the young people, were it not for the fact that (he claimed) Diego himself had pleaded with him to allow the marriage, saying that "she was his wife and she shouldn't marry anyone else." Encinas told Ribas that Diego had begged to be allowed to greet his mother-in-law; when she came out of the house, he got down on his knees, and she embraced him. María's brother Francisco de Encinas later stated that when the news of the engagement became public, everyone in town congratulated Anzures.[13] According to the story that Alonso de Ribas heard from María's father, after the latter agreed to the marriage, Diego departed for Brihuega to collect his clothes from his parents' house but then failed to return.

Diego de Anzures's version of events was malicious, perhaps in large part as a result of his father's anger and the humiliation of being the subject of widespread discussion and innuendo. He impugned María's virtue and alleged that her family had bribed a serving girl to testify falsely about the betrothal. He also implied that María's good looks (he disparagingly referred to her as "not too ugly") and presence in Sigüenza accounted for her success in winning the suit. His father, apparently having pardoned his son's romantic lapse, joined Diego in maligning the Encinas family, calling them "very converso, vile and of lowly occupation" ("muy conversos, viles, de ruin oficio"), in obvious contrast to his own very respectable family.

In writing to his friend Escudero in Mexico City in 1574, Diego de Anzures said that he had thought little of the matter at the time, a claim that scarcely seems credible, given the considerable stir it caused both within his family and in the larger community. He insisted that he had been free to marry after winning the appeal and also that he had heard that María de Encinas had died after he left Spain, which certainly would have removed any lingering doubts regarding his liberty to marry. As proof that there could not have been any further consequences of the episode or remaining obligations to María and her family, Anzures reminded Escudero that some ten years before he had planned to travel to Spain not only with his wife and family but accompanied as well by people whom he called relatives of María de Encinas's relatives, a number of whom (according to Anzures) were living in Puebla.[14] He argued, with some reason, that since his siblings in Brihuega were well aware that he had married in Puebla, they surely would have informed him if there had been any problems with his plan to visit home. The visit never took place, however, because a storm forced some of the ships in the fleet to turn back and also destroyed some of his property.

Possibly Anzures escaped any further repercussions of the matter largely because María and her family lacked the means or spirit to pursue it. For some years María seems to have continued to hope that Diego would return to Castile and fulfill his obligations to her. Alonso de Ribas testified that when he returned to Spain around 1561 he ran into one of María's brothers in Seville, who told him that she was still alive and waiting for Anzures to honor their marriage. Juan García Rodrigo said that at the time Diego de Anzures intended to return to Spain, María had gone to Seville to wait for him. After the early 1560s, however, her actions and fate are unclear. In 1573 her brother Francisco de Encinas said he had not seen her in twelve years. He testified that María had gone with their mother to Ocaña, where their mother died, leaving María in the service of the corregidor of the town. The corregidor possibly took her with him to Galicia. Other witnesses, however, thought she had gone to live in Andalucía, and during the 1560s Alonso de Ribas heard that she had died.

Although María's ultimate fate is unknown, the sparse evidence offered by witnesses suggests that the course of her life was irrevocably altered by her entanglement with Diego de Anzures. Considering herself legitimately married to him, she would not have felt free to enter into another marriage.

Anzures clearly felt no such compunction, and in the long run he suffered hardly any consequences from the episode. In his letter to Escudero he seemed more annoyed by the inconvenience occasioned by the revival of the old case than conscience-stricken; he worried that the outcome would affect his business affairs. In May 1574 he said that "because I've been someone who has held high office and many [people] have come to hate me" ("por ser persona que he tenido oficio principal y muchos me han cobrado odio"), he feared the financial damage that might ensue should the Inquisition appear to be denying him the license to go to Castile that he had requested. After a year or so, however, the officials of the Holy Office suspended the case pending further inquiries to be made in Castile, and Anzures duly received permission to depart. This decision was tantamount to dropping the charges against Anzures, for they were never pursued, either in Spain or in Mexico.

While at one level this episode has obvious relevance to the issue of how marriages were made and the role of parental authority in regulating their children's behavior and choices, it also sheds light on how a community—or better, two communities, in Brihuega and Puebla—responded to a situation in which an individual who belonged to a socially prominent and economically influential family appeared to flout certain widely held social and moral norms and expectations. Gauging that response, as reflected in the testimony of witnesses in the two Inquisition cases against Diego de Anzures and in Anzures's own statements, is not simple, however. Notwithstanding Anzures's admission that many people disliked him, public reaction in Puebla seems to have been limited; the only people who were very concerned were members of the Brihuega immigrant community who had some memory of or connection with the individuals who had been involved in the events that had taken place twenty years before in the towns of the Alcarria. Clearly the case engaged the attention of many of the immigrants in Puebla in the early 1570s and doubtless it became a topic of discussion among them; Cristóbal Escudero stated that he had first heard about the bigamy charges from the merchant Francisco Alvarez, one of his compatriots living in Puebla, who wrote to Escudero about the case. Yet María de la Paz's attempt to cause trouble for Anzures or perhaps foster some kind of social censure of his actions, at least within the immigrant community, obviously fell far short of achieving those objectives. The kind of condemnation or derision that Anzures's treatment of María de Encinas had provoked in Brihuega and Cifuentes by no means was replicated twenty years later in Puebla. Even in Brihuega, unless it is assumed that social or moral pressures in some degree compelled Diego de Anzures to leave for New

Spain—a dubious assumption at best, given the evidence— a collective moral authority that resulted in his ostracism can hardly be proved.

As it was, the revival of the old charges in a quite different setting in the 1570s clearly had little real impact on the still fairly small immigrant community in Puebla. While in many ways the members of that community were closely connected and interdependent, they were mainly concerned with making their way in a new society, not with reliving old scandals. Diego de Anzures's economic success, officeholding, and social connections made him a key figure in the immigrant community and hence not a man to be brought down without possibly serious repercussions. As seen, the case arose just at the time large numbers of people were arriving in Puebla from Brihuega, and their main preoccupation would have been with establishing themselves there as quickly as possible. In that process the advice, assistance, and connections of successful earlier immigrants such as Anzures were crucial. Thus while the fate of an innocent young woman who had the misfortune to become involved with a headstrong youth whose father had little sympathy for his son's romantic escapades occasioned some social censure in Brihuega, twenty years later in New Spain the episode constituted little more than half-remembered gossip that for the most part was not taken very seriously.

Nonetheless, the entire episode suggests certain patterns of individual and collective behavior as well as the ways in which people perceived and judged the behavior of acquaintances and relatives. For one thing, people did not hesitate to discuss, criticize, and question the actions and motivations of others, particularly when they felt someone had failed to fulfill social and moral obligations. This kind of judgment is evident in a letter of 1572 that Diego de Pastrana wrote to his uncle Juan Díaz in Fuentelencina, in which he discussed mutual acquaintances, presumably from their town:

> Tell señor Alonso Rodríguez de Encinas what is going on here with his brother Francisco Rodríguez, that there's no occasion on which we see him in my house that we don't attack him like a Moor, telling him that he already knows that his brother is very poor and blind, begging him to favor him and conveying to him the extreme need in which he and his wife and children live, being as he is blind and poor. And also his cousin Diego Rodríguez, the priest, wrote to him, pleading with and importuning him greatly, and what he answers is that . . . he shouldn't expect anything from him, . . . that he hasn't even wanted to write a letter, and besides he is such that he will not do good for anyone.[15]

The controversy over Diego de Anzures's involvement with María de Encinas demonstrates that marriage had a social or public dimension that went beyond the desires and priorities of prospective marriage partners and their families. Friends, relatives, and neighbors were aware of Diego de Anzures's engagement, and the vecinos of Cifuentes reportedly showed their approval of the match by publicly congratulating him. In Brihuega many people clearly felt uneasy about Anzures's repudiation of the engagement and thus of the norms, both customary and legal, that in effect equated a betrothal with marriage itself.[16] They worried about the spiritual as well as the social implications of such an act and questioned and teased Anzures about it.

A stable marriage fulfilled a social function as much as a familial one and thus became a collective concern. Members of the community played a role in upholding the sanctity and significance of betrothal and marriage by acting as witnesses to private vows. As such they often recalled having attended the weddings of friends and neighbors. Hernando Ruiz "el viejo" testified to having been present at the wedding of Pedro (and Diego) de Anzures's parents in the church of San Felipe in Brihuega.[17] In the 1573 deposition of Francisco Gutiérrez, who wanted to accompany fray Alonso de la Vera Cruz to New Spain, Francisco de Pastrana stated that he had seen Gutiérrez's parents marry in the church of San Miguel and that he was in a position to know everything about them "as their neighbor and a person who has had and has with them particular awareness and neighborliness and friendship." Another neighbor of the family, Andrés Alvarez, who also had attended the wedding in San Miguel, said much the same.[18]

Friends and Neighbors

Statements made by people in Castile and New Spain in the cases brought against Diego de Anzures as well as in many other instances reflect and underscore the emotional ties and shared experiences of friends and neighbors who grew up together and associated with one another over many years. The regidor Capt. don Francisco de Torija was born in Brihuega in 1637 and left for New Spain when he was around twenty years old. When he tried to secure a position as familiar in Puebla in 1694, inquiries were made in Brihuega. Lic. don Cristóbal de los Santos, a 66-year-old priest, said he knew Torija because he had lived near him. Don Mateo Ruiz, who was a lawyer at the royal court and jurado of the town council, said he knew Torija because they had been students together; Francisco de la Peña also said that he had studied grammar at the colegio with Torija when they were boys. Cristóbal Tartajo, a labrador, said that, since they were neighbors, when Torija left Brihuega they parted "with much affection." Juan Calleja said he accompanied Torija, perhaps all the way to Seville, to say good-bye.[19]

The ties of friendship, kinship, and compadrazgo often blended seamlessly in the relationships of people who lived in a fairly small town. Testifying in the deposition of Juan González in Brihuega in 1609, the returnee Diego de Anzures said he knew when Juan was born "because when his mother was giving birth to him this witness, as he has been her compadre for other children of hers . . . and because he lived close to their house," was aware of the event.[20]

As one would expect, these kinds of bonds carried over to Puebla, where the unusual size of the briocense immigrant community enabled many people who had grown up together in Brihuega to maintain their ties in Puebla. Juan Barranco mentioned that in Brihuega his family had lived next door to the family of Isabel de Ribas, who went to Puebla with her husband, Andrés de Angulo. In the deposition of Andrés de Angulo compiled in Puebla in 1572, Juan de Trixueque, then about 30 years old, said he had known Angulo for as long as he could remember. Diego de Anzures testified that he had known Angulo since they were children and that their families were good friends. Anzures's brother-in-law Juan de Roa also stated that "he has had much friendship with" Angulo and had known him for more than 25 years.[21] The Inquisition case against Diego de Anzures reflected his long-term friendship with Cristóbal Escudero. When officials questioned Escudero as to whether he harbored negative feelings ("odio") toward Anzures, he said that on the contrary, "he loves him very much."

Briocenses living in Puebla remembered and missed their friends back home just as they did family members. In a letter of 1572 to his brother (possibly his brother-in-law) Pedro García in Brihuega, Juan de Brihuega wrote that "to the reverend Juan García Navarro you should give my greetings [*besamanos*]. . . . To señor Juan Ruiz and all my neighbors in general give my greetings with all the rest of my señores and friends." To his uncle Juan Díaz in Fuentelencina, Diego de Pastrana wrote in the same year that he should give his greetings to people in the town, "and if you go to Brihuega, give my regards to Alonso de Ribas and his wife." He sent the letter with "Diego Rodríguez, vecino of this city, a great friend of mine." Also in a letter of 1572 Martín Hernández Cubero mentioned to his nephew in Fuentelencina

> Señor Alonso Hernández and señor Alonso de Ribas, of Brihuega, because we went around together while they were here, and we were great friends, as we were all from one place [*patria*], so that at the time each of them went to that country, it made all of us feel bad to separate. . . . When señor Alonso de Ribas left this country I wanted to go with him if I could, and he wished it even more.[22]

Letters, word of mouth, and travel back and forth all fostered a sense of continuing connection between people separated by time and distance and of meaningful involvement in the lives of friends and former neighbors. In 1590, for example, in the deposition of Juan Crespo, Diego de Anaya testified to the prosperity of Crespo's father-in-law, the barber-surgeon Francisco Hernández, in Puebla. Anaya stated that he was in a position to know about him because he had lived more than twelve years in Puebla and "had been the neighbor of the said Francisco Hernández and dealt with him a lot and with much familiarity, because of being from the same country [*tierra*]." Anaya apparently brought letters from Francisco Hernández to Juan Crespo when he returned to Brihuega in 1587, and his wife testified that before leaving New Spain she and her husband had gone to Mexico City and had seen Crespo's uncle there.[23]

Neighborhoods and Urban Life

Comments in letters and elsewhere reflect the close relations that immigrants maintained with one another, not least by virtue of their physical proximity. In Puebla they bought, rented, and built houses near one another. Their neighborhood of choice was the barrio of San Agustín and the area east of it, toward the Hospital de Nuestra Señora and the church of the Jesuits. The briocenses—and hence the city itself—were strongly affected by the nature and exigencies of their involvement in industry and trade. Since they preferred to live near or even in the same building as their textile shops or bakeries, many took up residence in the city's most commercialized zones, such as San Francisco; but briocenses also established obrajes in the more prestigious neighborhoods where they lived. As they prospered, some immigrants who started out living and working in less central and urbanized neighborhoods moved closer to their compatriots and the center of the city.[24]

Pedro Camarillo, who was in Puebla by 1593 and owned estancias near Cholula, which he sold to the briocense Cristóbal de Beguillas in 1608, stated in 1598 that he owned a house in the barrio of Santiago that had a garden with a pair of small houses and an enclosed yard. In the late sixteenth century he apparently lived there, which would have placed him close to his properties near Cholula. He and his wife also owned property in San Agustín, however: one house that they purchased for 1,335 pesos in 1597 on the street running from the church of Vera Cruz to the "pond of the slaughterhouse" and another located next to lots owned by the briocense obrajero Francisco del Castillo that they purchased for 1,100 pesos. By 1612 Camarillo and his wife owned a house on the plaza of San Agustín itself, next to that of another briocense obrajero, Cristóbal de la Carrera, and probably by then they resided there rather than in Santiago.[25]

Other briocenses who held property elsewhere in the city also lived in San Agustín. The brothers Jorge and Hernando de Sepúlveda owned houses next to each other in the barrio of Santiago, across the street from the house of Juan de Ortega Prieto; all three, however, also owned houses in San Agustín. In 1608 Jorge de Sepúlveda had a house next to one owned by the briocenses María García and Lorenzo de Pajares on the street that ran from the convent of Nuestra Señora de la Concepción to San Agustín, and his brother Hernando probably owned a house next to his. The dowry of Juan de Ortega Prieto's second wife, Jerónima del Aguila, included "casas de morada edificadas de altos y bajos" on the Calle de los Herreros (present-day Avenida 3 Poniente), which led to the monastery of San Agustín. Her brother bought this property in 1590 for 2,900 pesos, but she and her husband still owned houses and lots in the neighborhood. Late in 1605 Juan de Ortega sold to the obrajero Melchor Rodríguez a house next to his own in San Agustín in which Rodríguez had been living.

Many other immigrants lived close to one another in San Agustín, often operating their obrajes in the same neighborhood, including Pedro and Macario de Anzures, both of whom lived near the monastery; the brothers Gaspar, Gabriel, and Melchor Caballero (from Budía) and their uncle Cristóbal de Brihuega; Cristóbal de la Carrera and his brother Lope de la Carrera; and Gabriel de Angulo and his cousin Juan Pérez de Angulo. In the early 1590s Gabriel de Angulo bought a house from his father-in-law on the plaza of San Agustín, and he also owned "casas de obraje" on two lots next to the house. Angulo, together with another obrajero from Brihuega, Francisco del Castillo, who owned a house on the plaza, in 1593 petitioned the city council for permission to build *portales* (arcades or porticos) in front of their houses, which was granted.[26] The houses owned by María García and her second husband, Lorenzo de Pajares, one of which housed a bakery, were next to Gabriel de Angulo's obraje. In 1590 the briocense Cristóbal de Salas bought a house next to Francisco de Castillo's house. Salas also owned other properties in the neighborhood, including a house he rented to the briocense Juan Portugués in 1590 and another he sold to his son-in-law (also from Brihuega) Alonso de Enche, located next to a house owned by the briocense Pedro Barranco and his wife. The Barrancos gave part of a lot next to their house on the Calle de Cholula (present-day Avenida de la Reforma) in 1615 to their son Francisco Barranco. The list of briocense home or obraje owners in San Agustín also includes Juan Merino Carrillo and his

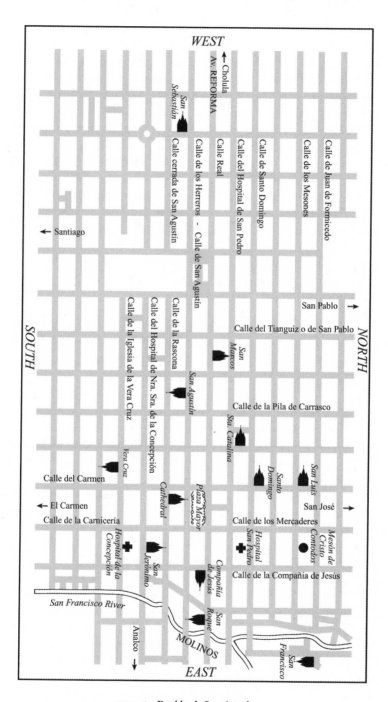

WEST

← Cholula
Av. REFORMA

San Sebastián

Calle cerrada de San Agustín
Calle de los Herreros - Calle de San Agustín
Calle Real
Calle del Hospital de San Pedro
Calle de Santo Domingo
Calle de los Mesones
Calle de Juan de Formicedo

← Santiago

Calle de la Iglesia de la Vera Cruz
Calle del Hospital de Nra. Sra. de la Concepción
Calle de la Rascona
San Agustín
San Marcos

San Pablo →

Calle del Tianguiz o de San Pablo

Calle de la Pila de Carrasco

Sta. Catalina

Vera Cruz

Santo Domingo

San Luis

Calle del Carmen

← El Carmen
Calle de la Carnicería

Cathedral
Plaza Mayor
San José

San José →
Calle de los Mercaderes

Mesón de Cristo
Contodos

Hospital San Pedro

Hospital de la Concepción
San Jerónimo

Compañía de Jesús
San Roque

Calle de la Compañía de Jesús

San Francisco River

Analco ↓

MOLINOS

San Francisco

EAST

SOUTH

NORTH

MAP 6. *Puebla de Los Angeles*

wife; the merchant and obrajero Hernando de Pastrana; Pedro de Cifuentes and his wife, Catalina de Cara, whose house was next to Juan de Angulo's obraje; and Alonso de Pedroviejo, who in 1598 bought "casas con su tienda" next to the house of his compatriot Francisco el Rojo.

Although one cannot draw a sharp distinction between the immigrants who owned or rented property in San Francisco and those who lived in or had businesses in more prestigious neighborhoods such as San Agustín or the area southwest of the plaza, still it is possible to discern a certain correlation between status and residence or work in one neighborhood or another. The briocenses who were most active in trade and transport—people such as Juan Llorente, his son-in-law Esteban Carrillo, his first cousin Bartolomé Tartajo, Miguel Toribio (probably also a cousin), and the brothers Miguel and Juan de Angón—lived primarily in San Francisco, and other very commercially active immigrants such as Pablo de Pastrana and Francisco el Rojo maintained their places of business there as well, even if they lived elsewhere.

It is not always easy to identify distinct circles of association within the immigrant community, although they certainly existed. Even lacking direct ties, virtually every member of the community would have known, or at least known of, every other and therefore would have had some sort of indirect connection. The extent of the ties among the immigrants thus makes it difficult at times to correlate choice of residence with other forms of association. Nonetheless, members of the group who had particularly close and enduring connections did reflect those ties in their choices of where to live or locate their businesses, and thus they would be neighbors as well as relatives, compadres, and business partners.

This residential clustering of briocenses in Puebla ensured a great deal of contact among the immigrants, who doubtless saw one another on a near-daily basis. People socialized by visiting the homes of friends and relatives, especially in the evenings after the workday had ended, to chat and pass the time playing cards and other games. Benito Sanz Bautista, for example, described how he spent the evening of January 16, 1608, the night his friend Francisco López was murderously attacked in Puebla. After working all day at his obraje in Cholula, Benito went to visit his compadre Cristóbal Rodríguez. Some other acquaintances, men and women, among them Diego de Simancas, a trader in cacao, were also there, and "they remained in good conversation until after eight o'clock." From there Benito Sanz Bautista went with Diego de Simancas to the house of the widow Teresa de Campos, Simancas's mother and Benito's *comadre*, and they stayed there visiting with her and some other people, including a tailor named Palma and his comadre's son-in-law, a schoolteacher, and his wife, until around ten.[27] During the day men would meet in public or stop by one another's shops to chat or to discuss business.[28]

The characteristic mix of residential and commercial-industrial uses of property in virtually all the city's neighborhoods created a busy and diverse urban milieu. The juxtaposition of private houses, business establishments, and religious and governmental institutions at times could produce friction. In 1565 neighbors complained to the alcalde mayor and city council about the dye mill ("molino de pastel") that Cristóbal de Ribas and another man had established in a house next to the Hospital de San Pedro, "which is the leading neighborhood of this city . . . and of houses of the most honorable vecinos." Production of the dye resulted in foul odors thought to be harmful to the health of the residents and damaging to the general character of the city. The council ordered the mill to be removed from the city proper and directed that no similar one be established in the future.[29] Regulating the supply and distribution of water was a constant preoccupation and could also lead to disputes. Perhaps surprisingly, however, the presence in prestigious neighborhoods of obrajes with dozens of Indian workers, many of them confined but others coming and going to their places of work, seems to have provoked little complaint. Since workers were mainly confined within the premises, these businesses on the whole probably caused relatively little outward disturbance.

Puebla was undergoing rapid urbanization in the late sixteenth and early seventeenth centuries, a development to which the briocenses contributed significantly. Areas that earlier in the century had gained formal recognition as indigenous barrios became increasingly Hispanicized.[30] In 1607, for example, Alonso de la Carrera and Cristóbal de Ribas, together with other vecinos, protested official efforts to prohibit the sale of wine in the barrio of San Francisco, where they claimed "more than eighty Spanish vecinos" were living, "with their houses and families."[31] The construction or expansion of residences and other establishments could lead to competition and conflict as available space in the city's prestigious central traza became increasingly scarce. In 1588 the Jesuits wanted to expand into a lot already occupied by a house belonging to Juan Barranco in order to create a small plaza and arcade for the "dignity and ornamentation of the said church." Barranco apparently was renovating his house, putting in high windows "to the detriment of the living and sleeping space" of members of the order who lived at the colegio. The Jesuits also complained of inconvenience and noise produced by the congestion from horses and servants, who had insufficient room to move about. The upshot was that the city ordered Barranco to exchange the house and property for a comparable one owned by the Jesuits.[32]

The varied and changing uses of urban space and residential and commercial patterns meant a great deal of contact not only among neighbors, kinspeople, and acquaintances within the immigrant and larger Spanish community but also between members of the Spanish sector of poblano society and the city's Indian, African, and mixed populations. Outside the arena of labor—in which Indians and other nonwhites invariably functioned as the subordinates of their Spanish employers and masters—information on the nature of relations between briocenses and the city's non-Spanish population is sparse. Not surprisingly, the rather infrequent recorded comments that briocenses made about their workers, servants, and slaves—the capacity in which they most often had contact with members of the non-Spanish community—tended to be negative and disparaging. In Diego de Anzures's letter to Cristóbal Escudero about the bigamy case, for example, when he promised to try to explain the events as completely as possible, he wrote: "I'll be like the Indians, who in order to tell something go in circles, so I won't leave anything out."[33]

The immigrants seem to have viewed Indians and other non-Spaniards in general as untrustworthy. Alonso de Viñuelas wrote to his brother Juan in 1583 complaining that the Indians could not be trusted and had to be watched all the time or they would not work.[34] In the suit between Pedro de Alcanadre and Alonso and Juan de Ribas, Alcanadre contended that his adversaries planned to prove their case "with Indians of their house" and other untrustworthy people who could easily be persuaded to lie. Such attitudes no doubt both fostered and reflected a real indifference to the experiences of their subordinates and the conditions in which they lived and worked. When Juan de Ribas testified about the state of one of the workers—an Indian named Lorenzo, who apparently had been badly beaten—in the obraje that he and his father purchased from Alcanadre, his main complaint was that Lorenzo had died almost immediately "without my being able to employ him, nor was he of any use to me at all."[35] General indifference and distrust did not preclude the existence of more particular antipathies as well. An Indian woman from Puebla named María Gómez brought charges against Manuel de Cuenca, the mayordomo of Pedro Gómez's obraje, in 1603, alleging not only that Cuenca commonly mistreated the Indian workers in the obraje, but that he had singled out her husband, Francisco Gómez, for particular abuse "just for hatred that he has taken against him." She accused Pedro Gómez's "calpixque" (majordomo) of forcing her husband to spin twice as much as the other workers and severely beating him.[36]

The prevailing attitudes of contempt and distrust did not, of course, prevent formation of ties of affection, trust, and intimacy. On the evening that Francisco López, the husband of Isabel Bautista's niece, was stabbed, the cries of the women who had been accompanying him alerted Juan de Mata, the mayordomo of Isabel Bautista's obraje, and he took two or three Indian workers with him to find out what the commotion was all about. In a situation of possible danger, surely he would have wanted men on whose loyalty he felt he could count to accompany him. Provisions in wills reflect the existence of affective bonds between masters and servants or slaves or with mestizo or mulato children brought into households who were often but not necessarily always the offspring of the master or another family member. The alférez Juan García Barranco freed Dominga, the daughter of his slave Juliana, "for services and good works that her mother has done for me and because I raised her." The wording does not, of course, preclude the possibility that Dominga was his own daughter, although likely she was not, as he made no financial provision for her future. He also placed María, the daughter of an Indian woman named María and his black slave Hernando, in the convent of San Jerónimo, founded by his relative Juan Barranco, stipulating that she was to receive 50 pesos a year for life.[37]

The development of bonds of trust and affection in some small degree may have tempered the social distance between Spanish vecinos and their Indian, African, and mixed neighbors, employees, and servants. Limitations on the socioeconomic and political control of people whom Spaniards considered their inferiors and therefore their subordinates, however, created tensions that also affected the unequal relationships between Spaniards and others. Obraje owners had little success in bringing back Indian workers who left, even when they knew where they were, unless they were in jail or another obraje. The "memoria de indios huidos" who were absent from the obraje that Pedro de Alcanadre sold to Alonso and Juan de Ribas included two men who were said to be in Mexico City, a mestizo who owed an exceptionally large debt of 160 pesos, a number of married couples (who probably had gone home, such as Juan Tepeaca and his wife, said to be in Tecamachalco), and people whose whereabouts someone was said to know (for example, Andrés Tepuzque de Tepeaca and his wife "están donde sabe Castañeda," and Simón de Tlaxcala, "sabe Juan Vázquez donde está").[38]

Despite such information, the rate of recovery of workers who fled seems to have been very low, especially if they left the city. Trying to bring back workers who had gone home to their own communities meant dealing with local officials whose priorities might be quite different from those of obrajeros. In one case a young obrajero named Cristóbal de Baeza (not a briocense) in Puebla sent his mayordomo, Juan Pérez, to Tecamachalco to bring back some workers who had left Baeza's obraje. When Pérez presented to the "teniente del dicho pueblo" a written order that the Indians be sent back, the official "read it and without saying a word went off toward the church," according to Juan Sánchez, an Indian from Texcoco who described himself as "capitanejo en el dicho obrador," who had accompanied Pérez. Another witness who was there, Juan Lázaro, testified that the "teniente real" crumpled up and threw away the order that Pérez presented to him.[39]

Spaniards' efforts to control and constrain non-Spanish workers, servants, and slaves generated tensions and priorities quite different from the kind of contention and competitiveness that could characterize relations between Old Christians and conversos in Brihuega. Resentment of conversos to a significant degree was rooted in their ability to participate fully in all aspects of local society—politics, religious life, and economic endeavors. Conversos functioned in society at the same level as their Old Christian peers, and sometimes with greater success, so that it was impossible to relegate them to an inferior or subordinate status. Had there been significant numbers of Moriscos in Brihuega, their position might have been more comparable to that of Indians and blacks in New Spain, as most likely they would have entered briocense society at its lowest levels. In the aftermath of the Alpujarras rebellion, however, Brihuega apparently received few if any Moriscos, although other places nearby, such as Pastrana, had substantial Morisco communities in the late sixteenth century.[40] Hence before going to New Spain most briocense emigrants had little if any experience in dealing on an ongoing basis with groups of people whom they would presume to be their social inferiors by virtue of their ethnic identity rather than their socioeconomic status. While they no doubt readily emulated the attitudes and behavior of Puebla's other Spanish vecinos in their treatment of the city's non-Spanish residents, it should be borne in mind that this particular arena of social relations constituted yet one more respect in which the immigrants' new home differed quite sharply from the old, not just in degree but in kind as well.

Conflict

Conflict within Spanish society certainly was not a new phenomenon specific to New Spain, but the nature and frequency of conflict may have differed there. One possible consequence of the social elevation, especially in relation to Indians, blacks, and mixed people, that Spaniards living in the Indies generally experienced was that many more Spanish men carried arms on a regular basis than was the case in Castile in the sixteenth century. Levels of violence quickly escalated when participants in disputes had ready access to weapons. Confrontations that otherwise might have ended up in fistfights or shoving matches perhaps more frequently resulted in fatalities, or at least serious injuries, when the parties involved brandished swords—"espadas desnudas," in the common phrase—and daggers.

One might consider in this light an incident that took place in Puebla at the end of June 1603. It involved "a fight and stabbings" that ended in the wounding of a young man named Juan de Portillo. A man named Francisco de Castañón testified that he, Alonso de la Torre, and another man were standing on the corner near his house after six o'clock in the evening when Andrés de la Fuente, one of the sons of the briocense obrajero Martín de la Fuente, passed by with Juan de Portillo, apparently arguing. Castañón and Torre (who probably was a briocense) followed and found them with their swords drawn trying to stab each other, and they tried to intervene. A carpenter named Juan Gómez Melgarejo arrived "saying 'peace, peace.'" At that point a friend of Fuente's showed up and wounded Portillo in the head or neck, and then he and Fuente took refuge in the church of Vera Cruz.

Andrés de la Fuente's confederate was Francisco López, a locksmith working in the shop of a man named Serrano, according to a mulato slave named Tomás de Aquino who witnessed the scene behind the church, where he saw "many men with unsheathed swords."[41] Juan Gómez Melgarejo, Juan Portillo's stepfather, testified that he had tried to keep Portillo from going out that evening because he knew Andrés de la Fuente was looking for him to follow up an earlier argument. Portillo claimed that Fuente tricked him into going out and led him to the area near the church where Francisco López, "his companion," had hidden. Andrés de la Fuente, who was 20 years old at the time, alleged that Portillo and his stepfather had attacked him, a version of the events no one else confirmed. López, who was 21, said that Fuente and Portillo had argued. He insisted that it was Fuente, not he, that had wounded Portillo. The two young men had to pay a fine of six pesos each. The alcalde appointed Andrés de la Fuente's cousin Benito Sanz Bautista to be their guardian, since they were under 25 years old.

Although this was a fairly minor episode, it suggests a ready disposition to resort to violence when bad feelings and disagreements arose. Alonso de Ribas made a criminal complaint in June 1584 against several men (Pedro Hernández; Cristóbal Pérez; Luis Hernández, mulato; and Domingo, negro) on the grounds that they had tried to kill his son Cristóbal de

Ribas.[42] Two years later the cloth shearer Juan Martínez and his wife, Floriana de Pliego, who had arrived from Brihuega only a year or so before, signed a letter of pardon in which a man named Gonzalo García agreed to pay 600 pesos in compensation for the murder of the couple's son Juan Martínez. He had been fighting with some men "about certain words they had said against the said Juan Martínez and injuries they had done him" when Gonzalo García joined in the fight and struck Martínez several times, wounding him fatally in the throat. The alcalde mayor had sentenced García to death, but Martínez's father opted for compensation because of the costs and lost work time he had incurred in pursuing the criminal complaint against García.[43] In 1600 one of the alcaldes ordinarios in Puebla brought charges against the obrajero Melchor Rodríguez and others for involvement in the murder of a man named Felipe de Santiago; Rodríguez's goods were sequestered.[44] In June 1609 the alcalde Alonso de Ribera Barrientos sent an alguacil to arrest the regidor Rodrigo García and Gabriel de Torija, both briocenses, the former to be confined in the cabildo building and the latter in jail. Rodrigo García, accused of having stabbed Torija in the head, stated that he had been standing at the door of the cathedral when Torija started to argue with him and placed his hand on his sword. He claimed that Torija previously had argued with his son Juan García del Castillo.[45]

Violence not only came into play in personal disputes but could be used to intimidate social inferiors and individuals wielding authority as well. In 1614 the notary Hernán Sánchez Gallardo accused the regidor Diego de Carmona Tamariz of having insulted and threatened him in the presence of the alcalde mayor while accompanied by his son Juan de Carmona Tamariz (son-in-law of the briocense obrajero Alonso Gómez), calling him "moro mulato y falsario."[46] Seeking a royal order of protection, Hernán Sánchez complained that Carmona was "so well connected, favored and rich and I alone without relatives and holding public office . . . and he is a vengeful man who carries out his passions."[47] Carmona's threats to the notary stemmed from an inquiry Hernán Sánchez was conducting into the death of Capt. Juan de Olivares Villarroel, purveyor of the royal navies and administrator (*juez administrador*) of the royal *noveno* (ninth part of tithes) of the bishop of Tlaxcala. A number of people, including several regidores and Marcos Rodríguez Zapata, close associate of some of the leading figures in the briocense community, had landed in jail on suspicion of some connection with this official's murder. Twenty years earlier Diego de Carmona had been implicated in another murder, having allegedly instigated "certain relatives of his" to kill a man named Francisco Granado Mercado.[48]

Although actual or threatened violence hardly was unique to Spanish society in the Indies, the frequency with which it erupted in everyday life is noteworthy. Its seeming banality should not disguise the underlying social tensions that both fostered and resulted from disputes that at this remove may seem trivial but at the time could be, quite literally, deadly serious. Violence by no means involved only adult men, although they probably most often were both the perpetrators and the victims.

Probably the most notorious crime of this era involving members of the briocense community took place early in 1608. Implicated in it, among others, were the two young men accused of stabbing Juan de Portillo in 1603. The circumstances were very different, however, as in the 1608 episode the locksmith Francisco López was the victim of a murderous attack, and Andrés de la Fuente was one of the accused perpetrators. Although only part of the testimony in the case has survived and its resolution is not known, the available information not only provides details about the incident but also sheds light on aspects of the interwoven relationships of kinship and acquaintance that bound the briocense community together—or sometimes fractured it.[49]

Francisco López was the husband of Magdalena Barranco, the niece of Isabel Bautista. Isabel was the widow of Martín de la Fuente, both of them from Brihuega. In 1608 López and his wife were living with Isabel Bautista, who still ran the obraje that she and her husband had established. Her house and obraje were located some distance from the center of town, on the way to Cholula. Around seven o'clock in the evening on January 16, 1608, Isabel Bautista went with her niece Magdalena Barranco and daughter Catalina de la Fuente to visit in the house of a fellow briocense, Juan Merino. According to Juan de Mata, Isabel's mayordomo and later her husband, the women had not yet returned home when he heard shouts in the street and in the field ("sabana") behind the obraje. Going outside, Mata heard Magdalena Barranco screaming that someone was killing her husband and imploring Mata to come help. When he reached the women, they told him that López, who had been accompanying them home, had been wounded in the meadow. Mata went back inside, took his cape and sword, and called a couple of workers to go with him. They went out looking for López but failed to find him in the dark. Mata professed innocence of any involvement in the crime. A neighbor named Julio César Napolitano confirmed his story, saying that he had been eating dinner when he heard voices calling for help. When he went outside, he saw Mata and the Indians leaving the obraje and went with them to look for López. The Indian portero of the obraje and two Indian workers who accompanied Mata all made statements to the same effect.

In his deposition a man named Domingo Guerra described what hap-

pened after López was wounded. Guerra stated that he was on his way—
"quieto y pacífico"—to his lodgings in the barrio of San Sebastián and had
reached the corner of the street going to San Agustín when he heard a voice
saying confession and saw someone coming down the street toward the
monastery. When the man got closer, he recognized Francisco López, who
was carrying a sword in his hand. López apparently begged Guerra to call
someone to confess him, saying that he was wounded and dying "with his
guts in his hand." "Moved by Christian charity and because of being a great
friend of the said Francisco López," Guerra rang the bell at the entrance of
the monastery, urging them to hurry because López appeared to be dying.
Some of the friars came outside and a priest of the order heard his confession. They asked who had attacked him and tried to comfort him.

According to Guerra, in response to their questions López told them
that as he was returning home from Juan Merino's house with his wife and
aunt, a man had come up and attacked him treacherously, and then another
man arrived and wounded him again. After he explained what had happened, they placed López in a chair brought from the house of the notary
Juan de la Parra, who lived nearby. Then Guerra, together with Melchor
Rodríguez (the obrajero from Fuentelencina) and Cristóbal Ponce, who
coincidentally were passing by the monastery, carried López to the house
of another obrajero, the briocense Juan de Angulo. Guerra went to sum-
mon the surgeon Blas Ortiz to treat him. López was later taken to his
mother's house. Critically wounded, López told Guerra, who visited him,
that he believed a man named Juan Antonio was responsible for the assault.
He described him as a tall man dressed in black whom he had met in the
shop of don Mateo de Nápoles and with whom he had "a quarrel and insult-
ing words over a game." Another witness, Juan Yáñez del Castillo, testified
that López had told him the same story that Guerra recounted about two
men attacking him. The mysterious Juan Antonio, allegedly "recently arrived
in this city from Chichimecas," seems to have left Puebla after the incident,
and López, who subsequently died of his wounds, apparently never identified the second man.

Granted that all the information on the case comes from the depositions
of some of the accused, who naturally sought to exonerate themselves, it is
difficult to explain why these men were suspected of being involved in the
murder. By both their own testimony and that of others, all of the accused—
Andrés de la Fuente, Benito Sanz Bautista, Juan de Mata, Juan García
Barranco, and Domingo Guerra—were López's friends or his wife's relatives. As López and his wife at the time were living with her aunt, presumably he was on good terms with his wife's family; there is no indication that

he was not. He and Andrés de la Fuente had been friends for many years, as the earlier incident in 1603 would suggest. The probable source of the charges against them was López's family.[50] Juan de Mata alleged that López's mother, Isabel Sánchez, and Lopéz's brother-in-law and sister, Tomás Ochoa and his wife, doña María de Viedesola, were "capital enemies" of Mata and Isabel Bautista "and their relatives" and that they had bribed witnesses to testify against him. Isabel Sánchez in turn sued the briocense Pedro Gómez de Arrieta, accusing him of threatening her so she would withdraw from the "suit that she is bringing against the people who are guilty of the death of Francisco López."[51] Pedro Gómez de Arrieta was the nephew of the obrajero and regidor Alonso Gómez and was himself also an obrajero and entrepreneur; there is no known kinship connection between him and any of the accused. Pedro Gómez's uncle Alonso Gómez had been close to Juan Barranco, however, and therefore very likely Pedro Gómez had ties with Barranco's nephew, Juan García Barranco, who was one of the accused. Juan García Barranco probably was a cousin of Francisco López's wife, Magdalena Barranco, and related in some degree to Isabel Bautista.[52]

Although the timing could have been purely coincidental, Isabel Bautista's apparently hasty marriage to Juan de Mata after the murder seemed to some observers to point to a possible cover-up for Mata's, or even her own, involvement in the crime. Isabel Bautista had wanted her daughter Catalina de la Fuente to wed Mata. When the three of them traveled together to Mexico City to testify in the murder case, the trip apparently gave rise to rumors that Mata had seduced Catalina. A woman named María de Corona, the wife of Isabel Bautista's neighbor Julio César Napolitano, testified that Isabel had taken Catalina with her to Mexico City to try to marry her to Mata there because in Puebla her relatives, especially her son Andrés, would have prevented her from doing so. Whether or not there was any truth to the gossip that her virtue had been compromised, Catalina adamantly refused to marry Mata and insisted she wished to enter a convent. Andrés de la Fuente took his sister's side and helped her to profess in the convent of Jesús María.

Another witness, Marcos del Castillo, stated that when Catalina refused to marry, Isabel Bautista decided to wed Mata herself "to restore the honor and reputation of her daughter and because it seemed well to her that the said Juan de Mata should not leave her house, because of being involved as he was in the affairs of the obraje she married him and not because there could have been any guilt . . . in the death of the said Francisco López." Castillo went on to insist that all the accused were "friends and very agreeable and they treated one another and spoke with much love." María de

Corona agreed that Isabel Bautista and Juan de Mata had no reason to kill Francisco López, as they "all ate and drank together" and "they treated him . . . with much love and friendship." Witnesses also testified that López was a close friend of Isabel's nephew Benito Sanz Bautista, also implicated in the murder. Teodor Delgado, who worked for Benito Sanz Bautista and subsequently for Juan de Mata, said that at Christmas of the previous year Isabel Bautista, Andrés de la Fuente, and Francisco López and others had been at Benito Sanz Bautista's house in Cholula "to enjoy themselves as relatives and friends."

The testimony, such as it is, points to no apparent motive for murder on the part of López's friends and in-laws. The real friction in this group of relatives, in-laws, and friends seems to have been between Andrés de la Fuente and his mother, hinging in particular on Isabel's relations with Juan de Mata, whom she wanted to marry to her daughter against Catalina's own wishes, and later on Mata's new position as Andrés's stepfather and part owner of the obraje. After the murder trial Andrés de la Fuente became involved in a protracted suit against his mother and her second husband over his father's legacy. If resentment and jealousy could lead to murder, certainly Juan de Mata seems to have been a better potential victim than Francisco López.

In the end, in the absence of testimony by the accusers, there is no evidence that any of the accused had a motive to kill López. During the period before and after the murder Juan de Mata had come to play an increasingly important role in this cluster of relatives and friends that centered on Isabel Bautista and extended to members of the briocense community who were somewhat on the margins of that tight-knit group. Isabel's efforts to marry her daughter to Mata and her subsequent decision to wed him herself raised questions in people's minds about both Mata's and Isabel Bautista's motives and led to bad feeling in particular between Juan de Mata and his stepson. López too was an outsider to the group, and possibly his presence also created tensions, although evidence on that score is lacking.

The case is interesting in that it demonstrates the existence of complicated relationships within the briocense immigrant community that seemed to justify an assumption of collective responsibility for any wrongdoing. Some of the accused—Juan García Barranco and Benito Bautista—clearly had been nowhere near the scene of the murder. That they figured among those thought to be culpable supports, the notion that close association in and of itself pointed to complicity, at least in the eyes of their contemporaries. The episode and its repercussions suggest the complex interweaving and layering of social ties that hinged on kinship relations, friendships, shared economic interest, and proximity of residence. Mortally wounded, López headed toward the monastery of San Agustín, the very neighborhood most densely populated by people from Brihuega, where several briocense acquaintances and other friends came to his aid. Although himself probably not from Brihuega, López had become deeply involved with members of the immigrant community, perhaps so much so that his relations with them seemed to provide the most likely explanation for his violent end. The cohesiveness, size, and strength of the briocense community in Puebla perhaps generated some degree of suspicion and resentment in poblano society, feelings that in this case found expression in an apparently unsustainable accusation of murder.

Social Standing and Aspirations

The preponderantly commercial nature of the briocenses' economic activities in Puebla and their limited participation in local government and politics suggest that upward social mobility in itself was not an important concern or goal of most of them, at least in the first generation or two, although obviously it was a preoccupation for some. The question of social status figured among the briocenses in two ways. An individual's or a family's standing or prominence within the immigrant community by no means was identical with perceived status in the larger society of Puebla. A man such as Pablo de Pastrana, a key figure among the briocenses, was well regarded in Puebla, but outside the briocense community his social status probably remained modest. His crude signature suggests that he had little formal education, and he never was a candidate for office in Puebla, an aspiration that typically went hand in hand with striving for social elevation and distinction.

The concern that Diego Toribio expressed about his lineage and that of his intended wife, María Carrillo, also points to the dual nature of social status in the briocense community in Puebla. Neither he nor his wife was from an hidalgo family, and in Puebla Toribio pursued a commercial occupation. In his deposition of 1602 in Brihuega his grandparents were called "labradores principales."[53] Surely, then, Toribio's concern about lineage would have had some meaning only to people in or from Brihuega and virtually none to other residents of Puebla. According to Toribio, he and María Carrillo needed a dispensation to wed because they were the children of first cousins. They wished to marry because they were of the same status ("ambos de igual calidad y nobleza"); they wanted to preserve their lineage and not marry outside of it ("conservar la limpieza de nuestro linaje en nuestra propia familia y que no salga fuera della").[54] Furthermore, Toribio suggested that it might be difficult for María Carrillo to find another suitable partner, given her family's means. Yet contrary to what he implied, María's family does not seem to have been poorly off. They provided María with a dowry of 2,400 pesos, to which Toribio added his arras of 2,000 pesos.[55]

Education played an important role in facilitating upward social mobility for some briocenses, such as Diego de Anzures and his younger brother Pedro de Anzures, both of whom served as notaries of the city council. Pedro de Anzures was said to have studied both with his notary father in Brihuega and at the University of Alcalá.[56] On the whole, however, at least among the first generation of immigrants, higher education was rare. There were several notaries among the immigrants, and Cristóbal de Ribas's son Lic. Diego de Ribas was a lawyer. The second generation, as we have seen, included many more priests and people who earned university degrees.

Even in the first generation there were, of course, those—a minority—whose ambitions epitomized the kind of aspiration for social rank that is often assumed to have been typical of emigrants and returnees. Perhaps no individual exemplifies those aspirations better than Diego de Anzures, who founded an entail, briefly held the señorío of a town in Castile, married his only daughter into a distinguished noble family, and himself entered the order of San Juan. Seeking office in local government or positions with the Inquisition, founding capellanías and sending sons and daughters into the priesthood or convents, and building and buying houses in Puebla's most prestigious neighborhoods, all, of course, reflected social ambition. Very few briocenses seem to have been much concerned about establishing a claim to hidalgo status, however; the only immigrant known to have pursued recognition as an hidalgo was the obrajero Andrés de Angulo, who initiated litigation regarding his status when he returned to Brihuega to live in the late 1570s. According to Juan Portugués, who grew up with Andrés de Angulo's son Gabriel in Brihuega, he had heard from his grandmother, who lived more than 90 years, and from other long-lived relatives and acquaintances that Angulo "was from noble and clean stock and came from people who were hidalgos and because of the poverty of his antecedents he had not been able to get the proof of his hidalguía." Other witnesses in the 1587 deposition, such as Pablo de Pastrana, who said he had known the family for 40 years, seemed less certain about the family's hidalgo background. Pastrana said his uncle Francisco de Pastrana, "a very old person with much knowledge of the lineages of the said town [Brihuega]," had told him that the Angulos were "of good clean stock," but he stopped short of calling them hidalgos. Gabriel de Angulo claimed that his family was from Córdoba; "its origin is very ancient and very high, said to come from the kingdom of Scotland," and indeed their surname may well be a variant of *anglo*.[57] Gabriel de Angulo, as seen, probably was the member of the family in Brihuega most concerned about attaining what he thought was appropriate social status and recognition, and he attempted to pursue his father's claim to hidalguía.

Over time the economic success of many briocense immigrants and their children and grandchildren ensured some degree of social elevation, regardless of the form their social ambitions took. Downward mobility was not, of course, impossible. In 1605 Lucas de Ribas, the son of the obrajero Alonso de Ribas, was living with a mestiza woman named Mariana and their son near the church of Nuestra Señora de las Mercedes, having lost his obraje.[58] No doubt his case was not unique, but this kind of downward spiral is much less likely to be documented than a trajectory of economic success, which usually brought with it social acceptance.

The topics addressed in this chapter—patterns of social behavior and interaction, including the significance of friendships and of conflict and discord, choices regarding residence, contact among different socioeconomic and ethnic groups, the nature of urban life, and social status and ambitions—are difficult to document and certainly impossible to quantify. Discussion of these questions must be impressionistic and anecdotal. Notwithstanding such limitations, however, it is useful to examine particular situations that may illuminate the significance of social ties, interactions, perceptions, and ambitions and so may impart a fuller understanding of how people conducted their daily lives and experienced and confronted crisis and change. The story of Diego de Anzures's early broken engagement demonstrates the intersection of familial, moral, and social concerns and values and how they reflected and shaped individual responses and desires. The accusation of murder brought against the people who were close to Francisco López suggests how bonds of loyalty rooted in kinship and friendship reinforced solidarity, although they did not altogether eliminate the potential for jealousy and strain within a close-knit group. The details revealed in the testimony in such cases serve well to evoke a sense of the rhythm and texture of daily reality, as well as pointing to the kinds of events and tensions that could punctuate or disrupt the flow of everyday life.

Conclusion

T he briocenses who went to live in New Spain in the latter part
of the sixteenth century left behind a society that was characterized by continuity and conservatism, on the one hand, and on the other a
significant degree of permeability—one might say vulnerability—to external forces that impinged upon and modified, at times quite rapidly, long-
standing traditions and socioeconomic and cultural patterns. Brihuega's textile industry, important since the Middle Ages, remained central to the
town's economy. Nonetheless, it had deteriorated to the point where merchants no longer bothered to visit the town to purchase cloth from local
producers, and the majority of townspeople who were directly involved in
textile production were, if not extremely poor, certainly far from well off.
Long a part of the archbishopric of Toledo and a favorite of the archbishops, in the late 1570s Brihuega faced involuntary removal from the archbishop's jurisdiction and found itself offered up for sale. The vecinos thus
were forced to choose between the unpredictable alternatives of living under
a new unknown lord and taking on the financial burden of self-purchase
and the political uncertainties of self-rule. The town also confronted more
gradual and subtle but very real changes in the sixteenth century as members of formerly Jewish families that remained in the Alcarria became New
Christians who were eligible to participate fully in politics and religious life.
Religious life itself reflected the impact of new trends and priorities that
reached Brihuega from the outside, especially after the Council of Trent,
resulting in the organization of new cofradías and founding of new reli-

gious institutions. Added to this complex mix were the notably high levels of emigration of the town's vecinos, to the Alpujarras and New Spain, and the consequent impact of remittances from immigrants abroad and the substantial new opportunities that their success in Puebla in particular offered to those still at home who might consider relocating.

Given all these forces that in rather dramatic ways were transforming the town, stability and continuity seem somewhat illusory. Yet were they? The behavior and activities of the briocenses in Puebla reflect a striking degree of conservatism in the most literal sense, as the immigrants strove to preserve social ties and patterns of economic activity familiar to them from home. Their choices of marriage partners, for themselves and their children, and of godparents and business associates, their residential patterns in Puebla, and their constant efforts to encourage and recruit friends and family members to join them in New Spain all suggest that they were at least as intent upon maintaining a distinctive briocense identity as they were in integrating into poblano society, even though on the whole they appeared highly satisfied with their choice of a new home. Few of them indicated any great desire to return to the Alcarria. Certainly the size of the immigrant community was a crucial factor in making this kind of conservatism possible, while at the same time its existence suggests that for the immigrants their hometown still represented tradition and continuity, notwithstanding the transformations that it was undergoing in their lifetimes.

Brihuega itself was far from being a consistently harmonious, insular community. There were significant tensions between farmers and tradespeople, between conversos and Old Christians, between the town's well-to-do minority, who tended to dominate local politics, and those whose voices and opinions had relatively little impact. For many of the immigrants in Puebla nostalgia and distance may have diminished the memory and experience of these conflicts and contributed to the impulse to maintain a distinct identity, just as the sheer numbers of people who emigrated to Puebla made it possible to do so. While conflict was not entirely absent among the briocenses in Puebla, it normally stemmed from personal disagreements and involved a limited number of individuals. The kinds of disputes that threatened to engulf all of Brihuega—over the town's self-purchase, or over admission to the Cofradía del Remedio—did not surface among the immigrants, who doubtless recognized that collective success in their new home hinged to a great extent on their ability to cooperate and to maintain a close-knit, functional community.

Achieving the seemingly delicate balance between conserving a sense of identity as a community originating in a particular place while at the same time establishing roots and attempting to integrate into a new society may have had precedents in Castile. Not only are there indications that Brihuega attracted migrants from other towns, but these transplants seem to have retained some notion of their distinctive origins, grouping themselves residentially in the town's parishes and maintaining their connections, bolstered by ties of kinship and friendship, with people in their places of origin and other communities as well. One may suggest, then, that for all the seeming uniqueness of the displacement of the briocenses to Puebla, they—and doubtless many other people in Castile as well—expected that people who relocated together could preserve their distinctive traditions and identity and at the same time become full participants in their new community.

In Puebla the consistently high levels of immigration from Brihuega, beginning in real force in the 1570s and continuing into the early decades of the seventeenth century, had a significant impact on the nature as well as the size of the briocense community. Sustained, substantial immigration had the effect of constantly renewing, multiplying, and emphasizing ties among briocenses both in Puebla and at home for several decades. The frequent arrival of people from home and their ready absorption into Puebla's briocense community makes it difficult to draw sharp distinctions between first- and second-generation immigrants, especially because many of the newcomers married the American-born children of their compatriots. The vitality of the connections maintained both within the briocense community in New Spain and with people at home in Castile is reflected in visits made to Brihuega not only by immigrants but by their children and even grandchildren as well.

It was the briocenses' considerable success in Puebla, of course, that encouraged this sustained migration. How does one account for that success? Part of the explanation doubtless lies in timing. The briocenses began to go to central New Spain during a period of political stability and accelerating economic development. The fate of the encomienda had been settled, the wealth of the northern silver mines was stimulating and supporting increasing economic activity in all sectors—agriculture, commerce, industry—and trade networks centered in New Spain were expanding to include Peru and the Philippines. Immigrants with even a minimum of expertise who invested in textile production, bread and biscuit baking, regional trade and transport, and stock raising quickly discovered that they could operate on a scale unimaginable back home. In Brihuega the wealthiest vecinos had flocks of sheep numbering a couple of hundred; well-to-do immigrants in Puebla easily acquired ranches with several thousand or more head of sheep.[1]

According to the testimony taken in connection with the padrón of 1585, fewer than a dozen labradores in Brihuega had teams of oxen; some of the briocenses in Puebla involved in farming and transport owned dozens or even hundreds of draft animals. Obrajes in New Spain were often large-scale establishments encompassing all stages of cloth manufacture (generally the fulling mill was, by necessity, a physically separate operation, although often under the same ownership) and employing 50 to 100 or more Spanish, African, Indian, and mixed free and coerced workers. In Brihuega, in contrast, textile manufacture mostly took place in small shops in which an artisan worked with perhaps a few apprentices, assistants, and family members, with much of the production still domestically based. The scale of the enterprises that the immigrants organized and operated in New Spain ensured a level of profitability and hence of comfort and even wealth that they could never have achieved in Brihuega.

Comparisons between the lives of the briocenses at home and in Puebla underscore how complex the actual transformations in cultural and socio-economic patterns and institutions from Castile to Spanish America often were. Especially as seen from the point of view of individual experience, these changes could be both subtle and dramatic. An overlay of shared Hispanic culture fostered a certain uniformity and familiarity that encouraged and facilitated relocation within the Hispanic world, but it also could disguise or obscure the transformations that were under way. Membership in cofradías offers a good example. Immigrants could, and did, readily join Puebla's cofradías, which generally were accessible to all who were willing to pay the usually modest dues. With the increasing popularity of certain brotherhoods in both Castile and Spanish America in the latter part of the sixteenth century, they likely could belong to cofradías dedicated to the same cults as those they had left behind. Notwithstanding this kind of continuity, however, the actual experience of participating in these organizations in Puebla, where the majority of one's fellow members would be relative strangers who lacked the shared traditions and ties of kinship and longtime acquaintance to be found in cofradías at home in Brihuega, would be quite different for immigrants.[2]

Local government offers another example of how an institution in colonial Spanish America could closely resemble its Castilian counterpart in both structure and function while at the same time its significance in local society differed notably. Political participation in Brihuega, as we have seen, was fairly broad, given annual rotation in office and the existence of a number of sometimes overlapping institutions for local representation at the level of parish as well as town. It probably is fair to assume that most middling and well-to-do briocense families would expect to have one or two members who held office on the town or parish council at some time (or even much of the time). In contrast, obtaining a seat on Puebla's city council required not only personal or political connections with someone in the city's exclusive inner circle of officeholders but also payment of a substantial fee, generally at least 4,000 pesos. Political office in Puebla was the closely controlled possession of the wealthy and well connected.

Structurally, of course, although Puebla's city council resembled Brihuega's, with regidores and alcaldes, it lacked the representative element of the jurados or diputados. More drastic yet, perhaps, was the difference in the meaning and function of parishes in the two places. Puebla's parishes had no formally organized political life or institutions, whereas Brihuega's parishes had councils and officials and were characterized by residential groupings based on kinship and origin. The notable clustering of the briocense immigrants in the San Agustín barrio, and to a lesser extent in San Francisco as well, may have reflected not only practical considerations but also the desire to replicate a pattern familiar from home, whereby related families and people from the same place settled together in a given parish. The disappearance of any kind of political organization in the parishes in New Spain may also have had implications for the relationship between the church and local communities. Although in Brihuega the secular and ecclesiastical parish councils were separate, parish priests tended to play an active role in parish politics, so that there appears to have been a fairly close if unofficial collaboration between clergy and laity in parish affairs. Very likely this kind of cooperation at the level of parish or barrio did not exist in Puebla in the absence of any formally constituted political bodies.

Considered in the larger context of the movement of people from Castile to the Indies in the sixteenth and early seventeenth centuries, the establishment of the briocenses in Puebla was unusual in the size and remarkable cohesiveness of the emigrant group. The briocense community in Puebla was large enough that the immigrants could maintain for some time a distinctive identity while simultaneously making important contributions to Puebla's history and economic development. Was the experience of the briocense immigrants simply anomalous, or does their story have significant implications for the history of expansion and development in the Hispanic world in the period? Obviously the implicit premise of this book is that it does. The briocense case provides an unrivaled opportunity to consider the collective experience of a substantial but clearly delimited group in two very different and distant parts of the Spanish empire that, because of the activities of the members of that group, became closely connected in the latter part of the sixteenth century.

The relocation of the emigrants from Brihuega to Puebla offers a window through which to view common people living in rather uncommon times. The immigrant community in Puebla encompassed individuals and families of varying background, status, wealth, and accomplishment. Nonetheless, the ties that bound the immigrants to one another had the effect of diminishing the socioeconomic disparities among them, and the relative homogeneity of the mainly working-class briocenses put a particular stamp on the migration movement itself. When we look to the other region I studied, it is clear that to a considerable degree emigration from the Extremaduran cities of Cáceres and Trujillo was shaped and driven by the activities and decisions of certain powerful, influential individuals. This was true not only in the early period of conquest and settlement, when men such as fray Nicolás de Ovando and Francisco Pizarro recruited people from their hometowns and region for their enterprises, but arguably all through the sixteenth century. As late as the 1570s, for example, the substantial movement of people from Trujillo to New Spain clearly owed much to the decision of Gonzalo de Las Casas, son of Francisco de Las Casas, an early encomendero and associate of Hernando Cortés, to establish himself permanently in Mexico.[3]

The Brihuega case was rather different. Certainly the success of the early emigrants who established obrajes in the 1560s demonstrated to people back home the considerable potential of Puebla and New Spain for entrepreneurial undertakings. As in the Extremaduran case, occasionally quite large emigrant groups formed around certain individuals such as Cristóbal de Ribas when he went to live in New Spain for the second time. But with very few exceptions, as perhaps in the case of Diego de Anzures, these men really did not have the kind of wherewithal or connections that could ensure their relatives and compatriots an easy entrée into society in the Indies. The direct benefits of Diego de Anzures's economic success, good marriage, and political connections probably did not extend much beyond his immediate family, and when Cristóbal de Ribas went to New Spain in the 1590s, neither he nor any other member of his extended family entered (or reentered) poblano society at its upper echelons. Like almost all other immigrants, they attained security and some measure of affluence through hard work and by looking to their already established compatriots, who had gone through much the same kind of process.

The story of the briocense immigrants in Puebla was very much a tale of success achieved through hard work and collective effort that unified the community. The briocenses in Puebla could offer newly arrived immigrants assistance in the form of credit, financial backing, employment, or marriage to daughters or sisters, which usually brought a decent dowry and business connections; but the new arrivals in turn were expected to contribute their work and expertise. Immigrants did not find an assured and easy living among their compatriots in Puebla, and doubtless they did not expect to do so. The artisans, entrepreneurs, and farmers of Brihuega largely continued to work directly in their accustomed occupations, although with significant adjustments and in circumstances quite different from those of home.

In a sense the briocenses colonized Puebla much as they did Mecina de Buen Varón in the Alpujarras. At first glance this hardly seems to make sense; Puebla was already an established city well on its way to developing a diversified economy based on agriculture, trade, and industry by the time the briocenses began to arrive in the 1560s. Yet from the point of view of the immigrants, it was a new land, and to a somewhat surprising degree they treated it as such. Although by the 1560s society in central New Spain was quite stable, and certainly ample information about the situation there would have been available to prospective emigrants, the trajectory of emigration from Brihuega greatly resembled migration movements of earlier times when conditions in the Spanish Indies were much less certain.[4] Thus like emigration from other places in Castile in earlier years, the movement from Brihuega was almost exclusively male at the outset, consisting of either single men or married men who left their families behind. Only after ten or fifteen years, when the first emigrants had begun to establish themselves successfully, did women and children begin to leave Brihuega for Puebla in some numbers.

This pattern has been characteristic of transatlantic emigration from the sixteenth century up to modern times, although of course it has not prevailed in all cases. Since the degree of development and stability in the chosen destination seems to have affected this two-stage pattern (men first, followed by women and children) relatively little, its persistence underscores the strong connection between a particular locality and the nature of the migration movement it produced. However attractive a destination might be, perceptions and conditions at home and the ties that existed among potential emigrants often had the most decisive impact on the organization, composition, and timing of migration and the objectives of people who chose to emigrate.[5]

All these factors, together with the size of the movement, had implications for the receiving as well as the home society. The briocenses were sufficiently numerous, concentrated, and unified that they created a distinctive niche for themselves in Puebla. The city was growing in the late sixteenth and early seventeenth centuries, attracting a rather diverse group of migrants from within New Spain and elsewhere as well. The briocenses' associates and neighbors in Puebla included Italians, Greeks, and Portuguese as well as people from all over Castile. None of these migrant groups, however, with the exception of indigenous ones from such places as Tlaxcala and Cholula, was large enough to form the kind of tightly knit, conspicuous community that the briocenses formed and maintained for a few generations. Thus although there was nothing extraordinary about the motivations, composition, organization, or activities of the emigrants from Brihuega, their cohesiveness and focus had significant and perceptible consequences for society in Puebla.

Unique though their situation may have been, the experiences of the briocenses reveal a great deal about the preferences and aspirations of quite ordinary people of their times and how they responded to new situations and choices both individually and collectively. In their willingness to incorporate new ways of doing things and confront new situations while at the same time maintaining long-standing traditions, the briocenses surely resembled many of their fellow Castilians and other transatlantic emigrants before and since. While their stories lack the drama and excitement of the careers of some of the individuals who participated in the early conquest and settlement of the Indies, nonetheless by virtue of their relatively humble background, pragmatic objectives, and largely unremarkable experiences the briocenses may well reflect the mainstream of the people who left Castile to make a new life in America.

This book may be said to represent the concluding half of a two-part inquiry into the nature of early modern transatlantic Spanish emigration and its implications for the development of society and culture in both Spain and Spanish America. In stating that the present study of Brihuega and Puebla brings to an end a project that began with the examination of emigration from Extremadura, I by no means wish to imply that these books cover and define the topic. Juan Javier Pescador's fascinating consideration of the impact of involvement in the Indies enterprise on the people, culture, and institutions of a Basque village is ample proof that the study of Spanish emigration will continue to yield significant new insights into the nature and consequences of the expansion of the Hispanic world and the many variants it encompassed.[6] Since most likely I will leave such further research to others, however, it may be appropriate to comment on the context and implications of work done to date.

My interest in the connections between Spanish and Spanish American society, the ways in which these ties were experienced and expressed by individuals and groups, and the human dimensions of socioeconomic and cultural transference and transformation from one side of the Atlantic to the other began with two studies I did on colonial Mexico. The first was a master's thesis on a family that came to be known as the Marqueses de San Miguel de Aguayo and their estates in the far north of Mexico; the second was a paper on Spanish society in Mexico City immediately after the Conquest.[7] Both of these studies pointed to the important role played by immigrants and the need to consider emigration in the context of Spanish society if we are to understand better its implications for society in the Indies. In the family of the Marqueses de Aguayo, which got its start in Mexico with a Basque named Francisco de Urdinola, a woman inherited the increasingly vast estates in one generation after another until the late eighteenth century.[8] These women all married immigrants from the Basque country or elsewhere in northern Spain. My research on early Mexico City revealed a Hispanic society that seemed to have sprung full-blown into life virtually overnight. The intensity and variety of economic activity under way within a few years of the Conquest raised questions that the existing literature on emigration and early modern Spanish society did not seem to answer adequately.

Certainly by the late 1960s and early 1970s there existed a significant body of scholarly work, especially on the Spanish American side, that shed light on these questions. James Lockhart's *Spanish Peru* provided a remarkably detailed picture of the early development of a Spanish colonial society. Peter Boyd-Bowman's massive compilation of data on emigrants and his analysis of the timing, regional origins, and socioeconomic and demographic composition of the movement to the Indies delineated and explained many of the basic patterns of sixteenth-century emigration from Spain.[9] Yet despite such important work, the essential connection between Hispanic societies on the two sides of the Atlantic had not been made in a systematic way. Studies such as Lockhart's of the participants at Cajamarca and Enrique Otte's of merchants and letters from people in the Indies back to Spain, however, did point in that direction.[10] It is no accident that my book on Extremadura in some ways seems like a sequel — or perhaps a prequel — to Lockhart's *Men of Cajamarca*, or that the present one in effect is an expansion of Otte's study of letters from emigrants in Puebla.[11] Clearly my debts to these scholars are considerable.

As I considered how to approach the subject of emigration, the idea of focusing on a particular locality seemed especially promising. In the case of Extremadura this approach worked perhaps better than expected. Abundant local documentation on the neighboring cities of Cáceres and Trujillo combined with the relevant records in the Archive of the Indies in Seville made it possible to demonstrate that emigration was inextricably tied to socioeconomic and kinship patterns and structures that were rooted in local society. The records also showed that the movement of people from these places had a perceptible, substantial impact on local society in Spain even as it contributed to the formation and development of society in the Indies.[12] The present study certainly sustains those conclusions. By showing how common origin, long association, shared economic interest, cultural expectations, and kinship relations figured in the lives and experiences of the people from Brihuega who settled in New Spain, this second inquiry into the implications of early modern emigration further demonstrates how patterns tied to local society in Spain could take hold, change, or fade away in the Indies. With their rather different emphases, then, the two books together argue strongly for the interrelatedness—indeed, the inseparability—of socioeconomic and cultural patterns in the early modern Hispanic world and the need to identify and examine these patterns in their proper context; that is, local society.

In some ways the places I studied and the emigration movements they produced could not have been more different. Cáceres and Trujillo were fairly small cities but important within their region. Their noble families were wealthy, powerful, and numerous. They dominated local stock raising and landholding, controlled the city councils, and maintained connections with the royal court. As I mentioned earlier, the early and intense involvement of these cities in the movement to the Indies to some degree hinged on the aspirations and connections of the provincial nobility. In the extremeño case, then, the importance of the provincial nobility in local society affected the nature and timing of emigration, as influential emigrants took with them entourages of relatives and retainers of various sorts to the Indies.

In the movement from Brihuega patronage also played an essential role, but it was patronage of a very different sort. Certainly many of the briocense emigrants looked to their compatriots for assistance and guidance. The considerable socioeconomic homogeneity of the town's population—and hence of the emigrant group—fostered the expectation that, through hard work and some good fortune, almost anyone could achieve much the same ends. Patronage in the briocense case, then, helped to generate a kind of collective upward mobility that both underlay and reflected the cohesiveness and relative homogeneity of the immigrant group in Puebla. Obviously the numbers of people who went to Puebla from Brihuega made it possible to create and sustain a strong ethos of collective progress. Yet arguably had such an outlook not existed, the briocense movement more than likely would have fragmented, and emigrants would have followed their patrons to varied destinations, as did the extremeños. Instead they virtually all went to one place that seemed to offer opportunities for as many as cared to come. This perceptible difference in the nature of the movements—"great men" and their entourages versus a more homogeneous and collective kind of relocation (characteristic not only of the briocense movement to Puebla but of their migration to the Alpujarras as well)—clearly reflected local patterns and circumstances.

Nonetheless, such tendencies did not preclude the kind of variability that would also foster similarities in the emigration movement more generally. The majority of people who went to Spanish America in the sixteenth century were artisans, farmers, or entrepreneurs, people accustomed to working hard for their living, and as such could be said to have had much in common, regardless of their origin or what propelled them there. They shared values that emphasized family interest and welfare; they displayed a ready economic flexibility that predisposed them to diversify and refocus their economic activities and expand them in scale; they sought to integrate themselves into their new communities through business dealings and partnerships, marriages, and participation in local political and religious life. All of these tendencies were rooted in their experience and background in particular localities, yet they suggest an overarching commonality that left a strong stamp on the development of a Hispanic society in the Indies. Thus however large, cohesive, and conspicuous the immigrant group from Brihuega was in Puebla in the late sixteenth and early seventeenth centuries, after two or three generations they had become more poblanos than briocenses.

If the overall thrust of socioeconomic and cultural development in Spanish America seems to point to increasing homogeneity, why then be concerned about the particularities of immigrant experience and background? For one thing, there was nothing inevitable about the process by which briocenses became poblanos or extremeños became Peruvians. Culture and social process cannot be divorced from human experience and choice, and the nature and direction of choice cannot be understood devoid of context. The emigrants' first context was their hometown, and they drew their values, aspirations, and understanding of how things could or should be done from that milieu. Their decision to relocate and place themselves in an often radically different context forced them to undertake a complex renegotiation of values and priorities; cultural and social change was the product of the process by which they compared, combined, chose, or discarded old and new ways and ideas.[13] Examining all the contexts in which emigrants functioned enables us to understand the entire process by which change and adaptation took place rather than just one part of it. This understanding in turn makes it possible to assess the implications of cultural and socioeconomic transformation for society on both sides of the Atlantic.

Reference Matter

Glossary

albacea	executor of a will
alberca	pond; reservoir
alcabala	sales tax
alcaide	governor of a castle; warden
alcalde	magistrate
alcalde mayor	presiding royal official in Spanish American municipalities
alcalde ordinario	magistrate of the first instance
alférez mayor	chief standard-bearer
alguacil	constable
alguacil mayor	chief constable
amancebado	living in sin
añil	indigo
aparejado	fit; ready
apellido	surname
arrabal	suburb (unincorporated community attached to a town)
arras	money given to a bride by the bridegroom
arroba	11.5 kilograms (ca. 25 pounds)
audiencia	high court
ayuntamiento	municipality; town hall
bachiller (Bach.)	holder of a bachelor's degree
barrio	neighborhood; municipal district

batán	fulling mill
batanero	fuller
bayeta	flannel
beata	laywoman living under voluntary religious vows
bizcocho	biscuit
bizcocho bazo	whole-meal biscuit
bodega	wine cellar
briocense	person or thing of Brihuega
bueyes	oxen
caballería	unit of agricultural land, slightly over 100 acres
cabeza	head
cabildo	municipal or ecclesiastical council
calle	street
cantería	stonecutting
capellanía	chantry; chaplaincy
cardador	wool carder
carga	three or four *fanegas*
carpintero	carpenter
carreta	cart; wagon
carretero	carter
carro	cart; cartload
caserío	homestead
cédula	warrant; decree
censo al quitar	redeemable annuity
censo perpetuo	fixed annuity
chancillería	high chancery court
chantre	choirmaster
clérigo	clergyman
clérigo presbítero	ordained priest
coa	digging stick
cochinilla	cochineal (red dye); also *grana cochinilla*
cofrade	member of a *cofradía*
cofradía	lay religious brotherhood
colegio	school
comadre	godmother of one's child
comisario	clerical commissioner for the Inquisition
compadrazgo	system of fictive kinship based on choices of godparents at baptism, Communion, etc.
compadre	godfather of one's child
compañía	partnership
contador	official receiver
converso	converted Jew or descendant of converts

corregidor	royal official presiding over a municipality
criado	servant; retainer
criollo	a person born in New Spain
cristiano nuevo	New Christian (i.e., converted Jew)
cruzada	indulgence
cuadrilla	team; gang
cura	parish priest
depositario general	general trustee
deshonestidad	indecency; lewdness
despinzador	burler
dieciocheno	woolen cloth of middling quality
diputado	representative on a parish or municipal council
don, doña	courtesy title used before the first name by members of the higher nobility in the sixteenth century
ducado	monetary unit worth 375 *maravedís*
dueño	owner; proprietor; master
emborrador	see *emprimador*
emprimador	person who did the second carding of wool
encerrado	"locked up"; worker confined to an *obraje*
encomendero	holder of an *encomienda*
encomienda	grant of right to collect tribute (in goods or labor) from a specified group of Indians
escribano	notary
estadal	four *varas*
estancia	estate, usually for raising stock
estanciero	rancher; small farmer
extremeño	of Extremadura; a person from Extremadura
familiar	lay informant for the Inquisition
fanega	unit of measure equal to approximately 1½ bushels; land measure equal to approximately 1½ acres, or 576 square estadales
feria	trade fair
fiel	inspector of weights and measures
fiscal	prosecutor
fuero	municipal charter; code of laws and privileges
ganado mayor	cattle
ganado menor	sheep; goats
ganado ovejuno	sheep
gañán	estate worker
grana	see *cochinilla*
hacienda de labor	agricultural estate
hermandad	league, brotherhood
hermano	brother

herrero	blacksmith
hidalgo	member of the privileged (noble) group in Spanish society
hidalguía	noble status
hierro	iron
hilador	spinner
hilar	to spin
indiano	returnee to Spain from the Indies
información	deposition; testimonial
ingenio	mill (sugar mill)
jornalero	day laborer
jurado	representative of a parish
juro	annuity tied to a particular source of revenue
labrador	farmer
ladino	Spanish-speaking person who is not a Spaniard
lana	wool
licenciado (Lic.)	holder of a master's degree
limpieza (de sangre)	purity of blood
madrina	godmother
maravedí (mr.)	basic monetary unit of account
mariscal	marshal
marjal	land measure equal to 100 square *estadales*
mayordomo	steward, manager
mercader	merchant
mesta	stockmen's association
mestizo	person of mixed Indian and European descent
molino	mill
morada	dwelling
Morisco	person of Muslim descent
mozo	youth (used to distinguish a son from his father of the same name)
mulato	person of mixed African and Indian or European descent
naboría	Indian servant or worker
obrador	workshop; textile shop
obraje	workshop; in Spanish America, usually a textile workshop
obrajero	textile manufacturer
obra pía	charitable foundation
oficial	tradesman; official
ovejas	sheep
padrino	godfather
padrón	tax assessment list
paisano	compatriot
panadería	bread bakery

paño	bolt of cloth (ca. 40–50 meters in length)
pastel	woad, a plant that produces blue dye
pastor	shepherd
patria	homeland
pechero	taxpayer; commoner
peón	laborer
perchero	teaseler (one who naps cloth with the prickly heads of the teasel plant)
perulero	returnee from Peru or the Indies
peso	unit of currency in Spanish America of varying value (a *peso de oro* was worth 400 maravedís; more commonly a peso equaled 8 *reales*)
poblano	of Puebla; a person from Puebla
pobre	poor
poder	power of attorney
probanza	legal proof
procurador general	general representative
promotor fiscal	prosecutor
propios	municipal properties; resources; means
quintal	100 kilograms (ca. 220 pounds)
racionero	prebendary (eccles.)
real	*noun* silver coin worth 34 maravedís; *adj.* royal
recua	string of animals (e.g., mules)
regidor	town councilman
regimiento	seat; administration
relación	report; account
reparto	apportionment
Sagrada Cruzada	see *cruzada*
Santo Oficio	Holy Office of the Inquisition
sayal	coarse woolen cloth
secano	unirrigated land
señorío	lordship
suerte	lot or grant of land
tabernero	tavern keeper; innkeeper
tanteo	matching bid for purchase of a town
tejedor	weaver
teniente	deputy
tercio	measure equaling 5 arrobas
tienda	shop
tierra	land; jurisdiction or district of a town or city
tierra caliente	hot country; lowlands
tierra firme	continent (*Tierra Firme*, isthmian region)

tierras baldías	crown or common lands
tinte	dye shop; dyeing
trabajador	laborer
tratante	trader
traza	center of a Spanish American city
trigo	wheat
tundidor	cloth shearer
vara	unit of measure of slightly less than a yard (33 inches, or 0.84 meters)
vecindario	census of households
vecino	citizen; neighbor
veedor	inspector; overseer
veintidoseno, *veinticuatreno*	high-quality woolen cloth
viejo	old; old man (used to distinguish a father from his son of the same name)
villa	town
visita	inspection

Notes

Archives and Collections

ACB	Actas del Cabildo de Brihuega
AGI	Archivo General de Indias, Seville
	Contrat. Contratación
	Indif. Gen. Indiferente General
	México
AGN	Archivo General de la Nación, Mexico City
	Civil
	Gen. Parte General de Parte
	Inquis. Inquisición
	Tierras
AGNP	Archivo General de Notarías de Puebla
AGS	Archivo General de Simancas
	Exped. Hac. Expedientes Hacienda
AHN	Archivo Histórico Nacional, Madrid
	Clero
	Cons. Consejos
	Inquis. Toledo Inquisición de Toledo
AJP	Archivo Judicial de Puebla
AMP	Archivo Municipal de Puebla
APSMP	Archivo de la Parroquia del Sagrario Metropolitano de Puebla
ARCG	Archivo Real de la Chancillería de Granada
ARCV	Archivo Real de la Chancillería de Valladolid
CONDUMEX	Centro de Estudios de Historia de México
FHCLDS	Family History Center, Church of Jesus Christ of Latter-day Saints
MNAH	Museo de Antropología e Historia, Mexico City
	Ser. AJP Serie Archivo Judicial de Puebla

RAH   Real Academia de Historia, Madrid
Tulane LAL   Tulane University Latin American Library
Vollmer   Günter Vollmer, unpublished data on the marriages of Spanish
               immigrants compiled from parish records in Puebla. Vollmer
               generously provided me with a copy of all his information on
               marriages in which at least one of the partners was from Bri-
               huega. The numbers are those he assigned to the cases.

Introduction

1. Otte, "Cartas privadas."
2. The major compilations are the *Catálogo de pasajeros* and Boyd-Bowman, *Indice geo-biográfico*. Mörner, "Migraciones a Hispanoamérica," reviews the literature on Spanish emigration.
3. Altman, *Emigrants and Society*.
4. J. C. García López, *El fuero de Brihuega*. García López's *Biblioteca de escritores* includes extracts of many documents and manuscripts. Rodríguez Gutiérrez's *Bosquejo histórico de Brihuega* is quite sketchy. Niño Rodríguez's *Organización social* is a study of Brihuega in the eighteenth century based mainly on the Catastro de Ensenada.
5. On Puebla's founding and early decades, see Hirschberg, "Social History of Puebla." On don Juan de Palafox, see Israel, *Race, Class, and Politics*, chap. 7.
6. Briocenses were subject to the Inquisition tribunal in Toledo, the records of which are housed in the Archivo Histórico Nacional (AHN) in Madrid.
7. In the 1960s Puebla's notarial records were microfilmed for the holdings of the Family History Center of the Church of Jesus Christ of Latter-day Saints. A recent project has made much of the colonial material in Puebla's municipal archive available on CD-ROM. Some records from Puebla's Archivo Judicial have been microfilmed and are available in the Museo Nacional de Antropología e Historia (MNAH) in Mexico City, as are the proceedings of the city council.
8. See, for example, Carabarán, *El trabajo y los trabajadores del obraje*.
9. See, for example, Prem, *Milpa y hacienda*; Vollmer, "La evolución cuantitativa de la población indígena"; Paredes Martínez, *La región de Atlixco*; Hoekstra, *Two Worlds Merging*; Weiland, "Economics of Agriculture."
10. Powell, *Puritan Village*. See also Allen, *In English Ways*, and Cressy, *Coming Over*.
11. Pescador, "New World Inside a Basque Village"; Angel, "Spanish Women in the New World."

1. *Settlement, Space, and Mobility*

1. The letters from Sebastián de Pliego to his wife and brother are in AGI, Indif. Gen. 2060, and have been transcribed and published in Otte, *Cartas privadas*, 161–63.
2. Passage as translated is from Lockhart and Otte, *Letters and People*, 127.
3. AGI, Contrat. 5538; *Catálogo de pasajeros*, vol. 6, no. 2767.
4. In 1583 he testified that he was "over 40 years old" and had been examined in his trade twenty years earlier in Brihuega, where he had kept a shop for over twelve years (CONDUMEX, f. XIV, carp. 14, doc. 304).
5. AGNP, Gabriel de Anzures, 1612: "El ni yo no teníamos bienes ningunos porque casamos pobremente en la dicha villa de Brihuega."
6. Vassberg, *Land and Society*, notes that after the expulsion of the Moriscos, "the crown dispatched commissioners to recruit families from Galicia, Asturias, Burgos, León, and Andalucía to come to the kingdom of Granada to farm the lands of the Moriscos. . . .

At royal expense 12,524 families were brought to populate 270 villages" (125). See also Barrios Aguilera and Birriel Salcedo, *La repoblación del reino de Granada*, which surveys the scholarship on the subject and includes transcriptions of some representative documentation.

7. In the 1585 *vecindario* (AGS, Exped. Hac., leg. 60) Alonso de Cifuentes was listed as producing 50 "cántaros de lino" (flax) and a "docena de paños bajos" (dozen bolts of low-quality cloth); Bartolomé de Trixueque produced twelve "cargas de lino." A *cántaro*, or pitcher, seems to have been a variable measure. A *carga*, or load, was equal to three or four *fanegas*; a fanega was equal to approximately 1½ bushels. Iradiel Murugarren, *Evolución de la industria textil castellana*, writes that in the Middle Ages "Brihuega se distinguía . . . por el cultivo de lino y elaboración de tejidos de esta materia" (22), but there is little evidence that this kind of cloth was produced in any quantity by the second half of the sixteenth century. Nor is there any indication of silk production in Brihuega, either in the ordinances regarding textile manufacture in the medieval fuero (charter) or in any other source, although there was some limited cultivation of flax, which presumably was processed locally. Furthermore, briocenses never involved themselves in Puebla's silk industry, further evidence that they had no experience in that sector of cloth manufacture.

8. The censo perpetuo functioned essentially as an annual tax or rent, since it could not be redeemed (unlike the *censo al quitar*, which was comparable to a mortgage in that the principal received eventually would be paid off). Vecinos were obligated to turn over one-tenth of their annual harvest, with the exception of the yield from olive and mulberry trees, on which they would pay one-fifth for the first ten years and after that one-third; see the Libro de Apeos in ARCG and also Vassberg, *Land and Society*, 125. Most vecinos received one *suerte*, which in Mecina de Buen Varón was defined as including 12 *marjales* of irrigated land (one marjal equaled 100 square *estadales*, which equaled 4 *varas* in length); 8¾ marjales of vineyards; and four fanegas (a fanega was around 1½ acres, or 576 square estadales) of *secanos*, or unirrigated land.

9. The information on the settlement of the towns of the Alpujarras comes from the Libros de Apeos in ARCG. The *libro* for Mecina de Buen Varón is a 1715 copy.

10. The *poder* appears in AGNP, Baltasar de Montoya, 1593. Pablo de Pliego's petition for a license and *información* appear in AGI, Indif. Gen. 2060, no. 76.

11. No Pliego appears in the tax lists of the 1580s or 1590s in Brihuega.

12. Archivo Histórico del Colegio Notarial de Granada, Protocolos de Ugijar, 1585. There are no remaining notarial records for Brihuega; these might, of course, have reflected what, if any, continued contact the people who had gone to the Alpujarras maintained with people in Brihuega, whether they returned, or whether others from the town later went to join them. Brihuega's notarial records ostensibly were destroyed during the Civil War in the 1930s.

13. AGI, Indif. Gen. 2061, no. 143.

14. Only one other person with the surname Pliego is known to have left Brihuega for the Indies in this era. This was Gracia de Pliego, whose husband, Alonso Díaz, a cloth shearer, left Brihuega for New Spain in 1573. In 1575 she asked for a license to join him with their seven children and a son-in-law, Andrés González, who was going with his wife and son. Gracia de Pliego very likely was a relative of the Pliegos discussed here, although the evidence for a family relationship is circumstantial: Andrés González testified for Pablo de Pliego, Gracia had married a cloth shearer—the Pliego family trade—and there is no record of any other Pliego family in Brihuega after the 1570s.

15. CONDUMEX, f. XIV, carp. 14, doc. 304.

16. Ibid., doc. 310.

17. Somewhat ironically, Melchor Rodríguez, an emigrant from Fuentelencina to Puebla who was closely connected with the briocense group, received assistance from the same men. He wrote to his brother in February 1594: "Yo vine a esta tierra y vine derecho a casa de Rodrigo García, el cual me ha hecho mucha merced, y dado mucho crédito, todo por respeto del señor Diego de Pastrana, porque se lo encargó en sus cartas" (Otte, *Cartas privadas*, 169). There was more than one Diego de Pastrana who went to Puebla. Probably the person mentioned by Rodríguez and the one who brought charges against the Pliegos was the man married to Juana Díaz; he was from Brihuega but became a vecino of Fuentelencina. At the time Rodríguez wrote to his brother, Pastrana and his wife appear to have returned to Fuentelencina to live. This is probably the Diego de Pastrana whose brother-in-law was Juan García Rodrigo, who was in the Indies by the early 1570s; one of his sons was Rodrigo García.

18. Alonso Gómez's antecedents are discussed below. He and his wife also were padrinos in 1584 for Gabriela, daughter of María Díaz and Andrés González and granddaughter of Gracia de Pliego, who, as mentioned in n. 14 above, probably was related to the other Pliegos. People often chose relatives as *compadres*.

19. AGNP, Marcos Rodríguez, 1593. The brothers do not appear to have worked together, nor is there any record of either having formed a partnership with any other briocense in New Spain, although Francisco did have business dealings with some of his compatriots, as we have seen.

20. She probably was a relative of his wife; AGNP, Baltasar de Montoya, 1593.

21. Bermúdez de Castro, *Teatro angelopolitano*, 189, says that Pliego was the mayordomo.

22. AGNP, Juan de Meneses, 1602. I have not identified the relationship between Diego del Río and the Pliego family. His first wife was named Mari Díaz, so the relationship may have been through María Díaz.

23. AGNP, Gabriel de Anzures.

24. The Alcarria is most strictly defined as the area lying between the Tajuña and Tajo Rivers, but the term is sometimes used to refer to a larger area encompassing much of the provinces of Guadalajara and Cuenca.

25. See J. C. García López, *La Alcarria*, 27, 40–41, for this story. Archbishop don Rodrigo Jiménez de Roda gave Brihuega its fuero, or code of laws and privileges, in the thirteenth century (45). In *El fuero de Brihuega*, García López concludes that the town received the fuero by 1242. He lists (21) Brihuega's *aldeas* as Gajanejos, Castilmimbre, Ferreñuela, Valdesaz, Tomellosa, and San Andrés in the thirteenth century. Ferreñuela (or Herreñuela) was given to the Jeronimite monastery of San Blas in the nearby town of Villaviciosa and by the early fifteenth century had been abandoned (63).

26. J. C. García López, *Biblioteca de escritores*, 615–16, 618. On the sale of towns see Nader, *Liberty in Absolutist Spain*. A town that was "self-purchased" belonged to no lord but the king.

27. In the vecindario of 1595 (AGS, Exped. Hac. 60) eight vecinos with the surname Alcalá and ten named Guadalajara lived in the parish of Nuestra Señora; neither surname appeared in the other parishes. Similarly all six Angóns lived in San Felipe, and twenty vecinos named Cifuentes lived in San Juan. There are other such examples.

28. AHN, Inquis. Toledo, leg. 289, exped. 9.

29. See Vassberg, *Village and the Outside World*. Naturally many of Vassberg's observations on village life hold for larger towns such as Brihuega as well.

30. AHN, Inquis. Toledo, leg. 146, exped. 31.

31. Ibid., leg. 79, expeds. 11 (Díaz) and 16 (Luis González).

32. J. C. García López, *La Alcarria*, 53.

33. Ibid. and J. C. García López, *El fuero de Brihuega*, 64–65.

34. AHN, Inquis. Toledo, leg. 79, exped. 16.

35. Ibid., leg. 137, exped. 13.

36. Certain inconsistencies in the testimony suggest he could not have been so old.

37. The weight of the testimony in favor of Beltrán seemed to be considerable. Although probably the majority of his witnesses were conversos and tradespeople like himself, many others testified for him as well, including people of some status and influence. The person who seems to have been the main force behind the accusations against Beltrán was also a converso. The negative judgment against him is perhaps not as surprising as the severity of the punishment, given the weakness of the case.

38. Naturally the opposite could occur as well: family members could lose all track of even close relatives.

39. Esteban Ballesteros's *información genealógica* is in AHN, Inquis. Toledo, leg. 275, exped. 14; it spans the years 1623–45. All the testimony related to Ballesteros's antecedents and relatives discussed or quoted below is included in this deposition.

40. He apparently had a less than sterling reputation and was known as "el crinoso marañero," trickster or schemer.

41. These offices are discussed in Chapter 3.

42. The statement is that Gonzalo Gutiérrez went "a hacer obras y trabajar al oficio de cantería en donde le había dejado." Witnesses stated variously that Gonzalo and his son worked in the Alcarria, in the *tierra* of Guadalajara, or in the Arzobispado of Toledo, which essentially coincide.

43. I have found no evidence that Diego Gutiérrez actually went to the Indies. If he did so, he would have been one of the first briocenses to emigrate and, obviously, one of the first to return, since all his children were raised in Brihuega.

44. Dr. don Joseph de Carmona Tamariz's información genealógica is in AHN, Inquis. Toledo, leg. 287, exped. 3; he wanted to become an official of the Santo Oficio in New Spain. His brothers Bach. don Antonio de Carmona Tamariz, who was the *cura beneficiado* of a town in the bishopric of Puebla, and Capt. don Juan de Carmona Tamariz also were contenders for positions with the Santo Oficio. Their informaciones appear in the same *legajo*, exped. 2 and exped. 4; all are identical. The informaciones initially done in Mexico are in AGN, Inquis., vol. 591, expeds. 5–6, and vol. 584, exped. 11. The brothers were the sons of Capt. Juan de Carmona Tamariz, who was regidor and *depositario general* in Puebla, and doña Agustina Gómez, daughter of the obrajero Alonso Gómez and Catalina de Pastrana.

45. This man apparently had a good recollection of Alonso Gómez because Gómez had been the executor of the will of Lucio's uncle Francisco de Brihuega, who had died in New Spain and left 4,000 pesos for an *obra pía* (charitable foundation) to provide dowries for his orphaned relatives in Brihuega.

46. See Pescador, "New World Inside a Basque Village," 140–63. Although law and tradition may have conferred on women in the Basque country advantages that were lacking elsewhere in Castile, Pescador shows that the experience of Basque women affected by emigration to the Indies certainly was not consistently positive; see his chapter "Basque Penelopes: Women and the New World."

47. See AGI, Indif. Gen. 2065, no. 32. Her deposition states that "habrá ocho años poco más o menos que por pasar mucha necesidad y trabajo y no poder sustentar el dicho Alonso de la Peña su marido a ella ni a sus hijos se fue a las provincias de Nueva España con deudos suyos que allí tiene en la Puebla de los Angeles, el cual ha sido nra. señora

servido de hacerle merced de darle en aquella tierra mucha hacienda en bienes raices y ganados." This Francisca Gutiérrez appears to have been related to the Gutiérrez family that was descended from Juan Gutiérrez el bueno.

48. Ibid., 2058.

49. On Melchor Rodríguez, see n. 17 above.

50. AGI, 2070, no. 50.

51. The documentation seldom explains why applications for licenses were rejected. In the case of these two women the refusal is difficult to understand, since they clearly had proof that their husbands were already in New Spain and had sent the money for their passage.

52. According to the letter that Melchor Rodríguez wrote to his brother Gaspar Rodríguez de Madrid in February 1594, he had sent 200 pesos so that his nephew Juan de Fuentes or his brother would bring his wife to New Spain. He also directed that a messenger be sent "to Alonso Rodríguez, my brother-in-law, to Jaén so that he will come with her and my children." See Otte, *Cartas privadas*, 169 (the letter is in AGI, Indif. Gen. 2070).

53. AGI, Indif. Gen. 2056.

54. In 1580 another cloth shearer named Francisco Sánchez sued Andrés González, alleging that González had rented his horses in order to go to meet his mother-in-law, then in Jalapa with other people who had arrived from Castile. Sánchez, who won his case, said that González had never paid him anything and returned only three of the four horses. González claimed never to have rented the horses and suggested that if someone did so for the stated purpose, it would have been his brother-in-law Juan Díaz. The episode certainly suggests that no one was especially interested in going to meet Gracia de Pliego. The whole scenario is rather strange. Alonso Díaz's son Juan Díaz went to Castile in 1580 to get his mother (see ibid., 2060, información of Beatriz de Villarreal, whose husband, Antonio Martínez, had authorized Juan Díaz to bring back his wife and children); why would he have left them in Jalapa and made no arrangements for them to get to Puebla? For Sánchez's suit, see AJP, 1580, exped. 133.

55. Juan García Rodrigo was listed as *soltero* (bachelor), the son of Juan García Rodrigo and Catalina Carrillo, in AGI, Contrat. 5537. He was about 30 years old at the time.

56. AGI, Indif. Gen. 2054, no. 75, and 2058.

57. Ibid., 2162A (1573), lists "Juan García y Rodrigo y Mariana Rodrigo" as going to New Spain with Diego de Pastrana and his wife. This listing could refer to two or three individuals. A brother of Rodrigo García, Juan García Carrillo, was in New Spain, and therefore the 1573 entry could refer to Juan, Rodrigo, and their sister Mariana García Carrillo, meaning that Diego de Pastrana did find his nephew in Seville.

58. Ibid., 2054. In the same year, when Juan García and his wife departed Brihuega for New Spain, he asked to take his orphaned sister, "que en mi poder tengo a cargo."

59. See ibid., 2072, no. 150, for their license to return; also AGI, Contrat. 5301, no. 2. For the money Peñarroja sent with Miguel Pérez, see AGNP, Juan de la Parra, 1605.

60. AHN, Inquis. Toledo, leg. 287, exped. 9.

61. For Pablo de Pastrana's statements about his origins and growing up in Brihuega, see AGI, México, 118, and AGN, Inquis. 452, exped. 2. Juan de Pastrana, who went to Puebla in the 1560s, returned to Spain, and then went back to New Spain with his wife and children in 1573, was Pablo de Pastrana's first cousin. Juan de Pastrana probably was directly responsible for Pablo's decision to go to Puebla, offering him a salary of 500 ducados to work in his obraje. The exact relationship between Pablo and María de Pastrana is not known; the terms "tío" and "sobrino" as used in this period do not necessarily mean uncle and nephew; they can imply an analogous relationship that spans two gen-

erations. There is no doubt the relationship was close, however; he provided 400 pesos for her daughter's marriage (to a man from Brihuega) and was the executor of María de Pastrana's estate; see AGNP, Nicolás Hernández de la Fuente, 1595.

62. AGN, Inquis. 591, exped. 5.

63. In 1602 Francisco Martínez and his wife, Isabel Toribio, and their children requested a license to go to "Peru por Nueva España." Isabel Toribio's brother Diego Toribio, who went with them, also wanted a license for Peru but stated that since at the time there was no way for them to go to "Tierra Firme" and they could not afford to wait in Seville, they would go to New Spain; see AGI, Contrat. 5271, no. 45. The wealthy brother that Diego Toribio said he had in Peru must have been the attraction, but in any case he remained in New Spain. A handful of other emigrants did go to Peru. Cristóbal de Salas's father, Francisco de Salas, died there around 1573, and in the seventeenth century two grandsons of Diego de Anzures—Hernando Pacheco, who left in 1612, and Lorenzo Pacheco, who left in 1615—went to Peru. Hernando left Spain as the *criado* of a man who was returning to Peru via New Spain, and Hernando apparently did continue on to Peru with him; in 1615, when his brother Lorenzo was planning to depart, his mother mentioned that Hernando was in Peru.

64. When he made his will in 1631, Pedro del Río, "vecino de la provincia de Tepeaca," left two pesos each to the "cofradías fundadas en el convento desta dicha ciudad de Tepeaca," but he asked to be buried in the "iglesia catedral" in the habit of San Francisco; see AGNP, Juan de Bibanco; Tulane LAL.

65. Vollmer, 1106.

66. This figure includes some individuals from Fuentelencina, Budía, and Romancos who were closely associated with the briocenses and for all intents and purposes functioned as part of the briocense immigrant community in New Spain.

67. In many cases it is impossible to know even approximately when someone emigrated. Those cases have been excluded. In other instances I have estimated the most likely date of emigration; this practice probably distorts the figures for the timing of emigration relatively little, particularly if one thinks in terms of averages over ten-year periods.

68. There were 53 solteros in the 1570s, 49 in the 1580s, and 41 in 1590s, representing 40, 32, and 25 percent of the migrant groups in those decades. Boys who emigrated with their parents have not been included in this category.

69. See the discussion in Chapter 5.

70. AGI, Contrat. 5380, no. 29.

71. See AGNP, Juan de Meneses, 1600, for the poder given to Hernando de Roa Anzures by his brother Juan de Roa Anzures to collect his share of their parents' legacy. For Hernando's applications for licenses, see AGI, México 270, Contrat. 5397, no. 38, and Indif. Gen. 2077, no. 127. For Juan and Diego de Roa Anzures, see Contrat. 5229, no. 6, ramo 8.

72. Residential patterns are discussed in more detail in Chapter 6 and in my article "De Brihuega a Puebla: Historias de fines del siglo XVI," in Cervantes, *Dimensiones del espacio.*

2. *The Economic Sphere*

1. The padrón is in AGS, Exped. Hac., leg. 60.

2. Iradiel Murugarren, *Evolución de la industria textil castellana,* 206, says that normally a paño was 40 or 50 meters in length.

3. In the dispute over the town's self-purchase, the issue of the sales tax paid when

cloth was sold elsewhere was raised. Some vecinos wanted to ask for exemption from the sales tax on cloth that they "and their criados or children and other persons make for them that may be taken to sell at the fair of the town of Torija which is on the day of San Lucas, October 18th of each year," and on all other merchandise they sold there; see AGS, Exped. Hac., leg. 901.

4. See Iradiel Murugarren, *Evolución de la industria textil*, 188–92, on the domestic organization of textile production and particularly on the importance of women's labor. He suggests that many of the trades involved in textile manufacture overlapped. "La mayor parte de las funciones eran diferenciadas más en teoría que en la práctica. Igualmente, aunque tales operaciones las podían realizar los hombres, la mano de obra femenina debía ser muy abundante, y en la mayoría de casos numéricamente superior" (192). This blurring of trades probably was significant in the organization of obrajes in New Spain, where workers were recruited who did not necessarily have any previous training.

5. Iradiel Murugarren refers to the "desarrollo de la tintura como empresa independiente, al margen del mercader fabricante" (ibid., 207; see 201–7 on fulling).

6. In August 1590 the council agreed to "proclaim that people who are children of vecinos of this town should not go to sleep at the batanes because of the great damage that results from it, nor should the bataneros receive them under a fine of 200 mrs" (ACB, 1590).

7. AGI, Indif. Gen. 2054.

8. See Iradiel Murugarren, *Evolución de la industria textil*, 109.

9. AHN, Inquis. Toledo, leg. 137, exped. 13.

10. Ibid., leg. 199, exped. 23.

11. RAH, 11-5-3, 8875-8, "Nuevas ordenanzas tituladas de esta villa de Brihuega y su tierra, confirmadas por el Illus. Sr. D. Bernardo de Sandoval, cardenal y arzobispo de la Santa Iglesia de Toledo, mi señor, año de 1617," no. 18. The ordenanzas essentially confirmed those of 1550.

12. Iradiel Murugarren, *Evolución de la industria textil*, says it could be used in conjunction with other dyes in treating lower-quality cloth (184).

13. In October 1582 the town council decided to request, through the corregidor, that the archbishop donate the "bread" (pan) that belonged to him "to plant and remedy in some part the great need this town has as a result of the small harvest that has been reaped this year" (ACB). In December 1582 the town took 1,000 ducados at censo and borrowed an additional 1,500 ducados "taken from private citizens of this town" to buy wheat. In August 1583 the council noted that "in this town very little wheat is harvested for which reason there is great need among the poor people . . . and this town has no properties [propios] or storehouse [depósito]. . . . In this town there are some rich and powerful people who should be compelled to buy wheat." On June 1, 1585, the council noted that the shortages of wheat were serious, "so much so that yesterday we were informed that many people went without eating and many others failed to go out to work for lack of bread."

14. AGS, Exped. Hac. 60, fol. 64.

15. AGI, Indif. Gen. 2065, no. 68.

16. AHN, Inquis. Toledo, leg. 289, exped. 9.

17. Ibid., leg. 275, exped. 14 (1623–45).

18. Diego Gutiérrez and Juan de Brihuega protested the town's self-purchase in the mid-1580s, "being as we are among the richest people in the said town," probably because they were concerned about paying a disproportionate amount of the costs; see AGS, Exped. Hac. 901. This is almost certainly the same Juan de Brihuega who in 1586 was called vecino of Alcalá de Henares as well as of Brihuega. He was a returnee from New

Spain who was involved in a suit with Isabel de Ribas, the widow of Andrés de Angulo, over the proceeds of the sale of 350 arrobas of cochineal that Brihuega had sent from New Spain, which Angulo had handled for him; see ARCV, Fernando Alonso, C293-9 (fenecido).

19. AGI, Indif. Gen. 2065, no. 32.

20. AJP, 1588, partition of María de Pastrana's legacy among her children.

21. See AGNP, 1595; microfilm no. 649692 of FHCLDS.

22. AGI, Indif. Gen. 2054.

23. AHN, Inquis. Toledo, leg. 287, exped. 3. The terms "mercader" and "tratante" appear to have been used interchangeably, although possibly "tratante" is more consistently associated with the cloth trade.

24. Niño Rodríguez's *Organización social y actividades productivas* focuses principally on the eighteenth century. His economic analysis is based mainly on the Catastro del Marqués de la Ensenada, compiled in the mid–eighteenth century, after the royal textile factory was established; hence in the period he studies the numbers of people directly involved in textile production were quite high, as were the numbers of merchants. Notwithstanding the lack of information for most of the intervening period, the appearance of so many merchants in a single deposition of the late seventeenth century suggests a high degree of continuity in the town's commercial and occupational structure.

25. For the most thorough study and analysis of Puebla's founding and early development, see Hirschberg, "Social History of Puebla." Her "Social Experiment in New Spain" summarizes much of her material and argument. See also her "Transients in Early Colonial Society."

26. Hirschberg, "Social History of Puebla," 416–17, notes that the city council recognized barrios for Indians from Cholula, Texcoco, Totomehuacan, Tlaxcala, and Mexico in 1546. Subsequently people from Huejotzingo, Calpa, Tepeaca, Tlatelolco, and Tecali formed communities as well. By the 1550s the Indian barrios were San Sebastián, San Pablo, San Francisco, and Santiago.

27. The tithe essentially was a tax on agricultural production. Israel, *Race, Class, and Politics*, points out that Puebla's agricultural wealth made it "twice as rich as the archbishopric of Mexico and several times richer than most of the other bishoprics" (291). See also Hirschberg, "Social History of Puebla," 200–201, on Puebla's success in the 1540s in extending its formal and informal spheres of influence.

28. Thomson, *Puebla de los Angeles*, 3–4. He writes that "Puebla became New Spain's first diversified region of settlement based upon small estate agriculture, balanced by trade and manufacturing, producing for a rapidly expanding regional, but, more importantly, extra-regional and overseas markets" (12).

29. On the routes connecting Puebla to the south and the ports on the Gulf of Mexico and the Pacific, see Borah, *Early Colonial Trade and Navigation*.

30. Puebla was an early center of silk production in New Spain; in the 1530s and 1540s mulberry trees were extensively cultivated in the valley of Atlixco and other areas close to Puebla (Huejotzingo, Tepeaca, the Mixteca). Although subsequently silk cultivation disappeared entirely from the valley of Atlixco, silk weaving continued to be important in Puebla in the 1540s and 1550s. The briocenses did not, however, become involved in this form of cloth production. See Borah, *Silk Raising in Colonial Mexico*.

31. On Puebla's premier position in the textile industry in New Spain, see José Ignacio Urquiola, "Distribución geográfica de los obrajes y su volumen de producción," in Viqueira and Urquiola, *Los obrajes en la Nueva España*, 136, 139.

32. Ibid., 132–33. Urquiola says that the report of the *oidor* Santiago del Riego, who

inspected Puebla's obrajes in 1595, mentioned 40 obrajes with a total of 2,200 Indian workers, for an average of 55 workers per obraje.

33. For the visita of Francisco de Brihuega's obraje, see AMP, l. 2676, f. 1/282, t. 221. Mateo Sánchez, a spinner from Tlaxcala, said that some Indians "salen al trocado con sus mujeres e hijos."

34. Ibid.

35. MNAH, Ser. AJP, reel 37, contains the records of the visitas of 1620.

36. AMP, l. 2676, f. 1/282, t. 221. His statement was that "cuando algún indio de los naborías no acude a trabajar . . . dicho Salaices va por ellos a sus casas y los trae al dicho obraje y los tiene encerrados una semana más o menos tiempo." The term "naboría" apparently refers to wage workers who were not confined. Salaices probably was from Brihuega.

37. All this testimony on the visitas of 1620 is from MNAH, Ser. AJP, reel 37.

38. AGNP, Marcos Rodríguez, 1591.

39. AJP, 1609, "bienes que quedaron por fin y muerte de Martín de la Fuente." In 1611 there were 12 tundidores, 21 cardadores, 5 percheros, 14 male spinners, and 41 female spinners in the obraje. I have not found any contracts for women working in obrajes. Women who contracted for domestic service seem typically to have earned two pesos a month, at least in the early seventeenth century; see the register for 1609 of "asientos de indios de diferentes oficios" in MNAH, Ser. AJP, reel 37.

40. Sarah L. Cline raised this interesting point.

41. These wages are within the range of what skilled and semiskilled Indian workers earned in other trades, although on the low side. The contracts registered in 1609 include a number of men who contracted to work for a blacksmith, most of them for five or six pesos a month (one who was called "maestro del oficio de herrero" was to receive ten pesos a month) plus room and board. *Panaderos* normally earned more, usually a little over eight pesos plus food. MNAH, Ser. AJP, reel 37.

42. Reyes García, *Indice y extractos*, nos. 1239, 1601.

43. All of these contracts are in the records of the third notarial series, AGNP.

44. See José Ignacio Urquiola's discussion of the significance and function of advances in "Los trabajadores de los obrajes," in Viqueira and Urquiola, *Los obrajes en la Nueva España*. He analyzes labor contracts made in Cholula, Tlaxcala, and Querétaro in the late sixteenth century (see cuadro 12, pp. 194–95); many of the contracts made in Cholula and Tlaxcala were with obrajeros from Puebla.

45. AJP, 1609, "Fiscal de la real audiencia contra Benito Bautista, Juan de Mata, Domingo Guerra, Juan García Barranco, vecinos de la ciudad de los Angeles." This case is discussed in Chapter 6.

46. Ibid., "Cristóbal de la Carrera, vecino de la ciudad de Los Angeles, dueño de su obraje contra Lucas Gaspar y Pedro Martín indios."

47. AGN, Civil, vol. 701, exped. 7. Escudero was fined but appealed the sentence; the result of the appeal is unknown. On Escudero's obraje, see Hoberman, *Mexico's Merchant Elite*, 133–35.

48. AGNP, Alonso de la Parra.

49. AJP, 1610. Alonso Gómez's will was made in 1601, and the list of slaves included nineteen men and four women. A list of 1608 revising the assessment of the slaves' value indicated a total of twenty slaves, including three little girls who were the daughters of two of the women slaves.

50. In 1663 Juan Bautista Sanz, who had emigrated to New Spain with his parents, Lázaro Bautista Sanz and Juana de Mena, owned an obraje in Cholula. In his will of

March 28, 1663, he stated that he owned 51 "piezas de esclavos" but did not say how many Indians were in his service (AGNP, Nicolás Alvarez; Tulane LAL).

51. In 1632 the *alguaciles* of Puebla charged Pedro del Río and María de Cifuentes, probably both children of briocenses, with keeping their workers confined and treating them badly; see AGN, Tierras, vol. 2945, pt. 2, exped. 432.

52. An Indian named Juan Lázaro, who in 1570 worked in the obraje of Cristóbal de Baeza (not a briocense), referred to another Indian named Juan Sánchez as "capitán de los indios del dicho obrador" (AGN, Civil 1290, exped. 24). The term "obrador" was used interchangeably with "obraje." Possibly the capitán was chosen by the workers as their representative rather than by the obraje owner or mayordomo. Juan Lázaro talked about an incident in which one worker who was late leaving for mass received a head injury when the mayordomo beat him; Cristóbal de Baeza said he would pay for the treatment. Juan Sánchez told Baeza that he (Sánchez) "ought to complain about that and other things to the judge."

53. AGNP, Diego de Anzures, 1570.

54. His letter to his brother-in-law Francisco Barbero (Iñigo's father-in-law) is in AGI, Indif. Gen. 2054, 1573. Anzures wrote: "Me dicen tiene casada una hija con Juan de Iñigo, el mozo, y es muy buen maestro de batán, y pues lo ha usado toda su vida, se venga con su mujer por acá, juntamente con v.m., que yo le daré mi batán. Y en él ganará muy bien de comer con su industria, porque acá se hallan muy pocos oficiales para los batanes" (Otte, *Cartas privadas*, 156). The letter to Rodrigo de Anzures is in AGI, Indif. Gen. 2057, and in Otte, *Cartas privadas*, 160.

55. AGI, Indif. Gen. 2162A. In 1573 Pablos [*sic*] de Pastrana asked for a license to go to New Spain with his wife, María la Cardera, to join relatives and cousins in Puebla, saying his "primo hermano" Juan de Pastrana would pay him 500 ducados a year to work in his obrador de paños, "con los cuales yo me puedo remediar y aprovechar a muchos hermanos y cuñados y sobrinos que tengo pobres." Juan de Pastrana said that "porque tiene a la continua dos otros españoles en su servicio y como ha de tener un extraño quería ocuparle y emplear al dicho su primo."

56. AJP, 1609.

57. Torijano's letter to his wife is in AGI, Indif. Gen. 2060, and in Otte, *Cartas privadas*, 163–64. The rental of the batán is in AGNP, Juan de la Parra.

58. AGNP, 1593, ante Nicolás Hernández. Ribas said, "Tengo de asistir durante los dichos dos años a las cosas que se ofrecen en el obraje del dicho Bartolomé García," and that Bartolomé García "ha de tener en el dicho obraje . . . un mozo que ayude a la administración dél, ayudando a mí."

59. AGNP, Francisco Ruiz.

60. AGNP, Baltasar de Montoya, 1594.

61. AGNP, Juan de Meneses, 1602.

62. Lucas de Ribas testified that "era obrajero y por falta de caudal y haberse ido los indios de presente no lo es" (AJP, 1605, exped. 665).

63. Juan Bautista Sanz, the vecino of Cholula who owned an obraje with 51 slaves when he made his will in 1663, was the son of immigrants Lázaro Bautista Sanz and Juana de Mena and the grandson of Juan Bautista Sanz and Catalina de Trixueque, who left Brihuega for New Spain in 1573. They may have returned to Brihuega. Their son Lázaro was born in 1585 and emigrated to New Spain with his wife in 1621, at which time their third child, Juan Bautista, was two years old (AGNP, Nicolás Alvarez; Tulane LAL).

64. AGNP, Marcos Rodríguez and Alonso Hernández, June 1591.

65. Benito Sanz Bautista frequently appears in the records as just Benito Bautista.

66. Reyes García, *Indice y extractos*, nos. 1485, 911.

67. AGNP, Juan de la Parra, Dec. 1608.

68. AGNP, Rodrigo Alonso de León, 1593; Juan de Meneses, 1602.

69. A copy of his 1601 will is in AJP, 1610.

70. AJP, 1603, exped. 638. Matías Pérez may have been from Brihuega. In January 1598 he said that Lope de la Carrera and his wife, María García, had leased to him and to Miguel Pérez, who was from Brihuega, a batán along the Atoyac River for four years and seven months for 600 pesos a year. Possibly the two men were related. The rental agreement was made in January 1596. With the rental they received the service of two "indios bataneros y una india" (Gaspar Santiago and his wife, María, and Gaspar Felipe), as well as equipment and ten asses, all of which they agreed to return as received (or replace if necessary) (AGNP, Nicolás Hernández de la Fuente, 1598; FHCLDS, 649691).

71. AGI, Indif. Gen. 2054; Otte, *Cartas privadas*, 156.

72. AGI, Indif. Gen. 2054; Otte, *Cartas privadas*, 152. The letter states that "se traiga consigo cincuenta o sesenta libras de añil que será buen principio para su ganancia, y otros cincuenta o cien pares de cardas desde Córdoba, que también se ganará con ellas."

73. AGNP, Marcos Rodríguez, 1591.

74. Various items in AGNP. "Paños de la tierra" apparently referred generally to locally manufactured cloth, not just to indigenous cloth, as "de la tierra" usually implies.

75. The types of cloth for which prices were specified included both high-quality *veinticuatrenos* and *veintidosenos* dyed red with "grana" (cochineal) for three pesos per vara; the same type in blue for two pesos four tomines; lower-quality black, green, blue, and yellow *dieciochenos* at eleven reales per vara; and *bayetas* (flannel) in black and other colors for six reales and six granos per yard (AGNP, Pedro de Anzures).

76. AGNP, Marcos Rodríguez.

77. AGNP, Juan de Meneses. Most of the cloth—47 paños—consisted of lower-quality dieciochenos, for which he paid 3½ reales per vara; the three bolts of veintidosenos sold at 3½ pesos per vara.

78. In Puebla the Llorente family, like the Ribas family, changed the spelling of their name, which in Brihuega was Lorente.

79. Some people with the surname Rojo used the article "el" but most did not; this particular individual, however, always appears in the records as Francisco el Rojo.

80. AGNP. Carrillo also said he had given Bartolomé Tartajo 400 pesos to take to Guatemala and invest in cacao for him. Carrillo's son Mateo Carrillo went with Tartajo.

81. AJP, 1603, exped. 651.

82. AGNP, Marcos Rodríguez. A quintal equals 100 kilograms, or about 220 pounds; an arroba equals 11.5 kilograms, or about 25 pounds; a tercio equals 5 arrobas. Bizcocho bazo was whole-meal biscuit.

83. AJP, 1590.

84. MNAH, Ser. AJP, reel 37, "Asientos de indios de diferentes oficios," 1609.

85. AGNP, Pedro de Anzures, 1573.

86. FHCLDS, reel 649669.

87. AGNP, Juan de la Parra. When Blas Carrillo was about to depart for Soconusco in January 1594, he gave his power of attorney to Rodrigo García and Martín de Viñuelas to purchase 300 pesos' worth of silver for him.

88. AGI, Indif. Gen. 2070; Otte, *Cartas privadas*, 169. "Díceme que es viaje que se gana de comer," he wrote. "Plega Dios sea así."

89. This was probably Juan Pérez de Angulo, not the Juan de Angulo who was the son of Andrés de Angulo and brother of Pedro and Gabriel de Angulo. That Juan de Angulo later was said to have gone to Peru.

90. AGNP, Alonso Hernández, 1592; Nicolás Hernández de la Fuente, 1597. María de Bonilla's will and the settlement of her estate (they had no children) are in AJP, 1615.

91. AGNP, Gabriel de Anzures Guevara, 1612.

92. García de Zúñiga had Tartajo's power of attorney; see AGNP, Juan de la Parra; FHCLDS, reel 649710. This may not have been the same Bartolomé Tartajo who is discussed below but another man of the same name who arrived in Puebla in the 1590s.

93. AGNP, Alonso Hernández.

94. AGNP, 1599, will of Francisco Carrillo. It is not clear when this trip took place. For Tartajo see AGI, Indif. Gen. 2162A, and various items in AGNP, notarial ser. 3. In 1594 another Bartolomé Tartajo left Brihuega for New Spain. His presence in Puebla makes it more difficult to trace the activities of the Tartajo who arrived twenty years earlier.

95. AGNP, Alonso Hernández; FHCLDS, reel 649673.

96. Vollmer, 156. The dowry was 850 pesos. In 1598 Llorente's daughter Isabel married a muleteer named Lucas de Yela, who was from the town of Valdesaz, near Brihuega. Her dowry was 981 pesos and his *arras* (money a bridegroom gives his bride) was 500 pesos (AGNP).

97. AGNP, Marcos Rodríguez.

98. MNAH, Ser. AJP, reel 6.

99. AGNP, Marcos Rodríguez.

100. AGNP, Marcos Rodríguez, Baltasar de Montoya, Nicolás Hernández.

101. AGNP, Juan de la Parra, Gabriel de Anzures.

102. AGNP, Gabriel de Anzures. Cristóbal de la Carrera was an obrajero and also owned a store; in May 1600 Hernando de Pastrana sold him a "tienda de mercaderías" for 7,000 pesos and also bought 3,188 pesos of merchandise for him in Mexico City. Carrera was to repay the money to Pablo de Pastrana, to whom Hernando de Pastrana owed it. See AGNP, Juan de la Parra, and also AJP, 1603, exped. 611. Although the briocenses do not seem to have been much involved in the trade with the Philippines, other merchants in Puebla were and even traveled there; in February 1600, for example, Melchor Gutiérrez stated that his two sons were in the Philippines (FHCLDS, reel 649693).

103. Diego de Anzures and Alonso de Ribera planned to send 9,000 "cueros vacunos" (cowhides) and 175 arrobas of cochineal (which Anzures had bought) to Castile in 1573, but instead sold the merchandise (which was already loaded on the ship) to the regidor, Diego Serrano (AGNP, Pedro de Anzures). Gabriel de Angulo sent more than 2,000 hides to Castile in 1604 (AGNP, Juan de la Parra).

104. All these transactions are in AGNP, notarial ser. 3.

105. AGNP, Juan de Bedoya.

106. AGNP, Juan de la Parra.

107. AGNP, Alonso de la Parra. In December 1613 Juan de Roa Anzures paid Cristóbal de Ribas 500 pesos that he owed for the remainder of the price of 820 pesos "en que . . . me vendio 12 mulas de recua aparejadas" (AGNP, 1613). He was one of the sons of Juan de Roa, an early merchant and obrajero and husband of Francisca de Anzures (the sister of Diego, Pedro, and Macario de Anzures), who returned with his family to Brihuega in the 1570s.

108. AGNP, Juan de la Parra. Of the seven Indian men listed, three were listed with their wives—the "capitán," Ambrosio, and his wife, Mariana; his son-in-law Antón and his wife, Mariana; and Juan Grande and his wife, Ana—so presumably the women traveled with them.

109. AJP, 1587, exped. 256.

110. AJP, 1615. Iñigo was the son of Juan de Iñigo, the *batanero* who had been recruited

by Macario de Anzures, the uncle of his wife, María de Anzures. He and his mother bought one of the estancias from his uncle Gabriel de Anzures Guevara. He stated in his will that after his father's death, since he was the only heir, he and his mother had never divided up the estate.

111. AGNP, Diego de Anzures.

112. AGNP, Juan de Bedoya.

113. AGNP, Pedro de Anzures.

114. AGNP, Baltasar de Montoya, Alonso Hernández.

115. AGNP, Marcos Rodríguez. The rental for two years was worth 364 pesos, the oxen 650 pesos, and the mares 350 pesos.

116. See Hoekstra, *Two Worlds Merging*, on the increasing availability of land in and near the valley of Puebla in the second half of the sixteenth century. Hoekstra suggests that the process of land acquisition in the region occurred in stages. After the conquest of central Mexico, "about 1550, many livestock haciendas came into being in the northern areas of Huejotzingo and Tlaxcala on the periphery of the valley of Puebla, in the Llanos of Ozumba and in the valley of Mexico. . . . Along the roads through the valley of Puebla proper, the Spaniards also started livestock haciendas" (85). Starting in the late sixteenth century, Indian land sales to Spaniards increased considerably; this trend continued for about a decade in the central parts of the valley of Puebla (100). Hoekstra comments that during the 1590s "everyone bought as much as he could, and we can almost speak of a run on land" (102). Land purchases in this period often led to the consolidation of larger estates in the early seventeenth century.

117. AGNP, Juan de la Parra. All told, the land measured about 6½ caballerías, or 600 acres.

118. Ibid.

119. AGN, Civil, vol. 216, exped. 1. She married her first husband in 1649, but the date of her second marriage is not known. Her second husband, Agustín Marín, had no money when they married, and they had no children together. Her dowry was the house in which she lived in Puebla, on the calle de los Mesones.

120. AGNP, Juan de Bibanco; Tulane LAL. Pedro del Río asked to be buried in Puebla's cathedral in the habit of San Francisco. The term "hacienda de labor" primarily meant an estate devoted to cultivating wheat.

121. Vollmer, 1106; witnesses were Cristóbal de Beguillas, Juan de Buena, and Diego Llorente, all briocenses.

122. His will of 1598 is in AGNP, Juan de la Parra; FHCLDS, reel 649689.

123. AGNP, Baltasar de Montoya.

124. In 1603 charges were brought against Benito López, called a "criado in the store of Hernando de Pastrana," who allegedly had struck a woman named doña Isabel de Medina when he had gone to her home looking for her nephew Alonso Gómez, who he claimed had taken 50 pesos' worth of merchandise from Pastrana's store; see AJP, 1603, exped. 611.

125. Pastrana referred to his properties and those of his father-in-law variously as estancias, sitios de estancia, haciendas de labor, and haciendas de ovejas or de ganado menor or ganado mayor.

126. AGNP, Juan de la Parra.

127. Ibid. The rental agreement was similar to the ones he made with Lorenzo Sánchez; i.e., that Pastrana would receive 73 arrobas of wool per 1,000 head of cattle; it probably was the same estate.

128. Ibid.; FHCLDS, reel 649715.

129. According to Gerhard, *Guide to the Historical Geography of New Spain*, 137, Guaza-

cualco is "a broad plain stretching from the Gulf coast" in what is today eastern Veracruz and western Tabasco.

130. AGNP, Juan de la Parra; FHCLDS, reel 649716.

131. AGNP, Gabriel de Anzures Guevara.

132. AGI, Indif. Gen. 2078. Juana Gutiérrez received a license to emigrate with her children, Juan, Sebastián, María, Juana, and Ana, in May 1578. In addition to her nephew Gaspar Gutiérrez she had other relatives in New Spain, including Gaspar's brother Juan Gutiérrez, who also apparently lived in Mexico City. What familial relationship, if any, existed between Cristóbal de Pastrana and the Pastranas who settled in Puebla is not known. His son Juan de Pastrana maintained close connections with the briocenses in Puebla, including Pablo de Pastrana and Juan de Pastrana and his son-in-law don Cristóbal Godínez de Maldonado. Hoberman, *Mexico's Merchant Elite*, 105, says that Juan de Pastrana was related to Hernando and Melchor de Pastrana. There were other Pastranas in Mexico City who were also involved in trade and textile manufacture—Melchor, whom Pablo de Pastrana called his nephew in 1593, Baltasar, and their second cousins Josephe and Mateo de Pastrana. In 1636 Josephe de Pastrana said he had taken over an obraje from his father, Alonso de Pastrana; Mateo de Pastrana was an "oficial de hilar lana" (AGN, Civil, vol. 1735, exped. 4).

133. AGNP, Juan de la Parra. See Paredes Martínez, *La región de Atlixco, Huaquechula y Tochimilco*, 103–4, on the cultivation of sugarcane in the region near Puebla; and Hoberman, *Mexico's Merchant Elite*, 103–10, on the history of the ownership and financing of the San José *ingenio*. By 1605 they had sold the obraje as well as a mine and refinery in Guantla together with some slaves and land.

134. AGNP, Juan de la Parra. María García's will is in AGNP, Juan de Zamora, codicil ante Gabriel de Anzures Guevara.

135. AGNP, Juan de la Parra.

136. Hoberman, *Mexico's Merchant Elite*, 105; the indebtedness was 50,540 pesos.

137. AGNP, Alonso Hernández.

138. AGNP, Juan de la Parra, 1604.

139. See will of María de Pastrana of January 1663, AGNP, Nicolás Alvarez; Tulane LAL. She called her husband, Hernando de Carmona Tamariz, "alférez." He probably was the brother of Juan de Carmona Tamariz, the husband of Agustina Gómez, daughter of the briocenses Alonso Gómez and Catalina de Pastrana. María de Pastrana and Agustina Gómez were probably distant cousins.

140. AGNP, Juan de Meneses, 1602.

141. AGN, Civil, 1310, exped. 2. The sale price of the obraje and batán, which included slaves and the debts of 150 Indians, was 10,704 pesos 6 tomines, which they were to pay in four installments between December 1582 and June 1584. They placed a mortgage on other obrajes they owned and on their houses. Alonso de Ribas owned estancias, six slaves, 15,000 head of cattle, and 400 horses, mares, and mules, a fifth of which would belong to Juan de Ribas at his father's death.

142. For comparison, see Pescador, "New World Inside a Basque Village": the "occupations of oiartzuarras on both sides of the Atlantic tended to be similar and associated with economic activities traditionally carried out by local families: iron production, smithing, and tasks involved in ship construction. Furthermore, . . . Valley men had experience in herding, building with stone and wood, and exploitation of woodlands" (38).

143. See his *información* in AGI, México 236, no. 19.

144. ACB, 1583.

3. Politics and Public Life

1. See the discussion of Sebastián de Pliego in Chapter 1 and the Libro de Apeos for Mecina de Buen Varón, where most of the people from Brihuega settled, in ARCG.

2. Francisco Gutiérrez, one of the merchants interviewed in connection with the padrón of the town done in the mid-1580s, attributed the low profitability of the cloth trade to the need to sell cloth outside the town. The merchants, he said, "pagan otra alcabala en las ferias donde van a vender los dichos paños porque a la dicha [villa] no vienen mercaderes a comprarlos y ansi tienen necesidad de irlos a vender a las dichas ferias" (AGS, Exped. Hac., leg. 60).

3. Niño Rodríguez, *Organización social*, 28–35, summarizes these events and their financial implications. The purchase price was nearly 31,000 ducados. Niño Rodriguez concludes (35–41) that the probable explanation for the town's resale lies in the close ties the archbishop maintained with the local clergy and the archbishop's offer to pay off 8,000 ducados of the town's debt. Some vecinos of Brihuega felt that self-government with elected alcaldes ordinarios had resulted in political dissent and discontent; see AHN, Con. 29.200. On the sales of towns, see Nader, *Liberty in Absolutist Spain*, 17 for Brihuega and 172–73 for Romancos, formerly under Brihuega's jurisdiction and for several years owned by a returnee from New Spain, Diego de Anzures.

4. This and the padrón of 1595 are both in AGS, Exped. Hac., leg. 60.

5. Nader, *Liberty in Absolutist Spain*, 36.

6. Lope de la Carrera was the brother of Alonso de la Carrera, who married Ana de Ribas, the daughter of Cristóbal de Arribas and his wife, Ana de Ribas. In Puebla the surname Arribas became Ribas. Cristóbal de Arribas apparently married Ana de Ribas in Puebla; her origin is not known. His marriage to her probably accounts for the modification of the surname Arribas to the more familiar (in Puebla) Ribas, the form that will be used here to avoid confusion. It should be noted, however, that in all the documents generated in Brihuega the family name is recorded as Arribas, not Ribas.

7. In the documentation of the dispute over the tanteo in 1584, Jerónimo Martínez, *escribano del ayuntamiento de pecheros*, appeared; see AGS, Exped. Hac. 901.

8. See the información of Esteban Ballesteros, who was married to Gutiérrez's sister María Gutiérrez, in AHN, Inquis. Toledo, leg. 275, exped. 14.

9. J. C. García López, *Biblioteca de escritores*, 615. As a land measure, a fanega was equal to about one and a half acres.

10. J. C. García López, *Fuero de Brihuega*, 87 n. 1. He did not note the nature of the suit between the pecheros and hidalgos.

11. This padrón, too, is in AGS, Exped. Hac. 60.

12. The Pastranas are a good case in point. The 1595 padrón lists sixteen vecinos with this surname, all of them in Santa María. In the lengthy inquiry into the antecedents of Catalina de Pastrana, maternal grandmother of don Joseph de Carmona Tamariz and his brothers, who in the 1660s were candidates to be familiares of the Inquisition in Puebla (AGN, Inquis., vol. 452, exped. 2), some witnesses stated there was only one Pastrana family, others two, others as many as five. The evidence seems to suggest that there was more than one lineage, but the fact that they all resided in the one parish suggests that they may have considered themselves as being related. The nature of many of the common clustered surnames—Cifuentes, Pastrana, Trixueque, Alcalá, Guadalajara (the last two all lived in Santa María)—also suggests the possibility that these families moved from other towns to Brihuega and settled near one another.

13. AGS, Exped. Hac. 901.

14. ARCV, register of Manuel Pérez Alfonso (fenecido), C1143.2.

15. The case was brought against Miguel Gómez, clérigo, for *deshonestidad* in 1592 when

he supported Juan de la Paz, a vecino of another nearby town, Almonacid de Zorita, who wanted to be a familiar of the Santo Oficio even though it was alleged that his wife's converso background was well known. The statement regarding conversos and officeholding was made by Juan de Soria, who was a familiar of the Inquisition in Fuentelencina; he stated that "los ascendientes de . . . María Hernández, mujer de Juan de la Paz . . . han tenido la mitad de los oficios de justicia desta villa, unos de alcaldes y otros de regidores por parte de los conversos que se llamaban mercaderes y oficiales porque en esta villa durante no hubo hidalgos estaban los oficios partidos y tenían la mitad los labradores cristianos viejos y la otra mitad los conversos mercaderes y oficiales" (AHN, Inquis. Toledo, leg. 71, expeds. 19).

16. See, for example, the testimony of Gabriel Colmenero, a familiar in Brihuega, in the información of Esteban Ballesteros, a native of Brihuega who in 1623 was a merchant and vecino of Tlaxcala and petitioned to become a familiar of the Santo Oficio (ibid., leg. 275, exped. 14, 1623–45). His maternal grandmother was Juana Roja; Colmenero asserted that all the Rojos were known as conversos. Ballesteros's grandfather Diego Gutiérrez ("el de San Juan") has been mentioned earlier (he was the father of Alonso Gutiérrez). See the discussion of this family in Chapter 1.

17. These deliberations are in the records of the ayuntamiento general in ACB. Brihuega has no archive as such; the surviving council records sit in the mayor's office. There is a hiatus in the records between the end of December 1584, when the negotiations were more or less complete, and April 1585, soon after which a council was appointed under the aegis of a royal corregidor.

18. AGS, Exped. Hac. 901.

19. "Como se acostumbran a consultar y han consultado de tiempo antiguo inmemorial a esta parte las cosas graves que en esta villa han sucedido."

20. AHN, Cons. 29.200. Diego de Anzures's grandson don Diego Pacheco de Anzures was alcalde ordinario in 1604, when the negotiations began, and alcalde of the hermandad of hidalgos in 1607. His mother, doña Catalina de Barrientos, married a noble who had served at court as a page and in Brihuega as the alcaide (governor) of the castle, which remained under royal control.

21. Peña, *Oligarquía y propiedad*, 162, 166, notes that in 1534 Puebla had two alcaldes and eight regidores, but by the early seventeenth century the number of regidores had grown to twelve.

22. Hirschberg, "Social History of Puebla," notes that in 1559 "Martín de Mafra Vargas's *regimiento* was disputed by the *cabildo* not only on grounds of youth, but also on the basis of his one-time service in his merchant brother-in-law's *tienda de mercaderes*" (329). Martín de Mafra Vargas himself was from a leading conquistador-encomendero family. His brother-in-law Juan de Formicedo, an obraje owner, served as alcalde ordinario in 1568, 1579, 1586, and 1589. Peña, *Oligarquía y propiedad*, observes that in the early seventeenth century "se advierte, en comparación con el siglo anterior, un indudable retroceso del grupo inicial de conquistadores y pobladores, como son los Díaz de Vargas, Reinoso, Ordaz, etc., aunque esta recesión no signifique ni mucho menor, como en el caso de la capital, su desaparición de los regimientos y, menos aún, del poder municipal" (166).

23. See Gabriel Caballero's información in AGI, México 36, no. 4.

24. The master's thesis of Guadalupe Pérez-Rivero Maurer at the University of Puebla (in progress) is on Puebla's regidores in the seventeenth century. She points out these marital ties between the briocense aspirants and members of the council, although in the case of Alonso Gómez the evidence is unclear. His daughter doña Agustina Gómez married Juan de Carmona Tamariz, who was the son of Diego de Carmona, a longtime regi-

dor and familiar of the Santo Oficio; but Alonso Gómez probably became a regidor before his daughter married. It should be noted that Agustina's future father-in-law, Diego de Carmona, was one of the regidores who voted against accepting Gómez on the council. The documentation on the controversy over the acceptance of Gabriel de Angulo, Alonso Gómez, and Rodrigo García as regidores and Juan García Barranco as alférez mayor by the council is extensive. In 1594, for example, Gabriel de Angulo's brother Andrés de Angulo was acting as administrator of his obraje, but Gabriel was still called the dueño; see AGN, Tierras 2967, exped. 142. Angulo sold his *regimiento* in 1602; see ibid., Gen. Parte, vol. 6, exped. 1338. On the 1595 visita of Dr. Santiago del Riego, see MNAH, Ser. AJP, LC, 1595.

25. See Guadalupe Pérez-Rivero Maurer, "Presencia peninsular en el cabildo poblano en el siglo XVII, 1640–1700," paper presented at the conference "Presencia Española en Puebla" (Puebla, 1995). She notes that Juan Bautista de Salaíces was married to Clara Gutiérrez de Aguilar y Castillo Villegas, who was the niece of two other regidores.

26. He was the son of the briocense immigrant Miguel Carrillo, who at some time served as alcalde ordinario of Puebla, and Francisca Barbero de Barrientos, daughter of the briocense immigrant Cristóbal Barbero and his wife, Ursula de Barrientos; on the Carrillo family, see AGI, Contrat. 422, no. 4, ramo 5 (bienes de difuntos), which concerns the legacy of Blas Carrillo, the husband of Miguel Carrillo's sister María Carrillo.

27. See AGN, Inquis., vol. 640, exped. 7. The dispute was over whether the members of the council would accompany the canon when he went to declare the decrees of the Santo Oficio. This may seem a trivial matter but it probably reflected some real antagonisms between city officials and the officials of the Inquisition. This conflict is discussed below.

28. Pedro de Anzures made a particularly distinguished marriage to doña Isabel de Vargas; his brother-in-law Francisco Díaz de Vargas was alguacil mayor and regidor. His wife's uncles Martín de Mafra Vargas and Alonso de Leiba Vargas were, respectively, regidor and canon of the cathedral. Pedro de Anzures served as alcalde ordinario four times as well as *alcalde de la mesta* and *contador de bienes de menores* (comptroller of the property of minors) but apparently never tried to acquire a regimiento. His son don Diego de Anzures, however, was regidor in the 1630s; see AGN, Civil, vol. 76, exped. 13.

29. These were Gabriel de Anzures Izquierdo, apparently not a close relation of Diego and Pedro de Anzures; Juan de Piña; and Juan Guerra.

30. According to Peña, *Oligarquía y propiedad*, 167, Marcos Rodríguez Zapata was credited by many regidores as having played a key role in mediating and settling disputes and discord that racked the cabildo in the late sixteenth century. He was an active entrepreneur who at times was involved in textile production, so his association with the briocenses is not surprising.

31. AGN, Inquis., vol. 452, exped. 2. The case against Juan de la Parra is not very clear; it is discussed in part in the proceedings against Francisco el Rojo, but I was not able to find the case itself in the Inquisition records. Despite Rojo's indiscretion in discussing the case in Puebla and the ties that at least some of the briocenses had with Parra, several people did testify to Rojo's good character and intentions, including the alférez Juan García Barranco. This case is discussed in Chapter 4.

32. See ibid., vol. 591, expeds. 5–6; vol. 583, exped. 11. See also AHN, Inquis. Toledo, leg. 287, expeds. 3–4. The Inquisition inquiry is discussed in Chapter 1.

33. Lic. Salmerón may have had fairly close ties to the briocense immigrant community. The surname seems to have been prominent in Fuentelencina, and Salmerón witnessed the wedding of Juan de Buena of Brihuega in Puebla in 1591.

34. Quoted in Peña, *Oligarquía y propiedad*, 167.

35. The document is in AGI, México 340. The list includes others who may also have been from Brihuega (Juan Díaz, Jerónimo Rodríguez) but cannot be identified definitely because their names were common, as well as people such as Alonso del Moral, who probably were not but were closely associated with briocenses (Moral was the son-in-law of Juan Llorente of Brihuega, whose name is also on the list).

36. These figures for each of the parishes include the two alcaldes and the procurador general. The parish priests also gave their poder (power of attorney). If the figures from the 1595 padrón are used for the number of vecinos in each parish, the percentage of veci-nos from each who participated ranged from roughly 8 (San Felipe) to 20 percent (San Juan)—in all cases a minority of vecinos, but a fairly substantial proportion of them nonetheless.

37. The briocense immigrants certainly had their share of conflicts as well, but the examples I have found give no clear indication that any of them resulted from long-standing antagonisms having their roots in Brihuega.

38. The office of depositario general was created in 1610 and held by Juan de Carmona Tamariz and subsequently by his son, hence by descendants of the briocense Alonso Gómez.

39. On the evolution of town and city councils in Castile from the Middle Ages, see, for example, Ruiz, "Transformation of the Castilian Municipalities" and *Crisis and Continuity*, chap. 6; Martínez, *Las comunidades de villa y tierra*; Lunenfeld, *Keepers of the City*; and Altman, *Emigrants and Society*, 33–37.

40. There is a growing literature on public ceremonies and rituals in colonial New Spain and especially on their implications for the reinforcement and sometimes subversion of social and political relations among different groups; see Beezley, Martin, and French, *Rituals of Rule*.

41. AGI, Indif. Gen. 1394.

42. The petition, and a somewhat crude picture of what he claimed to be his family's coat of arms, are in AGI, México 118.

43. The detail regarding the gold chain came from the testimony of Juan Portugués de Brihuega, a native of Brihuega close to Gabriel de Angulo in age, who said they had grown up together. Two other briocenses, Jerónimo de la Cruz, who had been in Puebla about seven years, and Alonso de la Torre, who testified in Puebla in 1590, also had witnessed the empress's visit to Brihuega and Angulo's part in it.

44. AMP, l. 2676, f.1/282, t. 221 (Visitas de obrajes).

45. Pedro de Angulo may have died as early as 1599, when he was ill and authorized his wife, Inés de Ochoa, and his brother Gabriel to make his will; he definitely had died by 1606 (see AGNP, Juan de la Parra, for those years).

46. This incident also is recorded in AGI, México 118. Alonso de la Torre testified in 1590 that Andrés de Angulo was litigating in the chancillería in Valladolid over his hidal-guía, and although he had died, Torres heard he had won the suit.

47. MNAH, Ser. AJP, reel 6 (Libros del Cabildo).

48. AGNP, Juan de la Parra.

49. AMP, Libros del Cabildo (no. 10), 1567. Peña, *Oligarquía y propiedad*, 145, writes that the primary and almost exclusive function of the office of alférez, which Anzures subsequently held, was "sacar el pendón en caso de guerra y en las ocasiones de fiesta que lo requerían."

50. Gómez was authorized to name "los oficiales necesarios," which probably referred to artisans to construct the set.

51. MNAH, Ser. AJP, reel 6 (Libros del Cabildo). According to Leicht, *Las calles de*

Puebla, 436, yet another briocense, Cristóbal de la Carrera, represented "el gran turco" in the fiestas for the reception of the viceroy, the marqués de Montesclaros, in 1603.

52. Many of the studies in Beezley, Martin, and French, *Rituals of Rule*, focus on relations between classes and groups rather than conflict within the ruling group itself.

53. Don Carlos de Luna y Arellano, mariscal de Castilla and señor de Ciria y Borovia, was the brother-in-law of don Luis de Velasco el mozo (they were married to the sisters doña Leonor and doña María de Mendoza, nieces of the first viceroy of New Spain, don Antonio de Mendoza); see Peña, *Oligarquía y propiedad*, 200, 203, 205, on Luna and his familial and political connections.

4. The Religious Realm

1. Barranco may have purchased the properties for only 10,000 pesos; the purchase price is not clear.

2. AGNP, Marcos Rodríguez, 1590.

3. A copy of the bull issued in Rome, translated into Spanish, is in CONDUMEX, f. XIV-1, carp. 1, no. 18. The title of the copy mistakenly refers to the alférez Juan García Barranco, a relative of Juan Barranco, as the founder of the Colegio de Jesús María, an error commonly made. Pérez Moreno, *Tradiciones religiosas de España*, also thought Juan García Barranco founded the colegio and convent in Puebla (27). There is absolutely no doubt, however, that they were two different individuals and that it was Juan Barranco who founded Jesús María in Puebla.

4. The term used is "labrar," to sew or embroider.

5. In this instance an orphan was considered to be a fatherless girl; her mother could still be living.

6. In the late sixteenth century dowries for young women entering convents generally were at least 2,000 pesos, so obviously the sum Barranco designated would not have been sufficient unless the convent had special provisions for accepting women who could not meet the standard dowry requirement. Convents might admit women who paid less than the full dowry, but they probably would never be allowed to take the black veil.

7. CONDUMEX, f. XIV-1, carp. 1, no. 18, fol. 34.

8. Cristóbal García was born in 1559. His name appears variously in the documents of the late sixteenth and early seventeenth centuries with the titles "bachiller" and (less frequently) "licenciado," but most often without any title at all.

9. AGNP, Marcos Rodríguez, 1590.

10. I did not find a complete copy of Barranco's will, and it is not clear what provisions, if any, he made for family members. Apparently he earmarked the income for six years (or at least part of it, since some of it went to the support of the colegio) from his fulling mills in Puebla for his niece Ana García, the sister of Juan García Barranco, who was married to Juan de Anzures Guevara, the son of Rodrigo de Anzures. Juan García Barranco had the poder of his brother-in-law, and he arranged to have the equivalent of 300 pesos sent to his sister in "añir y reales" (indigo and money; see AGI, Contrat. 339B, no. 1, ramo 18).

11. According to Pérez Moreno, *Tradiciones religiosas*, 25, San Ildefonso got its start in 1564 when several noblewomen established it "in some small houses of the parish of San Miguel," although it was not until 1596 that the convent was formally constituted and recognized by the archbishop of Toledo. An institution known as San Ildefonso did exist early in the sixteenth century, when doña Luisa de la Cerda was the prioress; see the case of Juan Beltrán in AHN, Inquis. Toledo, leg. 137, exped. 13, in which she testified.

12. MNAH, Ser. AJP, reel 6 (Libros del cabildo); AGN, Tierras, vol. 2980, exped. 157.

13. A copy of Juan García Barranco's will is in AGI, Contrat. 339B, no. 1, ramo 18 (part of the bienes de difuntos).

14. See Nalle, *God in La Mancha*, 113–14, on the foundation of "colegios de niños de la doctrina" in the sixteenth century, which probably were the model for Juan García Barranco's donation.

15. Juan García Barranco was related to the Ruiz family. In his will, which he made in April 1611, he named as his executors "mi tío padre Cristóbal García clérigo presbítero, Lope de la Carrera mi cuñado, Bartolomé de la Torre y Pedro Ruiz mi primo." His uncle Juan Barranco was the son of Ana Ruiz and Bartolomé García.

16. See Pérez Moreno, *Tradiciones religiosas*, 27.

17. All these provisions are in his will of 1611; see AGI, Contrat. 339B, no. 1, ramo 18.

18. AGN, Inquis., vol. 148, exped. 1. Juan Carrasco, who was born in Puebla in 1575 to a slave couple, both from Bran, had been arrested and punished previously by the Inquisition, in 1596. Carrasco stated that he had been baptized and confirmed, and that he attended mass, took Communion, and had confessed during Lent. He could recite his prayers but only half of the Ten Commandments. Alonso Hernández, an immigrant from Trujillo, testified that Juan García Barranco had said to Carrasco, "Perro, os haré quemar." A slave might curse God as a way of escaping punishment at the master's hands, but punishment by the Inquisition was nearly as certain, as we shall see.

19. AGNP, Juan de la Parra, FHCLDS, reel 649711.

20. AGNP, Juan de la Parra, FHCLDS, reel 649706.

21. AGI, Contrat. 339B, no. 1, ramo 18.

22. María de la Encarnación, the daughter of Lázaro Bautista Sanz and Juana de Mena, was a nun in the "convento de San Jerónimo" when her obrajero brother Juan Bautista Sanz made his will in 1663; see AGNP Nicolás Alvarez; Tulane LAL.

23. In her will of 1641 Mariana García Carrillo, the widow of Martín de Viñuelas, stated that her daughter Isabel de la Resurrección was a nun in the convent of La Concepción, as were her granddaughters, Mariana de San Juan and Isabel de San Matías, the daughters of her (deceased) daughter doña Juana de Durango and her husband, Hernando de Aranda Saavedra (AGNP, Juan Guerra).

24. Christian, *Local Religion in Sixteenth-Century Spain*. There are relaciones for some of the towns that had close ties with Brihuega, such as Tendilla and Fuentelencina. Possibly Brihuega was excluded because it was under the jurisdiction of the archbishop of Toledo.

25. Ibid., 165. Christian notes that "by 1615, after the diocesan prescription against long-distance processions, it was required each year to ask permission to fulfill its vow. Every year the permission was granted, but the net effect was that Brihuega each year acknowledged diocesan jurisdiction over its contract with Mary."

26. Pérez Moreno, *Tradiciones religiosas*, 15, 21, 23.

27. As late as 1571 San Pedro still had a parish priest, but it obviously was the smallest of the parishes. The other four had two or three other benefices besides that of the cura, but San Pedro had only "un beneficiado curado." See the Libro del Becerro for the archbishopric, fol. 280, in the Archivo Diocesano de Toledo.

28. Pérez Moreno, *Tradiciones religiosas*, 25. San Bernardo was sometimes called Santa Ana. It may be that San Ildefonso did not become a Jeronimite convent until later in the sixteenth century, but there is no doubt it existed as a religious establishment much earlier. In 1528 doña Luisa de la Cerda was called "madre de las religiosas y beatas de la dicha casa"; see AHN, Clero, 1986.

29. AHN, Clero, 1986.

30. AHN, Inquis. Toledo 287, exped. 3.

31. ACB.

32. Pérez Moreno, *Tradiciones religiosas*, 25–26.

33. Ibid., 138.

34. AHN, Inquis. Toledo, leg. 467, exped. 4. It is not clear when this individual lived (or died).

35. ACB. This effort perhaps was made in response to increasing pressure after the Council of Trent to verify and document local religious traditions, although Christian also points out that the practice of documenting miracles began as early as the mid–fifteenth century; see Christian, *Local Religion*, 103–5. Pérez Moreno, *Tradiciones religiosas*, fails to provide any details on the miracles associated with Santa María de la Peña.

36. AHN, Cons. 29.200.

37. In earlier times each parish might have had its own cofradía. Juan Beltrán, tried for Judaizing by the Inquisition in the early sixteenth century, said he was a member of the "cofradía de San Miguel."

38. See Nalle, *God in La Mancha*, 162–63, on the rise of cofradías dedicated to the Blessed Sacrament in Cuenca; she found that in the late sixteenth century about one-third of communities had them. "At mid–sixteenth century, the Catholic Reformation's promotion of the cult of the Eucharist led to the policy that each parish [in the city] should have its own confraternity devoted to the Blessed Sacrament." No doubt the same policies affected Brihuega as well. See Christian, *Local Religion*, chap. 6, on what he calls the "Christocentric nature of late-sixteenth- and seventeenth-century Spanish devotion" (190).

39. The ordinances of the cofradía are included in the suit in ARCV, Manuel Pérez Alfonso (fenecido), C1143.2.

40. Possibly this copy of the ordinances is incomplete. No women, however, are included among the "hermanos" listed in the suit.

41. Testimony in ARCV, Pérez Alonso (fenecido), C1143.2.

42. AHN, Inquis. Toledo, leg. 46, exped. 31. Sahelices was said to be the son of a man who had been reconciled by the Inquisition.

43. For Barragán, see AGI, Contrat. 5165, no. 1, ramo 55; for Lázaro Bautista Sanz, ibid., 5376, no. 12; for Alonso Bermejo, ibid., 5387, no. 37.

44. Ibid., 5263, no. 4.

45. Francisco Barbero's probanza is in AJP, 1616; for Justo Barbero, see AGI, Contrat. 5307, no. 2, ramo 7.

46. AHN, Inquis. Toledo, leg. 137, exped. 13. Francisco Ruiz still was the cura of San Juan ten years later, so his actions apparently incurred no very drastic disciplinary measures.

47. Ibid., leg. 470, exped. 11.

48. Alonso de la Torre does not seem to have been related to Benito Sanz Carpintero; there is some suggestion that he was representing a cofradía that apparently had some claim to the priest's estate.

49. In 1623 Lic. Alonso Cano was cura of San Miguel; Lic. Diego de la Casa was cura of San Felipe; Lic. Hernando Carrillo was beneficiado of San Juan; Lic. García de Salamanca was cura of San Juan; and Andrés Bautista Sanz was beneficiado of San Felipe Testimony in AHN, Inquis. Toledo 287, exped. 3 (probanza of don José Carmona de Tamariz) in 1662 was taken from Lic. Juan de Soria, cura of Santa María; Lic. Bernabé García, cura of San Miguel; Lic. Cristóbal de Soria y Velasco, archpriest and vicar of Brihuega; Lic. Gabriel de Alcalá y Medina, chaplain of the convent of Santa Ana; and Juan Carrasco, Pedro Alvarez del Villar, Paulino Alvarez, and Blas Pérez, all clérigos presbíteros,

all licenciados. Also included were Juan de Roa, Alonso de Brihuega, and Joseph de Pastrana, also clérigos presbíteros, who apparently did not have a degree.

50. Probably because of Brihuega's connections with Toledo, people from the town often went before the Inquisition to execute their informaciones genealógicas, not only because they aspired to hold office with the Inquisition but also in a number of cases because they wanted to emigrate to the Indies.

51. These statements were excerpted from Inquisition records regarding people with the surname Rojo as part of the información of Esteban Ballesteros, the briocense vecino of Tlaxcala who applied for the position of familiar in the Holy Office in 1623; see AHN, Inquis. Toledo, leg. 275, exped. 14.

52. Ibid., leg. 137, exped. 13, fol. 29. See Nalle, *God in La Mancha*, 129, on the efforts of many conversos in Cuenca to demonstrate the sincerity of their conversion by investing in religious education and purchasing indulgences and religious books.

53. AHN, Inquis. Toledo, leg. 137, exped. 13. Witnesses for Beltrán were asked if they were aware "that the year of the hunger, when other people were selling bread at four and a half [mrs.] a pound . . . Juan Beltrán sold all the bread he had to the town at three and a half." Doña Luisa de la Cerda testified that once Beltrán had given the wife of a man named Bartolomé Batanero a ducado to buy clothing and that Bartolomé had told her that Beltrán also gave them a fanega of wheat (fol. 46).

54. Ibid., fol. 42.

55. Ibid., leg. 275, exped. 14 (información of Esteban Ballesteros, testimony related to the Rojos).

56. Ibid., leg. 297, exped. 12. Alonso Cubero was accepted as familiar; in 1614, when Gabriel de Trixueque applied for the position, Bartolomé Cubero was still alive (ibid., leg. 470, exped. 11).

57. Ibid., leg. 287, exped. 9. Familiares were laymen, and comisarios were secular priests. Only comisarios could actually initiate inquiries about an individual.

58. Schwaller, *Church and Clergy*, notes that "the diocese of Puebla, originally called the diocese 'Carolense,' had precedence in the New World. The first constitution for New Spain was written for that diocese. The first bishop, don fray Julián Garcés, is credited with writing that document" (6).

59. Israel, *Race, Class, and Politics*, 291; also see Hirschberg, "Social History of Puebla," 200–201. Nonetheless, Mexico City still claimed precedence. According to Schwaller, *Church and Clergy*, "income differences created a hierarchy among the cathedrals. Mexico and Puebla sat at the pinnacle of the system, followed by Michoacán, Guadalajara, and lastly Oaxaca. Being an archdiocesan and viceregal capital, Mexico City had a higher status and enjoyed greater prestige than did Puebla" (130). The salaries of members of Puebla's cathedral chapter "from time to time . . . even exceeded those of the archdiocese but the latter's preeminence in all other areas assured it of primacy" (134).

60. According to Israel, *Race, Class, and Politics*, 48 (nn. 94 and 95), in the mid–seventeenth century ecclesiastical personnel in Mexico City numbered 2,500, including 1,000 nuns, compared to Puebla's approximately 1,400, about 600 of them nuns. In 1635, however, Puebla's diocese included 700 members of the secular clergy, and the number rose to more than 1,000 by the end of the century; the diocese of Mexico had about half that number.

61. Ibid., 247. Under Palafox, Puebla doubtless reached the height of its ecclesiastical and even political influence in the viceroyalty. He had arrived in New Spain in 1639 with appointments as both bishop of Puebla and visitor general of New Spain, and in 1642 he served as both interim viceroy and archbishop-elect.

62. See AHN, Inquis. Toledo, leg. 287, exped. 3; Alonso Gómez was responsible for

having the money sent back to Brihuega. Francisco de Brihuega also founded a *capellanía* in Puebla in the hospital of Nuestra Señora de San Juan de Letrán in his will of 1595, with his brother Cristóbal de Brihuega to serve as patron; see AGNP, Juan de la Parra, 1608.

63. AGNP, Marcos Rodríguez, 1590.

64. AGI, Contrat. 422, no. 4, ramo 5 (bienes de difuntos).

65. As relatively few wills have been found for the briocenses in Puebla, it is impossible to do a real survey of their religious and charitable bequests.

66. AGNP, Juan de la Parra. Cristóbal García de Zúñiga mentioned sending something with this box.

67. See Leicht, *Las calles de Puebla*, 288.

68. Pablo de Pastrana bought a "solar y medio cercado de piedra" (lot and a half walled in stone) next to the hospital on the Calle de los Herreros from María de Pastrana (the daughter of Juan de Pastrana) and her husband in 1592 for 1,023 pesos; Juan de Pastrana donated another "solar y medio" at the same time; see AGNP, Baltasar de Montoya. Leicht, *Las calles de Puebla*, 355–56, says that the hospital became known as San Roque in 1614. After suffering damage in the 1650s, it was rebuilt in 1662 with the financial assistance of Roque de Pastrana, Pablo de Pastrana's son. Roque de Pastrana was baptized in Puebla in August 1591.

69. Their mother, Mariana García Carrillo, made her will in 1641 (AGNP, Juan Guerra).

70. On Juan de Cifuentes, see AGI, Indif. Gen. 2162A, and on Francisco, see ibid., 2058, and AHN, Inquis. Toledo, leg. 293, exped. 9.

71. According to Juan de Pastrana, "Fray Juan de Cara frayle profeso de la orden de San Francisco descalzo que estaba en Indias en la ciudad de los Angeles este presente año vino a Brihuega y en presencia deste testigo trató con el dicho Gabriel Lozano y su mujer y hermanos que los quería llevar a las dichas indias y que solo venía a efecto de llevar a los susodichos a las dichas indias . . . y no a otra cosa" (AGI, Indif. Gen. 2071, no. 38).

72. See the discussion in Altman, *Emigrants and Society*, 80, 163–64.

73. AGN, Inquis., 374, exped. 16.

74. Antonio Tamariz de Carmona [*sic*] was author of *Relación y descripción del templo real de la ciudad de la Puebla de los Angeles en la Nueva España, y su catedral*, published in 1650 and reissued by the Gobierno del Estado de Puebla in 1991.

75. AGN, Inquis., vol. 591, expeds. 5–6.

76. According to Schwaller, *Church and Clergy*, "perhaps more priests served chantries than any other type of ecclesiastical office. Given the requirement that each cleric enjoy a minimum income before ordination, chantries grew in popularity toward the end of the sixteenth century. Many chantries were founded by parents for the ordination of a son. After that, later generations of family members could use the pious work as the basis for ordination" (124).

77. AGNP, Juan de la Parra, 1608. Josephe de Nava's will of 1602 establishing the chaplaincy named Pedro de Anzures as the first patron.

78. This document, found in AGNP, Gabriel de Anzures, 1612, is incomplete and may date from some time earlier.

79. AGNP, Alonso de la Parra, 1618. Diego del Río died in 1615. Members of this family used del Río, el Río, Ríos, and de los Ríos as their surname, apparently interchangeably.

80. AGNP, Gabriel de Anzures.

81. AGNP, Juan de la Parra.

82. AGNP, Gabriel de Anzures Guevara.

83. In her will of January 1663 yet another María de Pastrana, the daughter of Her-

nando de Pastrana and his wife, Catalina de Herrera, asked to be buried "en el entierro y boveda que tengo . . . en el altar del Sr. San Diego que está en la capilla mayor de la iglesia del serráfico padre San Francisco desta ciudad"; see AGNP, Nicolás Alvarez; Tulane LAL. All these María de Pastranas probably were related in some degree.

84. She made her will in 1595; see AGNP, Nicolás Hernández de la Fuente.

85. On Pliego, see Bermúdez de Castro, *Teatro angelopolitano*, 189.

86. See Destefano, "Miracles and Monasticism," 75, table I, and his chap. 3 on the family background of the holy people he studied. According to Destefano, 78, the biographer of the Jesuit Nicolás de Guadalajara, who was born in Puebla around 1631, stated that his subject was the son of a "general" and that his family owned an obraje. Most likely he was the son of the briocense immigrant Juan de Guadalajara, who married María de Alcanadre, the widow of the obrajero Pedro Gómez (the son of Alonso Gómez) in Puebla in 1625. According to Leicht, *Las calles de Puebla*, 278, Juan de Guadalajara was named "justicia and teniente general" of Puebla in the 1650s; see also Bermúdez de Castro, *Teatro angelopolitano*, 181. Little is known about the family of Cristóbal de Molina. Destefano writes that "his mother was of very noble lineage in the village of Uriguega" (79), which most likely is Brihuega. He was credited with healing powers and other miraculous acts, especially relating to food. María de Jesús also had some connection to the briocenses. Her father, Sebastián Tomellín, was an obrajero and the brother-in-law of the obrajero Juan de Ribas. On the topic of holy people in New Spain, see also Morgan, "Saints, Biographers, and Creole Identity Formation," which has chapters on two holy people of Puebla, fray Sebastián de Aparicio and Catarina de San Juan. In her will of 1641 the briocense Mariana García Carrillo left three pesos "para ayuda de la beatificación o canonización del siervo de Dios fray Sebastián de Aparicio de la orden del Sr. San Francisco" (AGNP, Juan Guerra; Tulane LAL).

87. Mariana de Piña was the daughter of Mancio Alonso de Piña and María de Urgelos, the parents of a large family that moved in several stages to New Spain in the 1580s and 1590s; the family is discussed in Chapter 5.

88. Salmerón, *De la vida de la venerable madre Isabel*, 12. Peace and quiet may have been at a premium, since in all likelihood Isabel was a member of a large family. It is not known how many children her parents had, but Isabel was the third child born in about as many years. According to Destefano, "Miracles and Monasticism," 23, Salmerón was a secular priest, born in Puebla, who served as chaplain in the Carmelite convent.

89. Salmerón, *De la vida de la venerable madre Isabel*, 14.

90. Destefano, "Miracles and Monasticism," 158–60, 164–66. According to Destefano, "there have historically been two kinds of saints, those who achieve holiness through their deeds and those who achieve it through their suffering. These latter, the 'passion saints,' in the sense that their glory lay not so much in what they do as in what they passively receive, are exemplars of perfection precisely because they approach an imitation of Christ's own passion" (175). Clearly Isabel belonged to this group.

91. Ibid., 118, 153, 156, 158, 179, 293, 299.

92. AGN, Inquis., vol. 271, exped. 18.

93. Ibid., vols. 281 and 343, exped. 29. Andrés Cetín was sentenced to receive 50 lashes.

94. Ibid., vol. 281, fol. 694.

95. Ibid., vol. 281.

96. Ibid., vol. 182, exped. 15. Apparently few people took the cruzadas very seriously, and donations in the wills for their purchase usually were minimal.

97. Ibid., vol. 452, exped. 2.

98. Ibid., vol. 368, exped. 68. According to Rojo, in early August 1604 he ran into Jerónima as she was about to throw her infant down a well, and he stopped her.

Jerónima allegedly yelled, "Be my witnesses that I have repudiated God." Her husband was there as well. He admitted they were having a fight and said he had asked her if she was drunk.

99. Hoekstra, *Two Worlds Merging*, mentions an interesting case that seems to demonstrate almost the reverse, with members of the cofradía of a pueblo near Tlaxcala questioning the orthodoxy of a local friar. The accused probably belonged to the briocense community, most likely the son of Alonso de Ribas and María de Pastrana. According to Hoekstra, "in 1603, in the *pueblo* of Atlihuetzian (Tlaxcala), the local Franciscan friar Fray Alonso de Rivas was inspired by 'Lutheran' thoughts. He refused to lead the local *cofradía* in processions and in services for the Virgin Mary. . . . He held the view that the Indians should not ask favour from the Mother of God, because '*she was a woman of flesh and blood, like all others.*' . . . The Indians lodged a complaint against the Franciscan with the court of the Inquisition when it had a sitting in Tlaxcala in 1603" (187). The outcome of the case is not known.

100. AGNP, Alonso Hernández.

101. In 1641 the immigrant Mariana García Carrillo, the widow of Martín de Viñuelas, stipulated that the "hermanos del hospital de San Roque" should bear her body on the day of her funeral and that they should receive five pesos in charity (AGNP, Juan Guerra).

102. Javier Pescador's discussion of the spread of the cult of the Virgin of Aranzazu in Spanish America provides an interesting counterexample. The cofradía of the "Basque-speaking Virgin," founded in the church of San Francisco in Mexico City in 1671, included members from all the Basque-speaking regions (Alava, Navarre, Gipuzkoa, and Biscay). Hence the cult was specifically Basque, while at the same time it was an "American" creation, having no counterpart in Basque society in Spain itself. See Pescador, "New World Inside a Basque Village," chap. 4, esp. 295–96.

5. Marriage and Family

1. AGI, Contrat. 5376, no. 12.

2. Ibid., 5263B, no. 1.

3. AHN, Inquis. Toledo, leg. 263, exped. 6.

4. AGI, Contrat. 5307, no. 2, ramo 7.

5. AGNP, Juan de Meneses.

6. *Catálogo de pasajeros*, vol. 6, no. 124; AJP, 1603.

7. AGI, Contrat. 5307, no. 2, ramo 8; Vollmer, 880.

8. AHN, Inquis. Toledo, leg. 276, exped. 6; Vollmer, 143.

9. AGI, Indif. Gen. 2065; Otte, *Cartas privadas*, 167.

10. AGI, Indif. Gen. 2054; Otte, *Cartas privadas*, 154–55.

11. AHN, Inquis. Toledo, leg. 33, exped. 51. The Inquisition charge hinged on these words, which both Cortés and Pedro de la Carrera repeated, although in slightly different form.

12. AGNP, Juan de la Parra.

13. AGNP, Alonso Hernández.

14. AGI, Contrat. 422, no. 4, ramo 5 (bienes de difuntos).

15. AGI, Indif. Gen. 2060; Otte, *Cartas privadas*, 164.

16. AGI, Indif. Gen. 2061, no. 151.

17. Ibid., 2063, no. 127.

18. Ibid., 2054; Otte, *Cartas privadas*, 155.

19. AGS, Exped. Hac., leg. 60.

20. In 1630 María de Aranda, the daughter of Juana de Durango and her second hus-

band, Hernando de Aranda Saavedra, married the emigrant Alonso Carrillo, brother of Blas Carrillo, who emigrated with his family in 1622 (Vollmer, 1312). María de Aranda's mother, Juana de Durango, was the daughter of the briocenses Martín de Viñuelas and Mariana García Carrillo. On Juana de Durango, see the will of her mother, Mariana García, of 1641 in AGNP, Juan Guerra; Tulane LAL.

21. Vollmer, 23.

22. Vollmer, 1096.

23. Vollmer, 234.

24. AGNP, Gabriel de Anzures, 1613.

25. Vollmer, 1157. Witnesses at the wedding were the immigrants Lope de la Carrera, Lázaro Gómez (Pedro Gómez's cousin), Miguel Carrillo, and Juan García del Castillo, son of the immigrant Rodrigo García.

26. *Catálogo de pasajeros*, vol. 4, no. 3726.

27. AGI, Contrat. 5308, no. 2, ramo 20.

28. AGI, Indif. Gen. 2054, 2162A; APSMP; FHCLDS, reel 0227520 (bautismos de españoles). Mariana de la Torre's will is in AGNP, Gabriel de Anzures.

29. AGI, Indif. Gen. 2060; APSMP; FHCLDS, reel 0227520; AGNP, Gabriel de Anzures. The family of Sebastián de Pliego and María Díaz is discussed in Chapter 1.

30. AGI, Indif. Gen. 2063, no. 127.

31. APSMP; FHCLDS, reel 0227520; Otte, *Cartas privadas*, 153.

32. APSMP; FHCLDS, reel 0227520; Otte, *Cartas privadas*, 156.

33. Otte, *Cartas privadas*, 153–54. Pescador, "New World Inside a Basque Village," describes a wealthy couple's reaction to the death of their seven-year-old daughter: "María Josefa's passing brought her parents great sorrow, in contrast to what has been said about adult indifference to child mortality in the Old Regime. Aldaco commissioned a full-body portrait of his daughter, dressed to marry" (229).

34. AGI, Indif. Gen. 2054. This is the same Diego de Pastrana discussed above; he was from Brihuega, where his parents were living, but apparently had become a vecino of Fuentelencina, which probably was his wife's hometown, before he went to New Spain.

35. AGI, Indif. Gen. 2054; Otte, *Cartas privadas*, 152.

36. AGNP, Juan de la Parra.

37. AGI, Indif. Gen. 2065, no. 52.

38. Vollmer, 173; AGNP, Juan de la Parra; FHCLDS, reel 649689. The statement was made in a will Camarillo prepared in 1598; he was still alive in 1612, however.

39. On adoption in Castile, see Vassberg, "Orphans and Adoption."

40. AGN, Inquis., vol. 452, exped. 2. In his will of 1591 Rodrigo García left 100 pesos for a girl named Juana whom Rojo was raising.

41. Cristóbal de Ribas el mozo was born in New Spain in 1562 and went to Brihuega with his family in 1573. He married María de Aguirre there and returned with her and the rest of his family to Puebla in 1593. In 1622 both he and his wife were around 60 years old and Juana was 11; see AGI, Contrat. 5380, no. 29.

42. AGNP, Juan de la Parra; FHCLDS, reel 649689.

43. AGNP, Marcos Rodríguez.

44. AGNP, Juan de la Parra.

45. AGNP, Juan de Zamora, Gabriel de Anzures.

46. Ibid.

47. AJP, 1609.

48. AGNP, Gabriel de Anzures, will of 1613. Isabel de Morales was the niece of Gabriel Caballero, the immigrant from Budía who was the son of the briocense Isabel de Brihuega. He provided 200 pesos toward her dowry when she married Alonso Caballero.

49. AGNP, Marcos Rodríguez.

50. An información for Lic. don Josephe de Anzures y Guevara done in 1625 is in AGI, México 236, no. 19. He made his will on board a ship going to Spain the following year; see AGI, Contrat. 368, no. 7, ramo 5.

51. AGI, Contrat. 5269, no. 27.

52. AGI, Indif. Gen. 2057; Otte, *Cartas privadas*, 160.

53. AGNP, Juan de la Parra; FHCLDS, reel 649706.

54. Otte, *Cartas privadas*, 153.

55. AJP, 1603, exped. 651.

56. AGNP, Alonso Hernández.

57. AGNP, Juan de la Parra. Isabel de Vallejeda probably was the daughter of María de Pastrana and Jerónimo de Vallejeda. María de Pastrana, who died in 1595, called Pablo de Pastrana her uncle, so Isabel de Vallejeda may actually have been Juana de Pastrana's grandniece.

58. AGI, Contrat. 422, no. 4, ramo 5.

59. I have found no documentation on the activities of Alonso de Anzures in Puebla, so possibly he died soon after arriving there.

60. Otte, *Cartas privadas*, 160.

61. AGNP, Pedro Caballero; FHCLDS, reel 649713.

62. AGI, Indif. Gen. 2061, no. 166.

63. AGNP, Juan de la Parra.

64. APSMP; FHCLDS, reel 227520 (bautismos de españoles).

65. In the case of this family, however, García was present in the maternal line as well, because Juan Barranco's brother the priest was Cristóbal García Barranco.

66. Juana de Durango's children by her second husband, Hernando de Aranda Saavedra, included a daughter called doña Juana de Durango; all the other children used the surname Aranda. See the will of Mariana García Carrillo of 1641 in AGNP, Juan Guerra; Tulane LAL.

67. Jorge de la Hoz received a dowry of 1,500 pesos and provided another 1,000 pesos as his arras when he married Juana de Durango (AGNP, Juan de la Parra, 1599; FHCLDS, reel 649691). The witnesses to the statement that he had received the dowry were his wife's uncles Rodrigo García and Juan García Carrillo and the briocense Juan de Buena. The dowry for her second marriage was considerably higher, 4,000 pesos.

68. See the discussion of naming patterns in Altman, *Emigrants and Society*, 138–40.

69. For example, doña María de Aranda, the granddaughter of the briocense immigrants María García and Martín de Viñuelas, married a man named Alonso Carrillo. He probably was from Brihuega or from a briocense family, but there is no proof that he was.

70. This information on the family's background comes from the testimony of Alonso de Villarreal in the deposition of Juan de Piña in 1577 (AGI, Contrat. 5226, no. 1, ramo 15).

71. Ibid., 2066, no. 100.

72. AGNP, Marcos Rodríguez, Alonso Hernández, 1590; FHCLDS, reel 649674.

73. AGI, Indif. Gen. 2162A; 2061, no. 151; 2065, no. 35.

74. Vollmer, 1321.

75. AGNP, Juan de Meneses.

76. Cristóbal de Salas mentioned him in 1590 but he may no longer have been living, or at least not living in Brihuega, in 1602, when María de Urgelos donated her houses to another son and daughter. Perhaps he too went to Puebla, although I have seen no record of his presence there.

77. For a distinct kind of migration that was almost exclusively male, see Pescador,

"New World Inside a Basque Village," who writes that "this pattern of men who migrate and women who worked locally [in Oiartzun] may represent the only constant in the history of the Valley's integration into the Spanish empire" (37). He notes that by the middle of the seventeenth century, "with iron's downfall and maize on the rise, men had more incentives than ever to leave the Valley, just as women had more reason to stay for the rest of their days" (65).

78. AGNP, Juan de la Parra; FHCLDS, reel 649712.

79. AGN, Tierras, vol. 2955, exped. 76.

80. AGI, Indif. Gen. 2066, no. 36.

6. Social Relations

1. The cases are in AHN, Inquis. Toledo, leg. 199, exped. 23, 1553, and AGN, Inquis., vol. 101, exped. 3, "proceso contra Diego de Anzures, natural de Brihuega, vecino de la ciudad de los Angeles, por casado dos veces," 1574. The case in Spain is peculiar. The principal charge was brought against Diego de Anzures's father, also Diego de Anzures, for "palabras escandalosas." He was "penitenciado" (penanced). The case against his son apparently was an addendum. Although some testimony was collected, there appears to have been no judgment made.

2. Escudero was 35 years old and a bachelor when he went to New Spain with Anzures; see AGI, Contrat. 5218, no. 81. He subsequently married in Mexico. On the obraje he owned in the pueblo of San Jerónimo, jurisdiction of Coyoacán, see AGN, Civil, vol. 687, exped. 1.

3. Members of the Anzures family were notably long-lived. Diego's brothers Rodrigo and Macario also both lived into their 80s; ages at death for the other siblings are not known.

4. AGN, Inquis., vol. 101, exped. 3.

5. All of María de la Paz's testimony as well as that of other witnesses and Diego de Anzures's letter to Cristóbal Escudero and his own statements are ibid. Andrés de Angulo and his wife, Isabel de Ribas, left Puebla to return to Brihuega in 1576.

6. "Se vino huyendo a estas partes." Whether this last was Pedro's or María de la Paz's observation is not clear. Pedro would have been around twelve years old at the time of the events in Spain, and some of his recollections could have been incorrect or incomplete, since he may not have known all the facts of the case.

7. Not surprisingly, Pedro de Anzures recalled that incident, which he witnessed. He was an adolescent at the time, and it must have been quite a memorable family scene.

8. Witnesses in the 1553 Inquisition case brought against Diego de Anzures (the father) recounted episodes over a period of years that reflected his bad temper; AHN, Inquis. Toledo, leg. 199, exped. 23.

9. Anzures's letter of April 18, 1574, to Escudero was included in the testimony in the Inquisition case in Mexico. Escudero testified in May 1574 that he had learned about the accusation of bigamy against Anzures three months before from a fellow briocense, Francisco Alvarez, who was living in Puebla. Escudero then wrote to Anzures asking him about it. Anzures replied that he would try to give Escudero as complete an account as possible. Not surprisingly, his tone and construction of events are quite self-serving.

10. "Que aunque los hubiera y [*sic*] Dios y Santa María y todos los santos no se casaría con ella sino que se metería frayle o se iría a Indias" (AHN, Inquis. Toledo, leg. 199, exped. 23).

11. Juan Rodrigo García was a contemporary of Diego de Anzures (el mozo), but he did not go to New Spain until 1571. He told the archdeacon in Puebla that Anzures's

father had spoken to him "diciéndole de otro negocio que ante le había sucedido al dicho Diego de Anzures diciendo por estas palabras, aún no he acabado este otro negocio de su hija de Alonso García."

12. Cristóbal Escudero specifically stated that Ribas was related to the Encinas.

13. Francisco de Encinas testified in October 1573 that people in Cifuentes came to greet Anzures, "dándole la enhorabuena todo el pueblo."

14. Anzures wrote that "como persona libre me iba a España a mi tierra con mis hijos y mujer y parientes de parientes de la moza, que hay en este pueblo muchos . . . los cuales iban conmigo a España" (AGN, Inquis., vol. 101, exped. 3).

15. Otte, *Cartas privadas*, 153 (my translation).

16. See Cook and Cook, *Good Faith and Truthful Ignorance*, on the complex question of the point at which a marriage was considered to have been contracted. "Before the reforms of the Council of Trent (1563) a marriage simply involved a verbal agreement between two freely consenting parties" (63). The Encinas family apparently believed that their daughter and Diego de Anzures had made such an agreement. Nonetheless, the Cooks also suggest that an agreement over the dowry was a crucial part of a betrothal (175 n. 5), and in the case of Diego's alleged marriage to María de Encinas no mention is ever made of a dowry having been offered, agreed upon, or paid.

17. AGI, México 98.

18. AHN, Inquis. Toledo, leg. 348, exped. 8.

19. Ibid., leg. 467, exped. 4.

20. AGN, Contrat. 5312, no. 24. González was around 30 years old and wanted to emigrate to the Indies. Diego de Anzures, who by then was fray Diego de Anzures y Guevara of the order of San Juan, testified that he had known González's great-grandparents.

21. AGN, Inquis., vol. 65, exped. 4.

22. AGI, Indif. Gen. 2054; Otte, *Cartas privadas*, 154–55.

23. AGI, Indif. Gen. 2065, no. 52.

24. Information on the location of immigrants' residences and places of business comes mainly from records of sales, rentals, and censos in Puebla's notarial archive and petitions and grants in the city council records. The most important published source on streets and urban development in the colonial period is Leicht, *Las calles de Puebla*. Leicht unfortunately does not include a great deal of information on the location of private residences, and his information on individuals in the sixteenth and early seventeenth centuries often is not reliable.

25. AGNP, Juan de la Parra. Camarillo made a will in 1598 but obviously survived his illness.

26. MNAH, Ser. AJP, reel 6 (Libros del Cabildo).

27. AJP, 1609, fiscal de la real audiencia contra Benito [Sanz] Bautista, Juan de Mata, Domingo Guerra, Juan García Barranco, vecinos de la ciudad de los Angeles, sobre que les acusa ser culpados en los heridos que dieron a Francisco López cerrajero de que murió.

28. Presumably Spanish women in particular were more likely to socialize within the house than in public places. On this subject, see Angel, "Spanish Women in the New World."

29. López de Villaseñor, *Cartilla vieja*, 101.

30. According to Hirschberg, "Social History of Puebla," "in 1546 the *cabildo* identified *barrios* for Indians from Cholula, Texcoco, Totomehuacan, Tlaxcala, and Mexico. In later years enough Indians migrated from Huejotzingo, Calpa, Tepeaca, Tlatelolco and Tecali to form communities within Puebla. By the fifties Puebla's Indian barrios had become formalized into the barrios of San Sebastian, San Pablo, San Francisco and Santiago" (416–17).

31. AGN, Tierras, vol. 2956, exped. 108.

32. López de Villaseñor, *Cartilla vieja*, 133–34.

33. "Para haberlo de decir seré como los indios que para decir la cosa traen rodeos por no dejarme cosa atrás" (AGN, Inquis., vol. 101, exped. 3).

34. AGI, Indif. Gen. 2061; Otte, *Cartas privadas*, 165.

35. AGN, Civil 1310, exped. 2, 1585.

36. AJP, 1603, exped. 591; AGN, Tierras, vol. 2948, exped. 110.

37. AGI, Contrat. 339B, no. 1, ramo 18.

38. AGN, Civil 1310, exped. 2, 1585.

39. AGN, Civil 1390, exped. 24, 1570. Baeza was only seventeen years old and had taken charge of the obraje for his mother and siblings when his father died. Members of the briocense community knew and worked with Juan Pérez, who said he had previously been the mayordomo of "Pastrana" (probably Juan de Pastrana). After Pérez was arrested in 1570 at the orders of Bach. Alonso Martínez, the "juez de comisión en la visita de los obrajes" in Puebla, on charges of mistreatment and wrongful confinement of Indian workers, the briocenses Juan Barranco and Cristóbal de Ribas testified on his behalf.

40. A. García López, *Moriscos en tierras de Uceda y Guadalajara*, 37, writes that although a group of 40 Moriscos apparently were sent to Brihuega, none were living there in the 1580s.

41. AJP, 1603, exped. 572.

42. AGN, Tierras, vol. 2948, exped. 79.

43. AGNP, Marcos Rodríguez; FHCLDS, reel 649668.

44. AGNP, Juan de la Parra.

45. AJP, 1609.

46. AGN, Inquis., vol. 584, exped. 1, 1614.

47. Hernán Sánchez said Carmona "es tan emparentado favorecido y rico y yo solo sin deudos ni parientes y ocupado en lugar y oficio público . . . es hombre vengativo y executivo de sus pasiones."

48. AGN, Inquis., vol. 211, expeds. 1–5.

49. AJP, 1609, fiscal de la real audiencia contra Benito Bautista et al. The records in the judicial archive include only the probanzas of Juan de Mata, Domingo Guerra, and Benito Sanz Bautista. The probanzas of Juan García Barranco and Andrés de la Fuente, also named in the accusation of murder, are missing, as is the testimony that implicated the accused as well as the final disposition of the case. It probably can be assumed that they were all acquitted. Juan García Barranco continued to serve as alférez mayor until his death in 1619, and Juan de Mata, who subsequently married his employer, Isabel Bautista, also is known to have been active in Puebla for many years after the case.

50. A man from Brihuega named Cristóbal de Espuela called Isabel Bautista his aunt. His sister María Ruiz, also known as María de Espuela, was married to Pedro Barranco, so Magdalena Barranco, said to be Isabel Bautista's niece, probably was María Ruiz's sister-in-law. Cristóbal de Espuela called Juan Barranco his uncle. Sometime before the incident Isabel Bautista was said to have had an argument with María de Espuela, but it is not clear what, if any, relevance it might have had to Francisco López's murder.

51. See AGN, Tierras, vol. 2950, exped. 52. The disparity in the names between López, his mother, Isabel Sánchez, and his sister certainly raises questions as to their exact relationship. Perhaps doña María de Viedesola was López's half sister.

52. There is insufficient information to reconstruct the whole Barranco family tree. Juan Barranco's mother was Ana Ruiz, and Cristóbal de Espuela, whose sister María Ruiz was married to Pedro Barranco, said that Juan Barranco was his uncle. Juan Barranco also was said to be the "primo hermano" of Juan Bautista Sanz, which probably points to

a relationship with Isabel Bautista and her nephew Benito Sanz Bautista. Juan Bautista Sanz was the son of Benito Sanz and Isabel Ruiz.

53. AGI, Contrat. 5271, no. 45.

54. Toribio gave his power of attorney to two men in Seville to ask for the dispensation; see AGNP, Juan de la Parra, 1608; FHCLDS, reel 649717.

55. AGNP, Gabriel de Anzures, 1612.

56. AGI, México 98, testimony of Juan Bautista clérigo.

57. Ibid., 118; my thanks to Juan Javier Pescador for pointing out the probable origin of the surname Angulo.

58. AJP, 1605, exped. 665, is a criminal complaint lodged by a woman named Leonor Vásquez who lived in the barrio of San Pablo. She alleged that Ribas's son and another boy had broken through a wall into her garden, where they caused damage. When she tried to run them off, the Ribas boy went to get his parents. She accused them of then coming and beating her.

Conclusion

1. For a good sense of the contrast in scale and environmental impact between raising sheep in Castile and in New Spain, compare Phillips and Phillips, *Spain's Golden Fleece*, and Melville, *Plague of Sheep*.

2. There is no evidence that the briocense immigrants were particularly active in any one cofradía in Puebla or that they organized any new ones.

3. See Ida Altman, "A New World in the Old," in Altman and Horn, *"To Make America,"* 40–46.

4. For more discussion of this point, see Ida Altman, "Moving Around and Moving On: Spanish Emigration in the Sixteenth Century," in Lucassen and Lucassen, *Migration, Migration History, History*, 267–68.

5. For a highly detailed and sophisticated analysis of a modern case, see Moya, *Cousins and Strangers*. In reference to the movement from one town he writes: "When it comes to understanding the process of emigration, national aggregates come perilously close to being meaningless. On the other hand, local singularity may pose a greater epistemological dilemma: if every village and town constitutes a unique case, a general understanding of the process becomes all but impossible. I am convinced, however, that what I discovered in Mataró was particular, not unique" (68).

6. See Pescador, "New World Inside a Basque Village."

7. My thesis was published in revised and condensed form in Altman and Lockhart, *Provinces of Early Mexico*. My "Spanish Society in Mexico City After the Conquest" is a revised version of the study of early Mexico City.

8. On Urdinola and his family, see Pescador, "New World Inside a Basque Village."

9. Boyd-Bowman, *Índice geobiográfico*.

10. Lockhart, *Men of Cajamarca*. For a bibliography of Otte's work, see his *Sevilla y sus mercaderes*.

11. Otte, "Cartas privadas."

12. For comparison, see Pescador, "New World Inside a Basque Village." He concludes that

> rooted in the values that protected the caserío in the sixteenth century, the network of paisanos ended up transforming the social weight attached to lineage and household in the Basque country. In the colonies, by contrast, the paisanos privileged individual merits, such as discipline, hard work, loyalty, and talent over local and family

values. In this process, a Basque network was created for the first time that transcended the boundaries defined by caserío, village and province. (321)

13. See Roger Rouse, "Mexican Migration and the Social Space of Postmodernism," in Gutiérrez, *Between Two worlds*, on a modern case of movement between a Mexican community, Aguililla, and the United States. He suggests that it is "inadequate to see Aguilillan migration as a movement between distinct environments. Today, it is the circuit as a whole rather than any one locale that constitutes the principal setting in relation to which Aguilillans orchestrate their lives" (254). Although the migration from Brihuega to Puebla in many ways does not equate with the one Rouse has studied, not least because of the much greater distance that separated the two localities, the idea that the movement was defined by an interactive dynamic that encompassed both places as well as lines of communication and personal and economic ties between people in the old home and the new one certainly is relevant to the briocense case.

Bibliography

Albi-Romero, Guadalupe. "La sociedad de Puebla de los Angeles en el siglo XVI." *Jahrbuch für Geschichte von Staat, Wirtschaft und Gesellschaft Lateinamerikas* 7 (1970): 76–145.

Allen, David Grayson. *In English Ways: The Movement of Societies and the Transferral of English Local Law and Custom to Massachusetts Bay in the Seventeenth Century.* Chapel Hill: University of North Carolina Press, 1982.

Altman, Ida. *Emigrants and Society: Extremadura and Spanish America in the Sixteenth Century.* Berkeley and Los Angeles: University of California Press, 1989.

———. "Spanish Society in Mexico City After the Conquest." *Hispanic American Historical Review* 71, no. 3 (1991): 413–45.

Altman, Ida, and James Horn, eds. *"To Make America": European Emigration in the Early Modern Period.* Berkeley and Los Angeles: University of California Press, 1991.

Altman, Ida, and James Lockhart. *Provinces of Early Mexico.* Los Angeles: Center for Latin American Studies, UCLA, 1976.

Angel, Amanda. "Spanish Women in the New World: The Transmission of a Model Polity to New Spain, 1521–1570." Ph.D. diss., University of California, Davis, 1998.

Barrios Aguilera, Manuel. *Moriscos y repoblación en las postrimeras de la Granada islámica.* Granada: Diputación Provincial de Granada, 1993.

Barrios Aguilera, Manuel, and Margarita M. Birriel Salcedo. *La repoblación del reino de Granada después de la expulsión de los moriscos.* Granada: Universidad de Granada y Grupo de Autores Unidos, 1986.

Bazant, Jan. "Evolución de la industria textil poblana (1554–1845)." *Historia Mexicana* 13 (1962): 473–516.

Beezley, William H., Cheryl English Martin, and William E. French, eds. *Rituals of Rule, Rituals of Resistance: Public Celebrations and Popular Culture in Mexico.* Wilmington, Del.: SR Books, 1994.

Bermúdez de Castro, Diego Antonio. *Teatro angelopolitano: Historia de la ciudad de Puebla.* (1746.) Puebla: Junta de Mejoramiento, 1985.

Borah, Woodrow. *Early Colonial Trade and Navigation Between Mexico and Peru.* Berkeley and Los Angeles: University of California Press, 1954.

———. *Silk Raising in Colonial Mexico.* Ibero-Americana 20. Berkeley and Los Angeles: University of California Press, 1943.

Boyd-Bowman, Peter. *Indice geobiográfico de cincuenta y seis mil pobladores de la América hispánica.* Mexico City: Fondo de Cultura Económica, 1985.

Carabarán G., Alberto. *El trabajo y los trabajadores del obraje en la ciudad de Puebla, 1700–1710.* Puebla, 1984.

Carrión, Antonio. *Historia de la ciudad de Puebla de los Angeles.* 2 vols. Puebla: Escuelas Salesianas de Artes Oficios, 1897.

Catálogo de pasajeros a indias durante los siglos XVI, XVII y XVIII. 7 vols. Seville, 1940–46, 1980–86.

Cervantes, Francisco, ed. *Las dimensiones del espacio en la historia de Puebla, siglos XVI–XIX.* Puebla: Gobierno del Estado de Puebla, forthcoming.

Christian, William A., Jr. *Local Religion in Sixteenth-Century Spain.* Princeton: Princeton University Press, 1981.

Cook, David Noble, and Alexandra Cook. *Good Faith and Truthful Ignorance.* Durham: Duke University Press, 1991.

Cressy, David. *Coming Over: Migration and Communication Between England and New England in the Seventeenth Century.* Cambridge: Cambridge University Press, 1987.

Destefano, Michael T. "Miracles and Monasticism in Mid-Colonial Puebla, 1600–1750: Charismatic Religion in a Conservative Society." Ph.D. diss., University of Florida, 1977.

Foster, George. *Culture and Conquest: America's Spanish Heritage.* Chicago: Quadrangle Books, 1960.

García López, Aurelio. *Moriscos en tierras de Uceda y Guadalajara (1582–1610).* Madrid: Gráficas Delón for Diputación Provincial de Guadalajara, 1992.

García López, Juan Catalina. *La Alcarria en los dos primeros siglos de su reconquista.* (1894.) Guadalajara: Institución Provincial de Cultura Marqués de Santillana, 1973.

———. *Biblioteca de escritores de la provincia de Guadalajara y bibliografía de la misma hasta el siglo XIX.* Madrid: Impresores de la Real Casa, 1899.

———. *El fuero de Brihuega.* Madrid: Manuel G. Hernández, 1887.

Gerhard, Peter. *A Guide to the Historical Geography of New Spain.* Rev. ed. Norman: University of Oklahoma Press, 1993.

Gutiérrez, David G., ed. *Between Two Worlds: Mexican Immigrants in the United States.* Wilmington, Del.: Scholarly Resources, 1996.

Hirschberg, Julia. "Social Experiment in New Spain: A Prosopographical Study of the Early Settlement at Puebla de los Angeles, 1531–1534." *Hispanic American Historical Review* 59 (1979): 1–33.

———. "A Social History of Puebla de los Angeles, 1531–1560." Ph.D. diss., University of Michigan, 1976.

———. "Transients in Early Colonial Society: Puebla de los Angeles, 1531–1560." *Bibliotheca Americana* 1 (1983): 3–30.

Hoberman, Louisa Schell. *Mexico's Merchant Elite, 1590–1660: Silver, State, and Society.* Durham: Duke University Press, 1991.

Hoekstra, Rik. *Two Worlds Merging: The Transformation of Society in the Valley of Puebla, 1570–1540.* Amsterdam: CEDLA, 1993.

Horn, James. *Adapting to a New World: English Society in the Seventeenth-Century Chesapeake.* Chapel Hill: University of North Carolina Press, 1994.

Iradiel Murugarren, Paulino. *Evolución de la industria textil castellana en los siglos XVII–XVI: Factores de desarrollo, organización y costes de la producción manufacturera en Cuenca.* Salamanca: Universidad de Salamanca, 1974.

Israel, J. I. *Race, Class, and Politics in Colonial Mexico*. Oxford: Oxford University Press, 1975.

Leicht, Hugo. *Las calles de Puebla*. (1934.) Puebla: Junta de Mejoramiento Moral, Cívico y Material del Municipio de Puebla, 1980.

Lockhart, James. *The Men of Cajamarca: A Social and Biographical Study of the First Conquerors of Peru*. Austin: University of Texas Press, 1972.

——. *Spanish Peru, 1532–1560*. Madison: University of Wisconsin Press, 1968.

Lockhart, James, and Enrique Otte, eds., *Letters and People of the Spanish Indies: Sixteenth Century*. Cambridge and New York: Cambridge University Press, 1976.

López de Villaseñor, Pedro. *Cartilla vieja de la nobilísima ciudad de Puebla*. (1781.) Mexico City, 1961.

Lucassen, Jan, and Leo Lucassen, eds. *Migration, Migration History, History: Old Paradigms and New Perspectives*. Bern: Peter Lang, 1997.

Lunenfeld, Marvin. *Keepers of the City: The Corregidores of Isabella of Castile, 1474–1504*. New York: Cambridge University Press, 1987.

Marín Tamayo, Fausto. *La división racial en Puebla de los Angeles*. Puebla, 1960.

Martínez, Gonzalo. *Las comunidades de villa y tierra de la Extremeña Castellana*. Madrid: Editora Nacional, 1983.

Melville, Elinor G. K. *A Plague of Sheep: Environmental Consequences of the Conquest of Mexico*. Cambridge: Cambridge University Press, 1994.

Morgan, Ron. "Saints, Biographers, and Creole Identity Formation in Colonial Spanish America." Ph.D. diss., University of California, Santa Barbara, 1998.

Mörner, Magnus. "Migraciones a Hispanoamérica durante la época colonial." *Anuario de Estudios Americanos* (Seville) 48, no. 2 (1991), suppl.

Moya, José C. *Cousins and Strangers: Spanish Immigrants in Buenos Aires, 1850–1930*. Berkeley and Los Angeles: University of California Press, 1998.

Nader, Helen. *Liberty in Absolutist Spain: The Habsburg Sale of Towns, 1516–1700*. Baltimore: Johns Hopkins University Press, 1990.

Nalle, Sara T. *God in La Mancha: Religious Reform and the People of Cuenca, 1500–1650*. Baltimore: Johns Hopkins University Press, 1992.

Niño Rodríguez, Antonio. *Organización social y actividades productivas en una villa castellana del antiguo régimen: Brihuega*. Guadalajara: Caja de Ahorro Provincial de Guadalajara, 1985.

"Nuevas ordenanzas tituladas de esta villa de Brihuega y su tierra, confirmadas por el Illust. Sr. D. Bernardo de Sandoval, cardenal y arzobispo de la Santa Iglesia de Toledo, mi señor, año de 1617." Manuscript in Real Academia de Historia, Madrid.

Otte, Enrique. *Cartas privadas de emigrantes a Indias, 1540–1616*. Seville: Consejería de Cultura, Junta de Andalucía, 1988.

——. "Cartas privadas de Puebla del siglo XVI," *Jahrbuch für Geschichte von Staat, Wirthschaft und Gesellschaft Lateinamerikas* 3 (1966): 10–87.

——. *Sevilla y sus mercaderes a fines de la Edad Media*. Ed. Antonio-Miguel Bernal and Antonio Collantes de Terán. Seville: Fundación El Monte, 1996.

Paredes Martínez, Carlos Salvador. *La región de Atlixco, Huaquechula y Tochimilco: La sociedad y la agricultura en el siglo XVI*. Mexico City: Fondo de Cultura Económico, 1991.

Peña, José F. de la. *Oligarquía y propiedad en Nueva España (1550–1624)*. Mexico City: Fondo de Cultura Económico, 1983.

Pérez Moreno, Camilo. *Tradiciones religiosas de España: La Virgen de la Peña de Brihuega*. Madrid: Asilo de Huérfanos de S.C. de Jesús, 1884. (Real Academia de Historia, caja 485, no. 11.046.)

Pérez-Rivero Maurer, Guadalupe. "Presencia peninsular en el cabildo poblano en el siglo XVII, 1640–1700." Paper presented at conference "Presencia española en Puebla," Puebla, 1995.

Pescador, Juan Javier. "The New World Inside a Basque Village: The Oiartzun Valley and Its Atlantic Exchanges, 1550–1800." Ph.D. diss., University of Michigan, 1998.

Phillips, Carla Rahn, and William D. Phillips Jr. *Spain's Golden Fleece: Wool Production and the Wool Trade from the Middle Ages to the Nineteenth Century.* Baltimore: Johns Hopkins University Press, 1997.

Powell, Sumner Chilton. *Puritan Village: The Formation of a New England Town.* Middletown, Conn: Wesleyan University Press, 1963.

Prem, Hanns J. *Milpa y hacienda. Tenencia de la tierra indígena y española en la cuenca del Alto Atoyac, Puebla, México.* Mexico City, 1988.

Reyes García, Cayetano. *Indice y extractos de los protocolos de la notaría de Cholula (1590–1600).* Mexico City, 1973.

Rodríguez Gutiérrez, Miguel. *Bosquejo histórico de Brihuega y sus pueblos.* Madrid: T. Sánchez, 1981.

Ruiz, Teófilo F. *Crisis and Continuity: Land and Town in Late Medieval Castile.* Philadelphia: University of Pennsylvania Press, 1994.

———. "The Transformation of the Castilian Municipalities: The Case of Burgos, 1248–1350." *Past & Present* 77 (1977): 3–33.

Salmerón, Lic. Pedro. *De la vida de la venerable madre Isabel de la Encarnación, carmelita descalza, natural de la ciudad de los Angeles.* (1640.) Mexico City, 1675.

Schwaller, John F. *The Church and Clergy in Sixteenth-Century Mexico.* Albuquerque: University of New Mexico Press, 1987.

Thomson, Guy P. C. *Puebla de los Angeles: Industry and Society in a Mexican City, 1700–1850.* Boulder: Westview Press, 1989.

Vassberg, David E. *Land and Society in Golden Age Castile.* Cambridge: Cambridge University Press, 1984.

———. "Orphans and Adoption in Early Modern Castilian Villages." *History of the Family* 3, no. 4 (1998): 441–58.

———. *The Village and the Outside World in Golden Age Castile: Mobility and Migration in Everyday Rural Life.* Cambridge: Cambridge University Press, 1996.

Viqueira, Carmen, and José I. Urquiola. *Los obrajes en la Nueva España, 1530–1630.* Mexico City: Consejo Nacional para la Cultura y las Artes, 1990.

Vollmer, Günter. "La evolución cuantitativa de la población indígena en la región de Puebla (1570–1810)." *Historia Mexicana* 23 (1973): 43–51.

Weiland, David J. "The Economics of Agriculture: Markets, Production and Finances in the Bishopric of Puebla, 1532–1809." D. Phil. thesis, University of Cambridge, 1995.

Zerón Zapata, Miguel. *La Puebla de los Angeles en el siglo XVII.* Mexico City, 1945.

Index